New Worlds

Ashley and Miles Baynton-Williams

New Worlds

Maps from the *Age of Discovery*

Quercus

Contents

Introduction

To beautify their Halls, Parlers, Chambers, Galeries, Studies or Libraries with ... [Collectors] liketh, loveth, getteth, and useth, Maps, Charts, and Geographical Globes ...

So WROTE THE ELIZABETHAN SCHOLAR, mathematician and mapmaker John Dee in 1570. Indeed, this is one of the most famous, and oft-quoted, references to old maps, but also one that exemplifies the fascination the modern collector has with them.

Maps have always had an immediate visual appeal, whether in the more elaborately engraved, highly decorative style so much loved by early mapmakers and publishers, or the elegant simplicity, but high technical accuracy, of the modern map.

More than that, maps are artefacts with which anyone, and everyone, can have an immediate rapport. The first instinct on seeing a map of a familiar area is to run your finger across its face, to seek out those areas that you know, to admire the accuracy, or decry the inaccuracy.

In this vein there is the famous story of the Flemish mapmaker Abraham Ortelius's misfortune. In 1570, he despatched a presentation copy of his atlas, the *Theatrum Orbis Terrarum*, to his royal master, Philip II of Spain. When the messenger arrived at Philip's palace, the king was away, so Cardinal Espinosa received the gift. The cardinal opened the atlas, turned to the map of Spain, and looked for his birthplace Martimuñoz to find, to his chagrin, that it was not marked. This was probably not an unusual occurrence on maps of the period, but Espinosa was of sufficient status to do something about it. Ortelius subsequently received a letter from an official in Brussels:

Cardinal [Espinosa] writes me from Spain that he regrets to find his native town Martimuñoz, omitted in the map in your 'Theatrum' and asks me to send him a coloured copy of it with the said name inserted. Therefore remove, if possible, the name of Palacuelos and insert Martimuñoz in its place. When this is done let some copies of the map of Spain be printed to satisfy the wish of the Cardinal ...

Amidst profuse apologies from Ortelius, the plate was reworked, Martimuñoz inserted, and a copy of the atlas sent to the cardinal.

The first meaningful printed maps were published in Italy in 1477, in Ptolemy's *Cosmographia*, the original printed atlas of the known world. Although the maps themselves were engraved in 1477, the geographical information used to compile the 26 maps in the atlas dates from about AD 150, drawn by the Alexandrian cartographer Claudius Ptolemy. Other publishers prepared editions of the *Cosmographia* in 1478, two in 1482, 1511, 1513, 1540, 1548, 1561 and onwards.

If the *Cosmographia* was important as the first set of maps of the world in print, it also underlined the lack of progress made by Europeans in mapping in the intervening centuries. Many Europeans recognized the classical Roman world view was much outdated, but it was the discoveries of the Portuguese mariners en route to the Far East, and Spanish-sponsored expeditions to the Americas, among them that of Christopher Columbus, that really drove home the inadequacy of the Ptolemaic world view.

Across Europe, cartographers set themselves the task of correcting and supplementing the inherited corpus of knowledge, and new generations of publishers disseminated that information in printed form.

The first steps were tentative and very much in the hands of individuals, not government agencies. It is surprising that, as an example, the UK's official mapmaking agency, the Ordnance Survey, and the body responsible for charting the oceans, the Admiralty Hydrographical Office, both came into being in the late years of the eighteenth century, over 200 years after the publication of the first national atlas of England and Wales in 1579, surveyed by Christopher Saxton.

The great difficulty that all cartographers faced was the expense involved in making the necessary survey – and seeing it finally into print. But, if the costs were the great handicap faced by cartographers, the solution they found underpins the appeal of the maps they made.

Faced with the expense of surveys, engraving and printing, many early cartographers were forced to look to patrons for finance. In return for their money, patrons not only wanted an accurate map but also a lavish visual artefact in keeping with, or even enhancing, their perceived status among their peer group. Large laudatory dedicatory cartouches, armorials and such like were a prerequisite of satisfying one's patron.

Also, given the difficulties of creating maps without the scientific paraphernalia available to twenty-first century cartographers, many publishers were forced to recycle – pirate is another way of putting it – existing materials and present it as new survey. Faced with the similarity of information used by competing publishers, the publishers tried to set their work apart with high production values, but also by embellishing and emphasizing the decorative features of their maps, even at the expense of the cartographic element.

When, as in the case of the great era of Dutch cartography, there was a parallel surge in the markets for paintings and fine art, many of the talents, images and tastes found their way into the decorative display found on contemporary maps, blurring the distinction between art and cartography.

Indeed, R.A. Skelton commented 'that maps should please the eye has been accepted even by scientific cartographers. A map, remarked the French military engineer [Rigobert] Bonne about 1800, is so "dry" an object that opportunities for treating it as a picture must not be lost' (Skelton 1965, p.16).

When contemporary taste dictated that not an inch of space within a map should be left blank, it is hardly surprising that many became more pictorial than cartographic. Ortelius's map of Iceland, for example, is one extreme, where the map itself is subsidiary to the elaborate vignettes of mythical sea creatures, reported by superstitious sailors returning from voyages on the North Atlantic. On many of the maps of the period, South America is filled not with place names, mountains or rivers but with small ethnographic scenes, frequently depicting cannibalism. On the other hand, other mapmakers, married the need for decoration with the need to inform, including exquisite miniature town plans and views, to enhance the geographical representation.

In his *On Poetry, A Rhapsody* in 1733, Jonathan Swift complained, in a slightly tongue in cheek fashion, in a quatrain (lines 177–80):

> *So Geographers in Afric-maps*
> *With Savage-Pictures fill their Gaps;*
> *And o'er uninhabitable Downs*
> *Place Elephants for want of Towns*

Yet, this was the same man that used this very type of pictorial element on the maps commissioned for his books, including *Gulliver's Travels*, so that the reader could follow the text.

But, as Swift used maps to illustrate his fiction, so too publishers commissioned maps to illustrate accounts of the great discoveries and voyages of their period. The Englishman John Farrer, who compiled an important map of Virginia, first published in 1651, added a manuscript note in the margin of his copy of Edward Williams's *Virgo Triumphans* (1650): 'But a map had binn very proper to this Book. For all men love to see the country as well as to heare of it' and in 1607, William Camden, the antiquary, noted the problem with early editions of his account of the antiquities of England:

> *many have found a defect in this worke that Mappes were not*
> *adioined, which doe allure the eies by pleasant portraiture, and*
> *are the best directions in Geographicall studies, especially when*
> *the light of learning is adioined to the speechlesse delineations …*

Joseph Conrad, in his *Heart of Darkness*, talked of his fascination with maps: 'Now when I was a little chap I had a passion for maps. I would look for hours at South America, or Africa, or Australia and lose myself in all the glories of exploration'.

To look at an old map is also to see the world, or one of its parts, as it would have been seen by the kings, aristocracy, government, the military, merchants and navigators of the day. It is to step into the past to see countries, places and people as they once were. Maps above all tell of our strivings, the quest to see what is on the 'other side of the hill', across the river, or over the sea, and then his desire to record where the traveller had been and what he had seen.

Maps are the visual record of the story of European expansion, firstly within domestic borders, and then into the tentative beginnings of the early colonial period. Henry Briggs's map is an example, marking the English settlements of 'James Citie' (Virginia) and 'Plymouth' (Massachusetts), but without any real sense of the interior – not even the Great Lakes – and prominently displaying the contemporary conception that California was an island. At the other end of the spectrum, John Young's map of Texas, during its short-lived period as a republic, displays the expanding settlement pattern, as new counties are laid out to accommodate immigrants to the area.

Just as one can take pleasure in the accuracy, so too there can be pleasure in the inaccuracy – towns wrongly sited, coastlines wrongly charted and rivers wrongly routed. Equally charming are the anachronisms, the travellers' tales and fables adopted as fact by gullible mapmakers – sea-monsters that inhabit many early charts, or fanciful medieval creatures and distorted images of more factual animals that populate the empty areas of maps of far-flung areas outside European experience.

Then there are the misconceptions. As well as California as an island, there are: the fictitious islands of Brasil and Frisland; the legendary Seven Cities of Cibola, in the unsuccessful quest for which Spanish Conquistadores expended so much blood and sweat; and Raleigh's mythical lake Parime, with the city of Manoa, the site of El Dorado.

It is all these things, and many more, that make maps such a popular collectable, but perhaps the most intriguing element of this is the diversity of delights that different viewers can find in a single image.

To capture this rich diversity in 120 maps is impossible. We have selected maps that illustrate the development of geographical knowledge over the centuries, giving as wide a geographical coverage as possible, but also illustrating changing styles of cartography such as the shift in balance between art and science. We have selected maps that have their own story to tell and ones that are a little bit different, with examples not only of the mapmaker at work but also at play, with some of the famous curiosity maps, drawn for entertainment.

Within this challenge, we have endeavoured not to make this book a summary of the rarest maps ever made known, found only in institutions. Every map in this selection has been supplied from a 'trade' source, and has been bought and sold within the last 20 or so years.

1475

Untitled circular map of the world

Lucas Brandis de Schass
From: *Rudimentum Novitiorum sive Chronicarum Historiarum Epitome*, Lübeck, 1475. Woodcut with type lettering, 375 x 375 mm

The *Rudimentum Novitiorum* was a history of the world, in chronicle form, designed as an educational tool. It contained two maps, which are the two earliest printed maps that are anything more than schematic diagrams, this map of the world and a map of Palestine (the next entry).

The world map falls at the tail end of the Christian medieval tradition of circular mappaemundi, with Jerusalem placed at the centre of the map and east at the top of the page. Within the map the individual countries are depicted in a stylized form, as hills, with the Pope prominent in Rome and the Roman Emperor in Constantinople.

Working within the confines of this format, the designer of the map, possibly the publisher Lucas Brandis de Schass, has struggled to include the countries in their correct geographical relation, with the British Isles placed next to Dacia (modern Romania) and Livonia, and bordering on Spain.

The country of 'Vinla[n]d' is marked along the lower left border, and thus apparently on the outer reaches of Europe, leading some to speculate this refers to knowledge of Viking voyages to Greenland and beyond but, in view of the random placing of countries on the map, it is judged more likely to depict Finland.

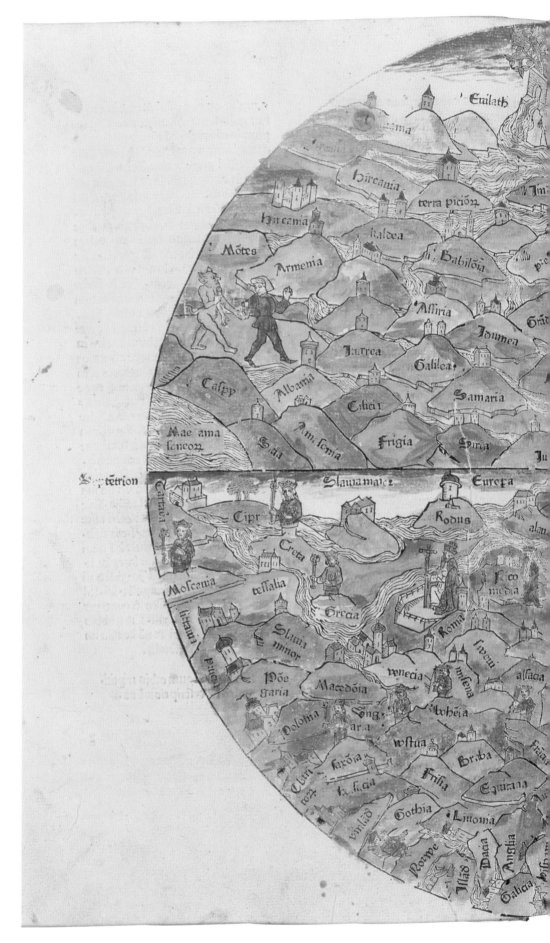

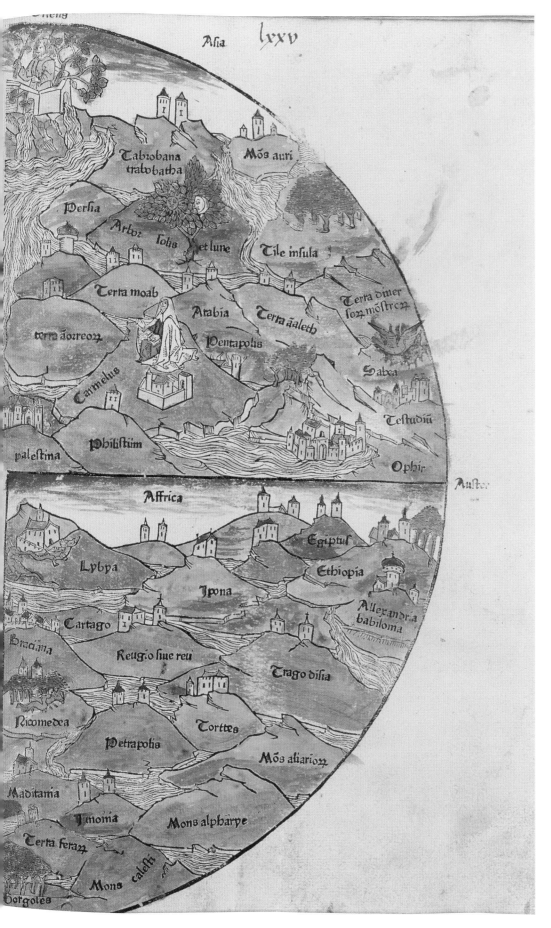

Asia *lxxv*

Tabrobana trabobatha

Móns auri

Perlia

Arbor solis et lune

Tile insula

Terra moab

Arabia

Terra äaleth

Terra dmer soꝛ mostreꝛ

terra äozreoꝛ

Pentapolis

Sabea

Carmelus

Testudiu

palestina

Philistim

Ophir

Auster

Affrica

Egiptus

Lybia

Ethiopia

Ipona

Cartago

Allexandria babiloma

Bradäna

Reugio siue reu

Trago disia

Nicomedea

Tortres

Pettrapolis

Móns aliarioꝛ

Maditania

Imonia

Mons alpharpe

Terra feraꝛ

Mons calesti

dorgoles

Untitled map of Palestine

Lucas Brandis de Schass
From: *Rudimentum Novitiorum sive Chronicarum Historiarum Epitome*, Lübeck, 1475. Woodcut with type lettering, 410 x 580 mm

The second map from the *Rudimentum* depicts Palestine. While the companion map of the world (the previous entry) is part of a medieval tradition, this map of Palestine is regarded as 'the earliest modern printed map, since it is the first to break away from the tenets of the medieval schoolmen' (Campbell, p.146).

Palestine is depicted in a heavily stylized pictorial form, almost in the form of a bird's-eye view, taken from an imaginary vantage point over the Mediterranean looking towards the east, with Jerusalem prominent at the centre of the map. The map extends from Damascus and Antioch in the north (at left), south to Egypt and eastward to the Sea of Galilee.

The map is derived from an original survey carried out by the traveller Burchard of Monte Sion, resident in Palestine for ten years during the thirteenth century, who wrote an account of his experiences there. Although he prepared a map from his travels, none of the manuscript versions extant today contain a map, so it can only be reconstructed from derivatives such as this.

(see overleaf) ↓

Amorite

area
polis

Cades bar
ne nu xiii

Amozrei

Tertamoab · Petradeferti

Mons seyr gñ
xiiii et deu iiii

Deferrtu phares

Mons syna

Mare mortuu

Iericho ier vl

Betagla

Statua falis muh
er loth gñ xix

tra amalech xxv

Herodiu

Ballis
bñdcois

collis achile

Engadi i re
xxiii

Carmelus i re
xxv

Tecua cinitas
ii re xiiii

Natatoriu syloe
io ix

achelce
mach

Betleem

Batachar et
Ramauilla

Ebronnoua

turris gregis

Ebron retus

Betlech

Mambre
gñ xviii

Caluaria

Bethsu
ra

ager damasce
nus

Sochot i ra
xvii io xxi

Beelefel
nu xiii

dõs zacharie

vallis lac riam

Cariathiarim
archa xx ãme

xiiii re

Roba i re xxi

Raphaim

azotus

Berfabee

Egiptus

accaron

afcolona

Mare rubzu

Baumia

Gaza

1482

Untitled Ptolemaic world map

Nicolaus Germanus
From: the Ulm edition of
Ptolemy's *Geographia*, 1482.
Woodcut, 420 x 575 mm

Claudius Ptolemy composed his *Geographia* in Alexandria, *circa* AD 150. It was a compilation of knowledge about the world as known to the Romans, with a list of co-ordinates of places, and a guide to creating maps. Lost to western Europe during the Dark Ages, the book was rediscovered by Maximus Planudes (*c.* 1260–1330), who translated a manuscript copy from the original Greek into Latin for dissemination. As an important work on geography it was inevitable that maps would be created to illustrate the work and these were among the first maps to be printed, starting with a copper-engraved edition published in Bologna, Italy, in 1477. This woodcut edition was the first German atlas, and this world was the first map to be signed by the maker, 'Johannes woodcutter of Armsheim'.

Making the most western land he knew, the Canary Islands, zero longitude, and the equator zero latitude, Ptolemy's co-ordinates have been put together to create this map of the world. Because he over-estimated the length of the Mediterranean the result has been distorted: Scotland has had to slant to the east to fit. It is likely that the eastern reaches of the map come from sources later than Ptolemy who have added new discoveries to the manuscript.

Even as the maps were printed they were known to be incorrect and in need of updating. Nicolaus Germanus, who edited the maps for the Ulm edition, has extended the map northward beyond Ptolemy's original borders to include Scandinavia. The separate map of Scandinavia is the next map to be described.

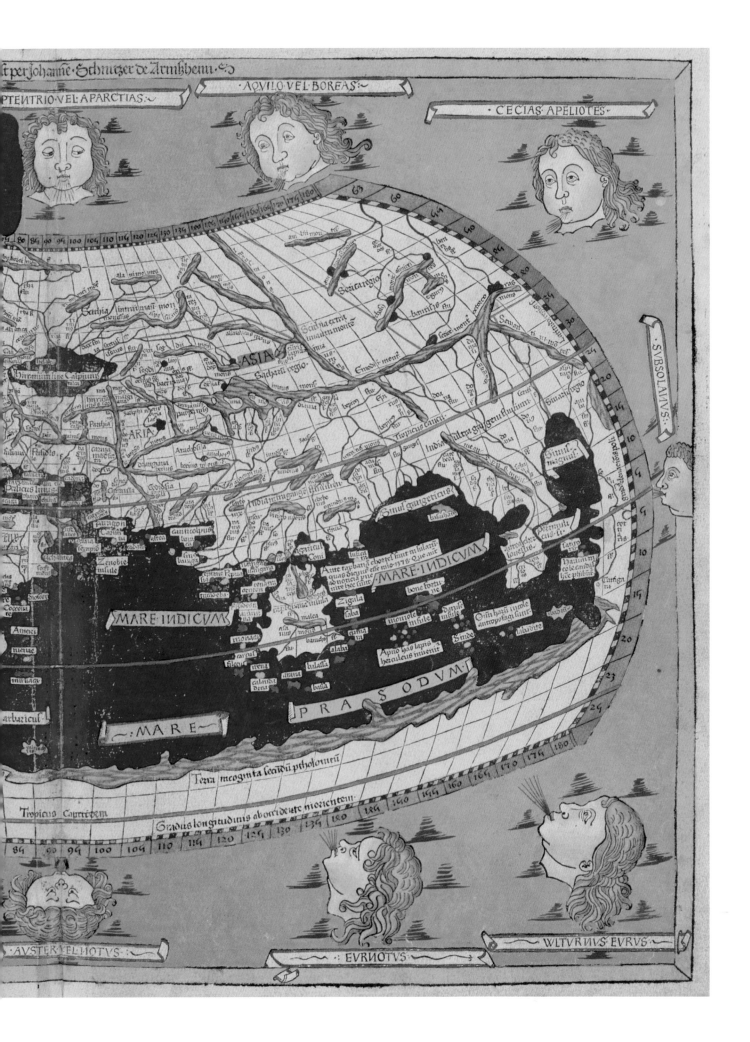

st per Johanne Schnitzer de Armßheim

ASIA

Sachari regio.

ARIA

MARE INDICVM

MARE INDICVM

Simul gangeticus

PRASODVM

~: MARE ~

Terra incognita secundu ptholomeu

Tropicus Capricorni

Gradus longitudinis ab occidente in orientem

SVBSOLANVS

AVSTER VEL NOTVS ·   · EVRNOTVS ·   · WLTVRNVS EVRVS ·

13

1482

'Tabula Moderna Prussie Livonie Norbegie et Gottie'

Nicolaus Germanus
From: the Ulm edition of
Ptolemy's *Geographia*, 1482.
Woodcut, 320 x 575 mm

The 'Tabula Moderna Prussie Livonie Norbegie et Gottie' is the first printed map of northern Europe. It was published in the first German edition of Ptolemy's *Geographia* containing maps, which were prepared by Germanus.

Most of the maps in the atlas were drawn to illustrate the archaic geography written by Claudius Ptolemy of Alexandria, *circa* AD 150; this is one of five 'modern' maps added to the Ulm Ptolemy, taken from newer sources, with this map drawn by the Danish clergyman Claudius Clavus *circa* 1425.

However, the map still shows the British Isles in its Ptolemaic format, with Scotland with a severe east–west slant, while Norway, Sweden and Iceland are virtually unrecognizable. At the top of the page is 'Greenland', connected by a narrow isthmus to the rest of Scandinavia; confusingly this is not Greenland, as we know it today, but Svalbard or Spitsbergen, the island that became an important whaling station in the seventeenth century.

Iceland is placed in 'Mare Congelatum' or 'Frozen Sea'.

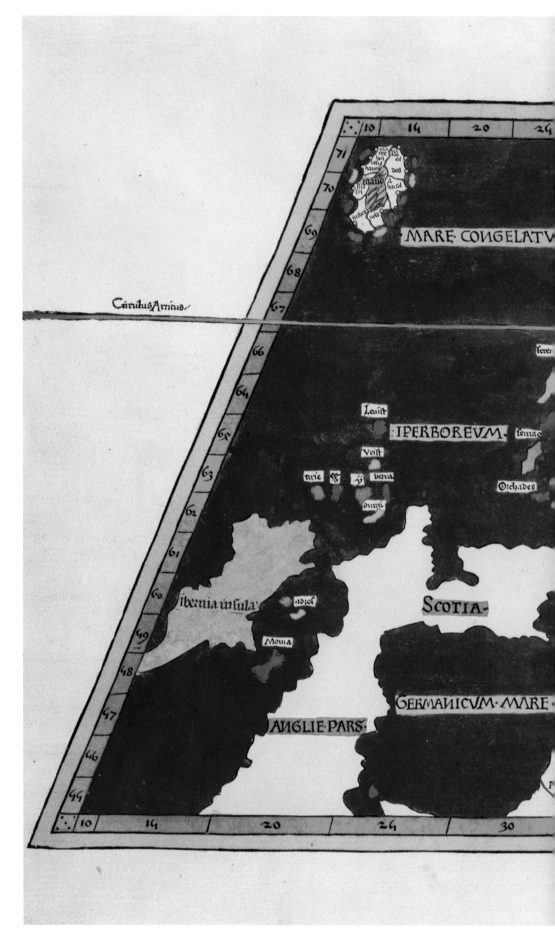

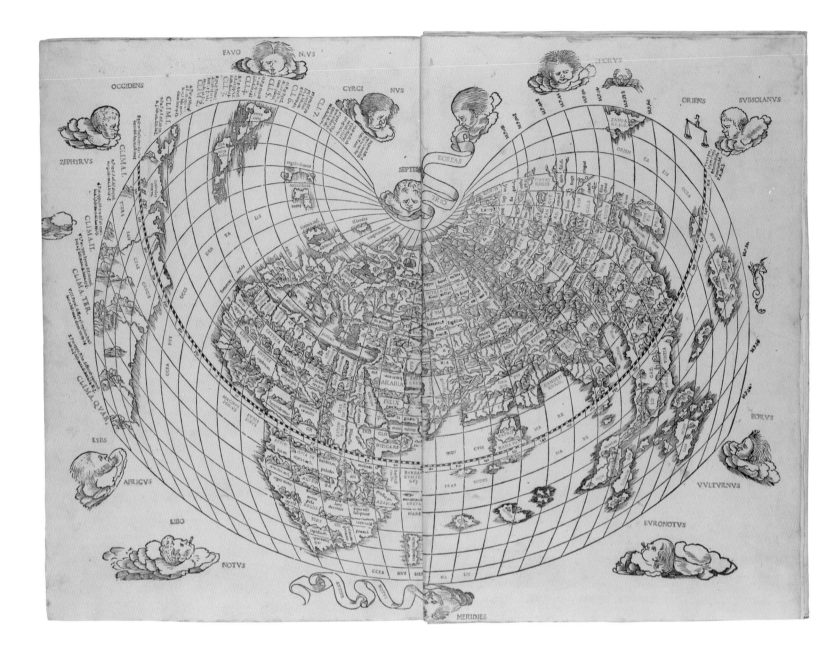

1511

Untitled world map on a cordiform projection

Bernard Sylvanus
From: the 1511 Venetian edition of Ptolemy's *Geographia*.
Woodcut, 415 x 565 mm

Sylvanus's world map is unusual as being from the only Italian edition of Ptolemy's *Geographia* illustrated with woodcut maps rather than copper engravings. It is also one of the first examples of two-colour printing, with the place names printed in red from movable type letters inserted into the woodblock.

What makes this map particularly distinctive is that Sylvanus has used an unusual cordiform, or heart-shaped, projection.

Sylvanus has attempted to modernize the Ptolemaic world view to take into account the latest discoveries. This is one of the earliest atlas maps to show the Americas, with the West Indies and South America visble on the left. In the east 'Zampagu Ins.' is Japan, the second time it appears on a printed map. Scotland has lost its distorted outline, and the Cape of Good Hope is shown in South Africa, whereas earlier maps showed Africa connected to the Great Southern Continent.

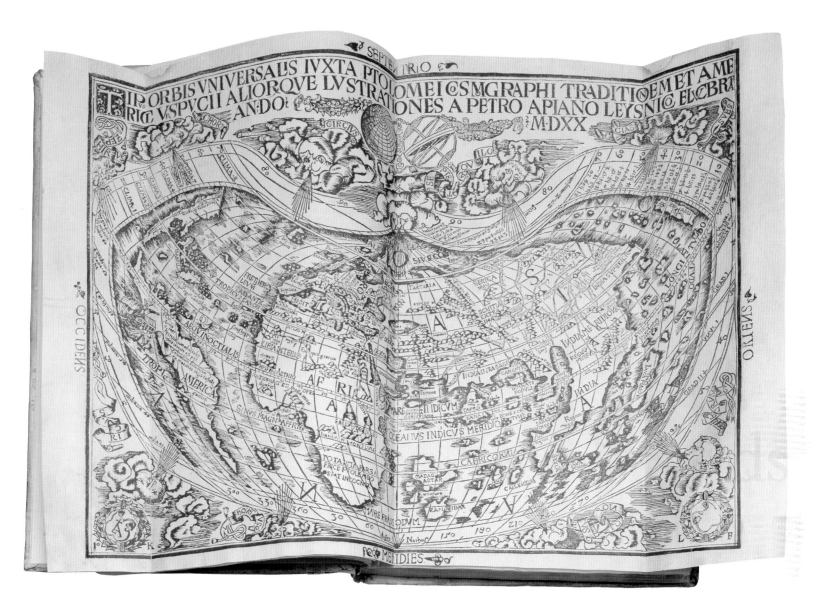

1520

'Tipus Orbis Universalis
Iuxta Ptolomei Cosmographi
Traditionem…'

Peter Apianus
From: Caius Julius Solinus's
Enarrationes…, Vienna, 1520.
Woodcut, 285 x 410 mm

Peter Apianus produced what is an essentially Ptolemaic map of the world but, as noted in the title, updated with the discoveries made by Amerigo Vespucci in South America from 1499 to 1504. Apianus's map is derived from the wall-map of the world map by Martin Waldseemüller, published in 1507, whose use of the word 'America' on South America led to Vespucci's name being adopted to describe the whole continent, at the expense of Columbus. Following that model, Apianus has inserted the name 'AMERICA' in large lettering within South America; with the Waldseemüller map known in only a single example, this is the earliest map available to a collector naming 'America'

Published at a relatively early date, before explorers had mapped the entire eastern coastline of America (let alone the western coast), there is a prominent passage between North and South America, probably in the unexplored Gulf of Mexico, perhaps in the region of the Isthmus of Panama.

1531

'Nova, et Integra Universi Orbis Descriptio'

Oronce Finé
From: Simon Grynæus's *Novus Orbis Regionem*, Paris, 1532.
Woodcut, 290 x 460 mm

Oronce Finé produced a very unusual double-cordiform world map on a polar projection, with the two hemispheres linked through Africa. On the left is the Northern hemisphere, with one huge landmass connecting Europe with Asia and then America. Florida is named, just a decade after its discovery by Juan Ponce de León in 1513. In Central and South America many new names have been added, reflecting the explorations of the Conquistadores.

The Southern hemisphere is filled with the 'Terra Australis', a concept that originated with the belief that there had to be a landmass in the Southern hemisphere to balance the weight of the countries of the Northern hemisphere, and keep the world stable on its axis. 'Terra Australis' is separated from South America by the Straits of Magellan, with the South Pacific named 'Mare magellanicum', a decade after their exploration by Magellan.

The outline of Antarctica has been claimed to be an extremely accurate delineation of the rock of Antarctica before it was encased in ice, and so used to 'prove' that an earlier civilization had mapped the region before the ice formed. However, this has been shown to involve redrawing features of the map to fit and, in the absence of an explanation of how Finé might come by such information, a simple cartographic coincidence is more likely.

In the upper cusp is the arms of the French royal family, supported by dragons.

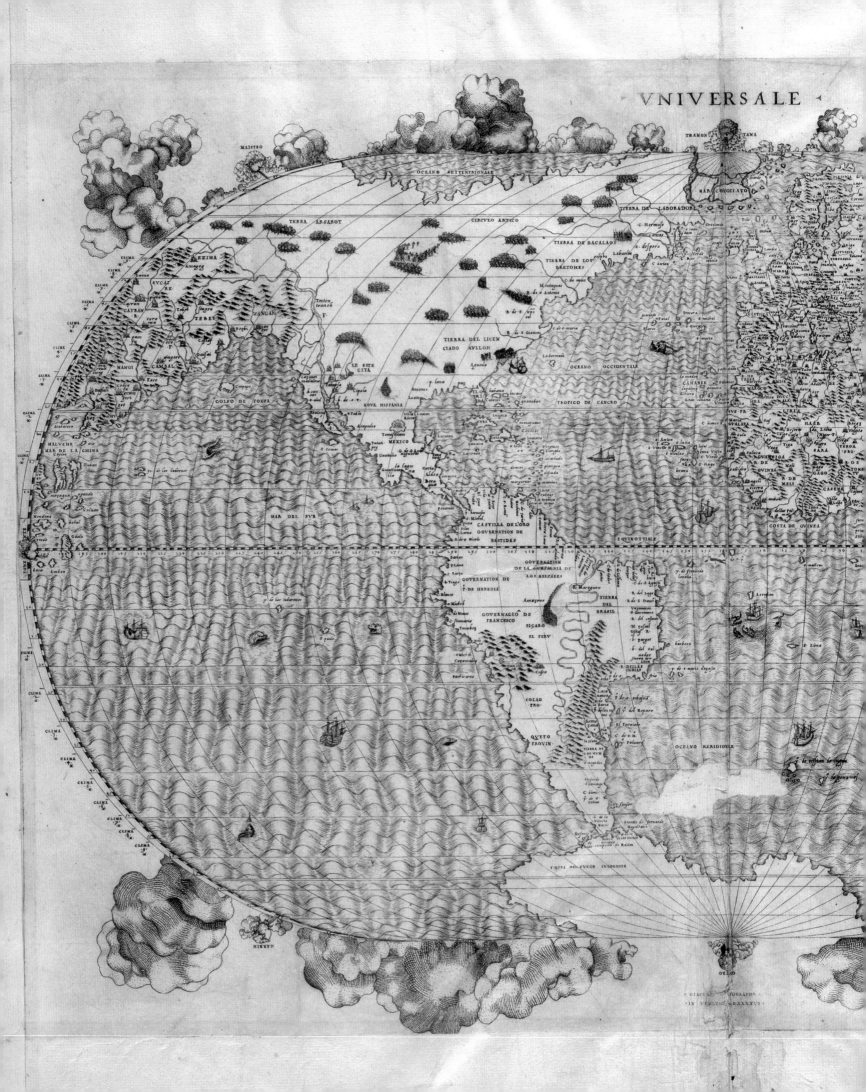

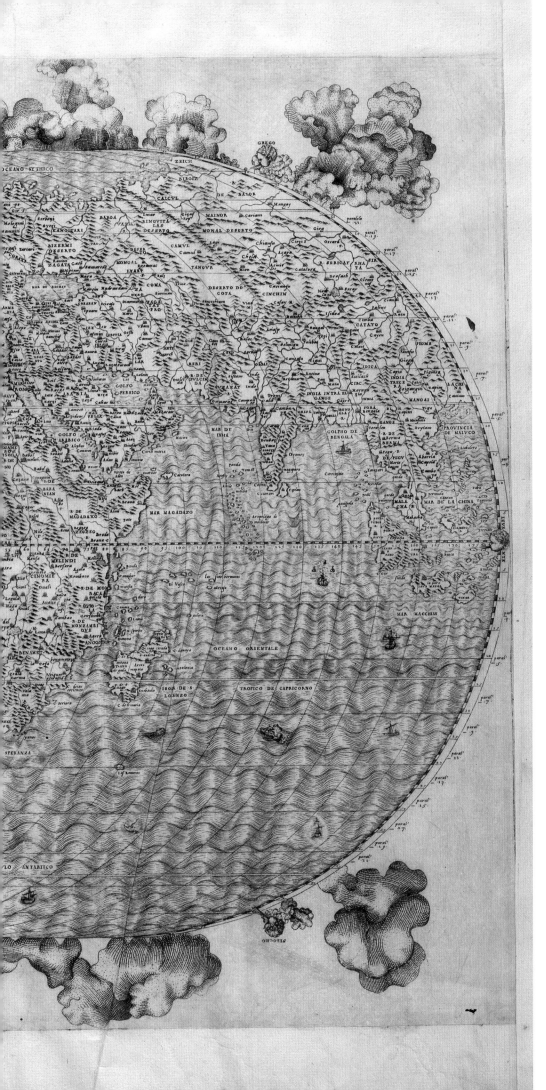

1546

'Universale'

Giacomo Gastaldi
Separate publication,
Venice, 1546.
Copper engraving, 365 x 530 mm

One of the most important cartographers of the mid-sixteenth century was the Piedmontese Giacomo Gastaldi. His skill graced the works like the miniature 1548 Venice edition of Ptolemy and Ramusio's *Raccolta di Navigationi et Viaggi* of 1556.

However, his most important works were the many maps that appear in the Italian composite atlases of the period. These were collections of maps made by different publishers and assembled to the individual requirements of the buyer, so no two examples are the same. Because the composition was so haphazard, some of the maps are now very rare.

This is one such rarity – it is Gastaldi's earliest recorded world map. Although the detail is not as clear as on some of his later, more accomplished, works, it is notable for raising the theory that Asia and America were one landmass, joined in the North Pacific, just north of the Peninsula of California. Other cartographers followed Gastaldi's lead, publishing similar maps even after Gastaldi had revised his opinion and prepared a new map, the first to show the Straits of Anian between Asia and America, published *circa* 1561.

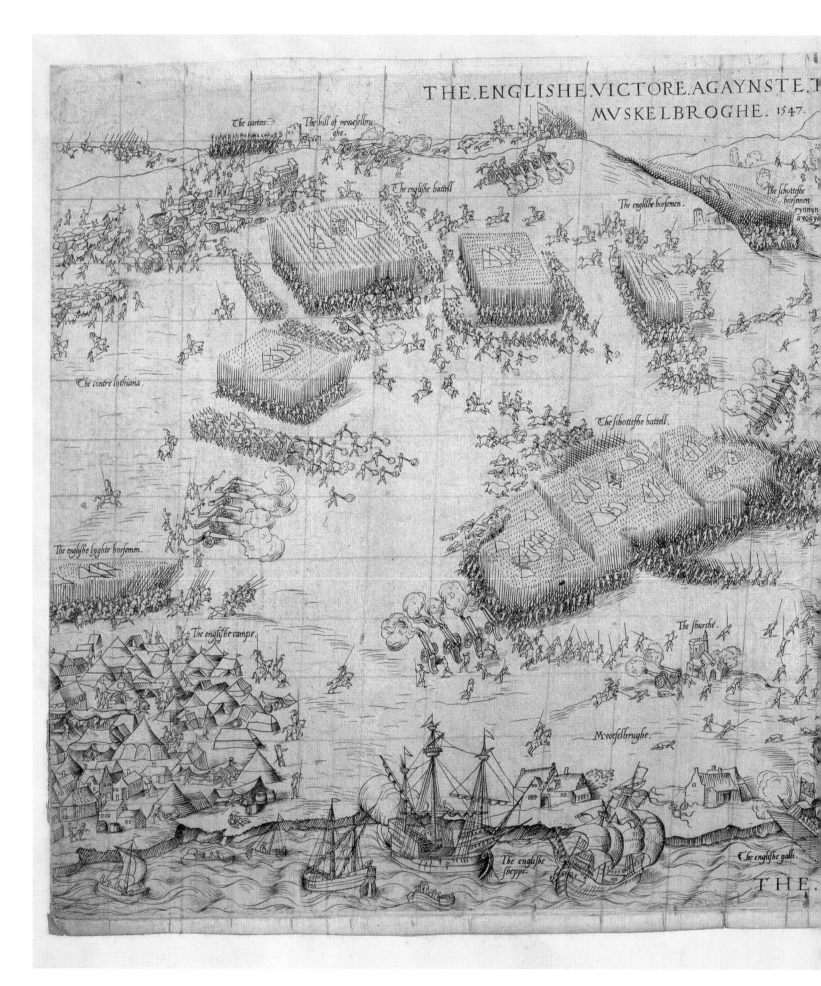

THE.ENGLISHE.VICTORE.AGAYNSTE.T[...]
MVSKELBROGHE. 1547.

The cartes. The hill of mvoeselbrughe. The englishe battell. The englishe horsemen. The schottishe horsemen gynyn a way

The contre lothiana.

The schottishe battell.

The englishe lyghte horsemen.

The englishe campe.

The shurche.

Mvorselbrughe.

The englishe sheype.

The englishe gall.

THE.

22

HOTTES.BY.

The hill.

The abbie of Edenburge

The castel.

Edenburge.

The grene hill.

The englishe campe.

the schottesche campe.

Litte.

SCHOTTES CHE SEE.

c. 1548

'The Englishe Victore agaynste the Schottes by Muskelbroghe. 1547.'

Anonymous
Separate publication,
[Reyner Wolfe, London, 1548].
Engraving, 315 x 505 mm

There is just a single surviving example of what is believed to be the earliest map engraved and printed within the British Isles.

This map/view depicts the battle of Pinkie Cleugh, fought on 10 September 1547 between an English army commanded by Edward, Duke of Somerset, Lord Protector (Regent) of England and the Scots. Somerset's plan was to marry the boy-king Edward VI to Mary Queen of Scots, to seal an alliance between England and Scotland. The Scots were unwilling, so Somerset determined to force the issue and invaded Scotland, winning a decisive military victory near Mussleburgh, outside Edinburgh.

The battle can be regarded as the first modern battle fought in the British Isles, with Somerset bringing to bear infantry, cavalry, artillery and naval bombardment against the Scots' forces.

Although the authorship of this map is uncertain, the engraving is apparently based on a series of manuscript plans of the battle drawn by the Scotsman John Ramsay, with the various stages of the battle combined on this plate. It seems likely that the engraving was specially commissioned by Somerset – he is the only individual named on the map – to commemorate his victory, probably from the King's Printer Reyner Wolfe, an émigré from Gelderland, and engraved by Thomas Geminus, a Flemish engraver also resident in London.

Although Somerset held the field of battle, the Scots sent Mary to France, out of his reach. In light of the failure of his grand strategy, it is plausible that Somerset never circulated this map, hence its rarity today.

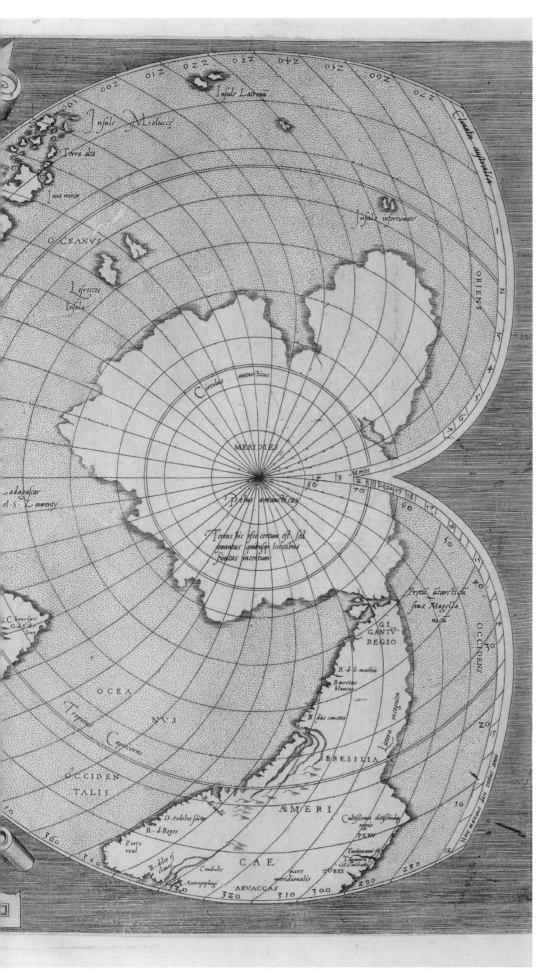

1550

Untitled double-cordiform world map

Antonio Salamanca
Separate publication,
Antonio Laferi, Rome, *c.* 1564.
Copper engraving, 325 x 520 mm

In the mid-sixteenth century, the twin Italian centres of Venice and Rome came to dominate European map-publishing. The most important figure in Venice was Giacomo Gastaldi (see p.21) and in Rome the print-seller and publisher Antonio Lafreri (see also p.27), although there were a large number of other figures active in both centres.

The 1540s saw an increasing number of new maps being published replacing the Ptolemaic corpus, but many of these are best known today through the derivatives of them published in Italy, and some are even otherwise unknown.

This superbly engraved double-cordiform world map is a close copy of a 1538 map by Gerard Mercator, today known in only two extant copies, both in American libraries. In turn, Mercator followed the 1531 woodcut by Oronce Finé, but made considerable improvements. America is now separated from Asia, although it would be almost 150 years before Vitus Bering crossed the Straits that bear his name in 1728.

At the North Pole there is a single landmass connected to Asia, not the group of four islands that Mercator was to depcit in later maps (see p.55 for example). In southern Asia are three promontories: India, the Malay Peninsula and an extra one south of China.

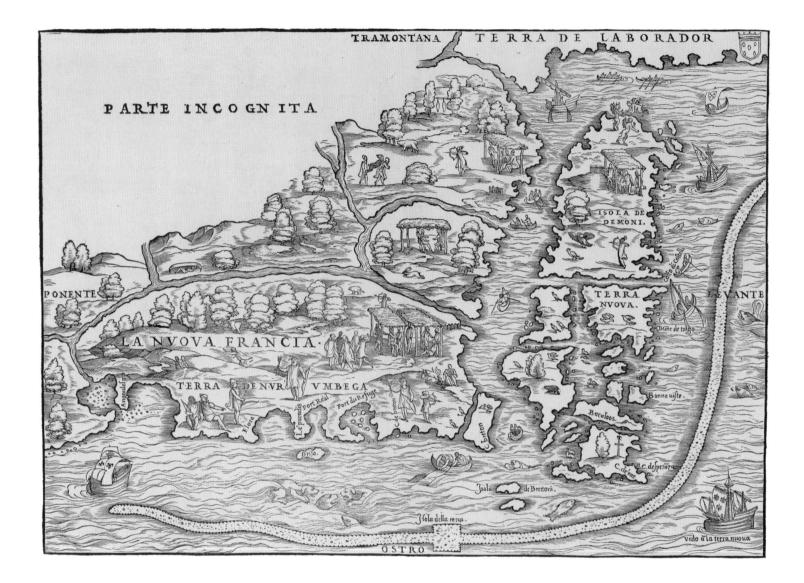

1556

Untitled map of
New England and
maritime Canada

Giovanni Battista Ramusio
From: Ramusio's *Raccolta di
Navigationi et Viaggi*, Venice, 1556.
Woodcut, printed area
280 x 375 mm

The first map devoted to New England and New France was published in 1556, marking the first appearance of the name 'New France' (*La Nuova Francia*). The map was probably designed by the great contemporary cartographer Giacomo Gastaldi, but the woodblock was cut by Matteo Pagano. Although it is based on Gastaldi's map of the region ('Tierra Nueva' from 1548), the larger scale allows better detail. The Hudson River and the St Lawrence are shown as one large loop; the New York area is named 'Angoulesme', with 'Flora' believed to be the south part of Long Island; 'Port Réal' is Newport Bay and 'Port du Refuge' Narragansett Bay. The importance of the

Grand Banks is highlighted by the number of fishing boats decorating the seas around Newfoundland.

This map is an example of the rare printing from the first woodblock, which was destroyed by a fire in the printing house of Tommaso Guinti after only one year's use. The second block, cut in 1565, can be recognized by the addition of the weeping willows along the left hand border. Another enemy of wood attacked this version: when another edition was printed in 1606 the printed surface had been ravaged by woodworm, leaving blank scars across the map.

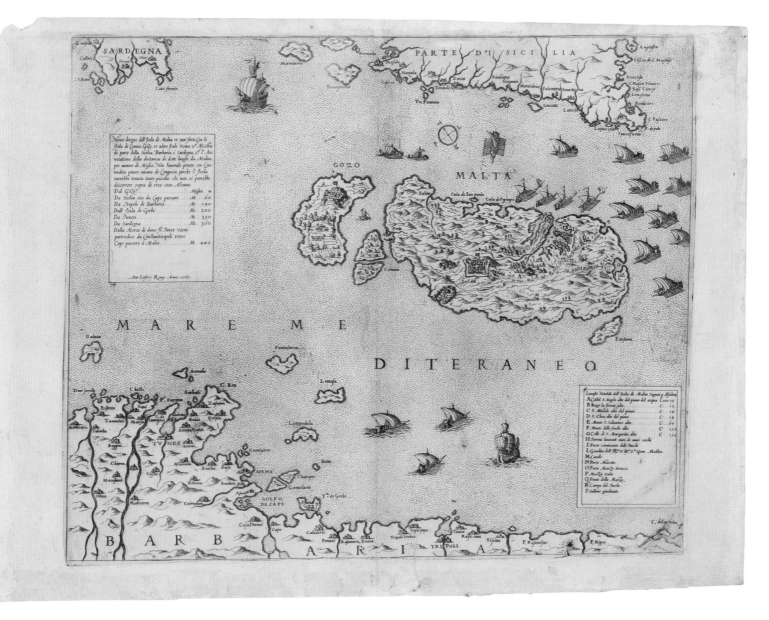

1565

'Nuouo disegno dell'Isola di Malta et suoi forti…'

Antonio Lafreri
Separate publication, Rome, 1565.
Engraving, 370 x 450 mm

The history of the eastern Mediterranean and southern Europe in the sixteenth and seventeenth centuries is dominated by the confrontation between Turk and Christian. The Turks sought to dislodge the Christians, most frequently the Venetians, from their strongholds in the eastern Mediterranean, and to drive up through the underbelly of Europe towards Vienna.

Of the many military confrontations between the rivals, perhaps none caught the contemporary popular imagination like the siege of Malta in 1565, and many contemporary print- and map-sellers rushed to feed the appetite of the public with news-maps depicting the unfolding events of the siege.

This map was published by Antonio Lafreri (properly Antoine Lafrère) who was the largest and most important of the print-sellers in Rome. It is unusual in that it places Malta in its geographical context within the central Mediterranean, but enlarges the island itself out of all proportion to allow a detailed delineation of the island. The map shows the stages of the siege from the initial Turkish landing on the island and the subsequent siege of Valetta.

Engraving a map plate was an expensive business so, when new information became available, publishers such as Lafreri simply engraved the new information onto existing plates; in the case of this map, Lafreri added a depiction of the ships of the Christian fleet sent to relieve the island landing troops on the western coast. This example of the map is apparently the only recorded example of the first state, without the presence of this fleet.

1566

'Cosmographia universalis ab Orontio olim descripta'

Giovanni Paolo Cimerlinus
Separate publication,
Venice, 1566.
Copper engraving, 520 x 580 mm

As noted on p.21, the Italian mapmakers of the sixteenth century copied, and disseminated, many maps printed in other countries that are very rare today. This Italian map, by the Veronese mapmaker Cimerlinus, is a close copy of Oronce Finé single-cordiform woodcut published in Paris in 1534, of which only two surviving examples are known.

The switch from woodcut to copper has allowed Cimerlinus to include far more detail, although this is most apparent in the ornate column borders. One of the angels carries a tablet with the publication line, while the base of the left pillar has a dedication to Henry Fitzalan, Earl of Arundel in England, with his crest on the base of the right pillar.

The map itself has no significant changes from Finé's original, with Asia and America still linked by a land-bridge.

Orontio olim descripta.

29

1570

'Septentrionalium Regionum Descrip.'

Abraham Ortelius
From: Ortelius' *Theatrum Orbis
Terrarum*, Antwerp, 1570–1612.
Copper engraving, 360 x 495 mm

Abraham Ortelius created this map of
northern Europe, showing Scandinavia in
detail, based on the 'Carta Marina' map of
Olaus Magnus, a Swedish historian and
geographer, published in Venice in 1539.
It also shows Greenland and part of North
America. In the North Atlantic, among
decorations which include a merman playing
a lute, are a host of mythical islands,
including Frisland, Estotiland, Icaria, Drogeo,
St Brendan and Brasil. It seems surprising
that Ortelius, who picked his sources carefully,
should have chosen to include them.

Most of the islands are derived from a 1556
book also published in Venice, which
purported to be the true account of the
voyages of the Zeno Brothers, Nicolas and
Antonio, in the 1390s, published by one of
their descendants. Their adventures took
them across the North Atlantic, leapfrogging
from island to island until they landed on
Estotiland. On this map Estotiland appears to
be Labrador: if the Zeno brothers had
reached there they would have made the first
recorded voyage to America. However it is
more likely that the story was a fabrication,
based on existing accounts, in order to claim
those discoveries as theirs.

Also marked is 'Brasil', southwest of
Ireland, which some believe to be Rockall,
a small 25 by 30 m (80 by 100 ft) wide, 20 m
(70 ft) high rock; and St Brendan, on which
the Irish monk that gave the island its name
landed in the sixth century. In his *Geography*
of 1130, Honorius of Atun called it the Lost
Isle, writing:

'There is in the Ocean a certain isle
agreeable and fertile above all others,
unknown to men but discovered by chance
and then sought for without anyone being
able to find it again and so called the "Lost
Isle." It was, so they say, the island whither
once upon a time St Brandan came.'

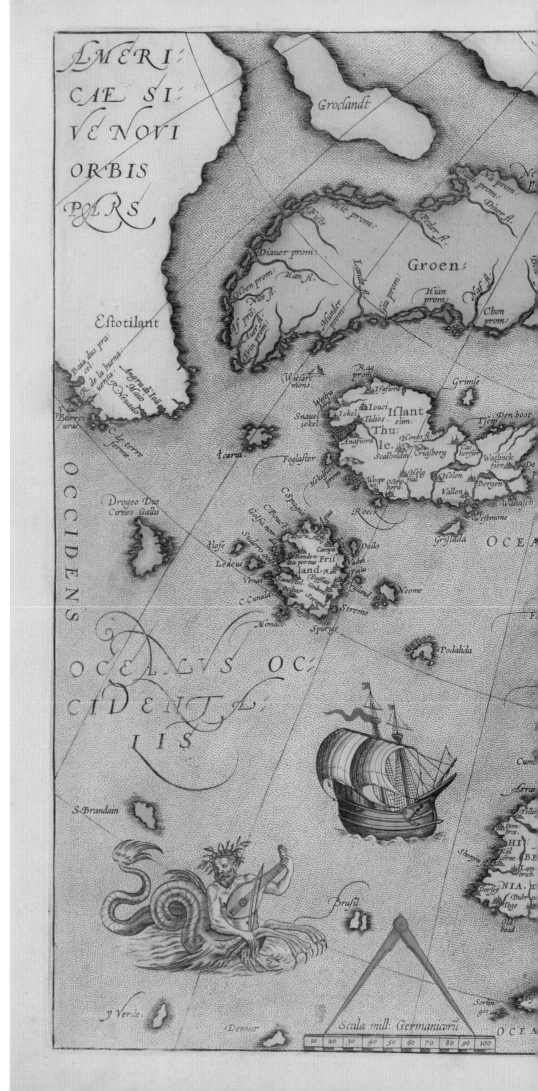

SEPTENTRIO

Parall: 80. gradus lat:

Pigmei *hic habitant.*

MARE CON-
GELATVM
Petzorke *vulgo*

Colgoieue
Pechora
Permia
Piesza fl.
Wolstick
Camenkh
Stanuwische
Condora
Apmi
Canlonscho
Stanckwische
C.S. Ioäis
Lampas
Slowoda
Mezen
Mezen fl.
Morzouecz
C. bone fortune
P. Penticost
Zolotizza
Foxinos
Polda
S.Michel
Pinego
Kouloai
Nicolai

S.Thome
cenobium

Margas-
ter

OCEANVS HYPER
BOREVS.

Biarmia
Tetreue
Diaun fl.
Colmogro
Pinego fl.

Santi
Rustene

Motka
prom.

Semes saxum
& prom: nau-
tis formida-
bile.

Sericfinnia.

Berge
Scarsigur
Norden
borg
Owna
S.Nicolas

Lacus Albus
Varziga fl.
Onega fl.

RVSSIA.

Caienska
semla
Pele
Olsbi

Kegory
Kildma
Pola fl.
Warbus
Swentinos
prom.

Caribdis

Helsin
gabri
Chalir
Lacastri
Pirki
Perna
Vista
Varta
Trofel
Vista

Kielanga
Varm
Loiru
Igma

Nisiot

OCEANVS GER-
MANI-
CVS.

Wardbuys

Vildal

Domschaf

BOD-
Vero DIA.
Persom

Nesbis
Vero
Nerbis

Iegobor
Onegaborg
Kexholm

Lapauesi
Kiuaneh
Ecclesia noua
Corela

Finlandt.

Parall: 60. grad latitud

Pirki
Kauanc

Kebela
Pskoue
Nouogrod

Lodoga

ORIENS.

Femo
Scetlant
ini

Orcades
Feril

SVEDIA.

Liuoniae
pars.

Riga
Deblin
Curuia
Vskil

Marienborch

Wolmar

OCEANVS GER-
MANI-
CVS.

GIA

DA

Bornholm
Oolsee.

Prussiae
pars.

Memmel
Ragnet
Coningsberg

SEP
TEN
TRI
ONA

Pomeraniae
pars.

ANNICVS

Ger
maniae
pars.

Cum priuilegio

MERIDIES.

LIVM RE
GIONVM
DESCRIP.

VENETIA.

CANAL DE LA GIUDECA,

LA GIUDECA

PIAZZA DE S. MARCO DI VENETIA

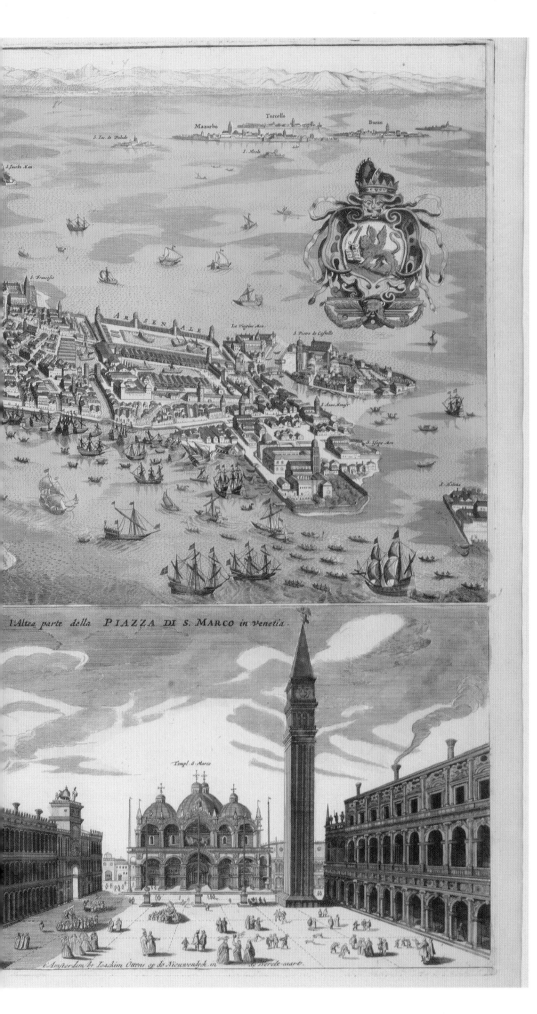

l'Altea parte della PIAZZA DI S. MARCO in Venetia.

1572

'Venetia'

Georg Braun & Frans Hogenberg
From: Braun & Hogenberg's
Civitates Orbis Terrarum,
Cologne, 1572.
Copper engraving, 270 x 475 mm

Venice is detailed in this map, as viewed from the south, with its important buildings shown in profile, and named in a 153-point key under the map. In the inset is a depiction of the Doge, the ruler of Venice, with his entourage.

Braun and Hogenberg's *Civitates Orbis Terrarum* was the first systematic book of city plans. The first volume was published in 1572; the sixth and final volume came out in 1618. Georg Braun was the editor of the text, and Frans Hogenberg compiled and engraved the plans. Even though the *Civitates* was published in Cologne in Germany, it was considered a 'sister' publication to the Ortelius atlas, the *Theatrum Orbis Terrarum*, published in Antwerp: Hogenberg engraved a large number of the maps in the *Theatrum*.

The conventions of mapping cities had not yet developed, so the 546 cities are shown variously as prospects, bird's-eye views and stylized map-views as well as in plan format. Many of the early plates also had figures in local dress placed in the foreground: not only was this supposed to be informative, but also, according to Braun, necessary for national security. In his introduction to Book I, he stated that he believed that 'his plans would not in consequence be scrutinized for military secrets by the Turks, as their religion forbade them from looking on representations of the human form'.

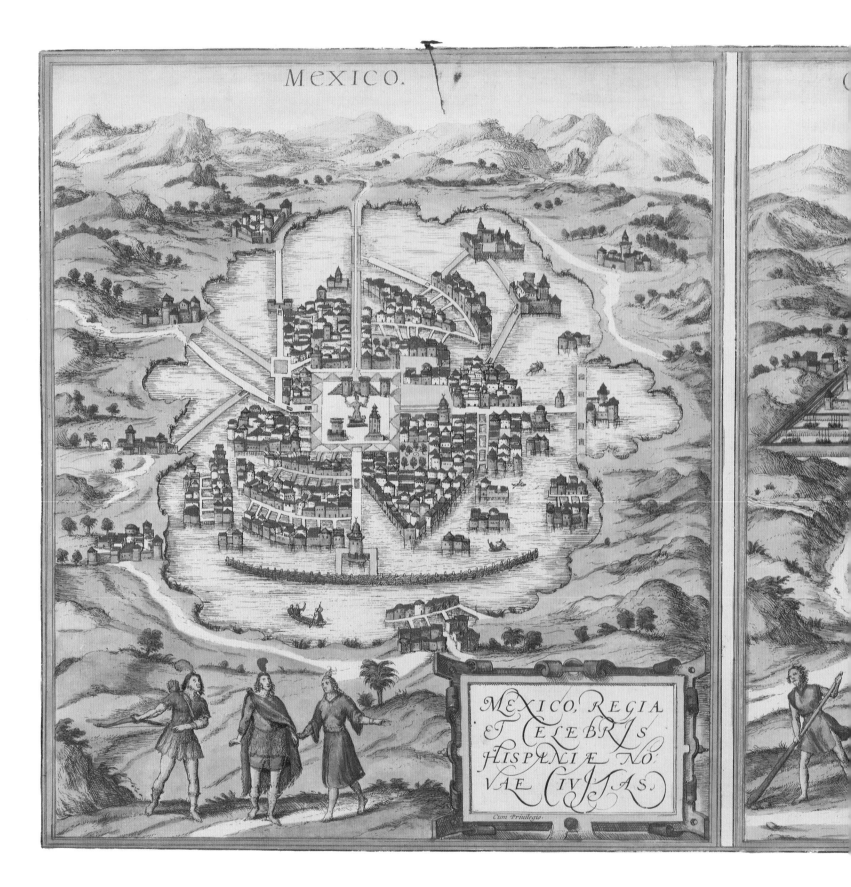

MEXICO.

MEXICO, REGIA ET CELEBRIS HISPANIÆ NOVAE CIVITAS.

Cum Priuilegio.

1572

'Mexico, Regia et Celebris Hispaniæ Novae Civitas' [&] 'Cusco, Regni Peru in Novo Orbe Caput'

Georg Braun & Frans Hogenberg
From: Braun & Hogenberg's *Civitates Orbis Terrarum*, Cologne, 1572.
Copper engraving, each image *c.* 270 x 475 mm

Two early map-views on one sheet, this is the only plate in the Civitates Orbis Terrarum to show cities in America.

On the left is Mexico City, which had been the Aztec capital Tenochtitlan: some of the Spanish Conquistadores, who had seen the European cities of Venice and Constantinople, said that it was as large and fine a city as any they had seen. However, when it was captured by Hernán Cortés in 1521 much of the city was destroyed, and the Mexico City of the Spanish built over the ruins.

On the right is Cusco, the capital city of the Incas in Peru, captured by Francisco Pizarro in 1533. Again the sheer size impressed the invaders. Pizarro's officers wrote to King Charles V of Spain:

'This city is the greatest and the finest ever seen in this country or anywhere in the Indies… We can assure your Majesty that it is so beautiful and has such fine buildings that it would be remarkable even in Spain.'

In the foreground of each image are depictions of Aztec and Inca figures, probably the defeated leaders of the two races, Montezuma and Atahuallpa.

1576

'Promontorium hoc in Mare proiectum Cornubia dicitur'

Christopher Saxton
From: Saxton's untitled atlas of England and Wales.
Engraving, 370 x 490 mm

Christopher Saxton was the first to publish an atlas of the English and Welsh counties, the maps engraved between 1574 and 1579, when they were assembled and sold as an atlas.

Although he is known as 'the father of English cartography', little is known of his background and early life. It seems likely that he learned surveying and draughtsmanship as an assistant to a local vicar, John Rudd who, in the 1560s, travelled through England carrying out survey of the county.

Saxton's survey, while ostensibly a private project, was sponsored by the inner circle of the government of Elizabeth I, under the supervision of Lord Burghley, her Chief Minister. There were many reasons why the Crown was interested in accurate surveys of England. The Protestant Crown was threatened by Catholic enemies both at home and abroad. Furthermore, with the Protestant Reformation in England, large amounts of land had been seized from the Catholic Church and been granted to friends of the Crown, forming power bases that could protect or threaten the Crown, and Burghley was clearly anxious to identify the threat, as the copious annotations on his personal copy of the atlas, now in the British Library, attest.

If the maps were a tool of government, they were also a propaganda tool; the dedication to the queen, the lavish decoration found on each map, give a sense of unity, unity under the Crown, at a time when threat of civil war, which had scarred the history of England in the previous century, was never far away.

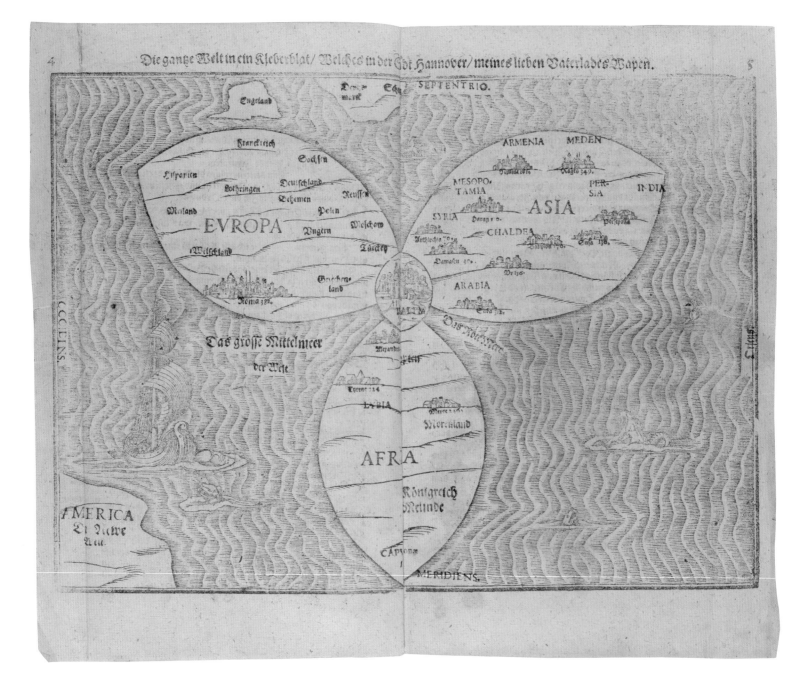

1581

'Die Ganze Welt in ein Kleberblat…'

Heinrich Bünting

From: Bünting's *Itinerarium Sacrae Scripturae*, Darmstadt, 1581.
Woodcut, 260 x 360 mm

Bünting's symbolic map of the world has the three continents of the old world depicted as a clover leaf. Bünting's use of a clover leaf may have been influenced by the fact that it was the civic symbol of his home city, Hamburg. His book was a retelling of the Bible as a travel account, so it is not surprising that he placed Jerusalem at the centre of the world. Bünting did include lands off the clover leaf: in the north are England and Scandinavia, and in the bottom left, America.

The book contained two other curiosity maps: Europe depicted as a maiden, and Asia depicted as Pegasus, the winged horse, which we will be discussing next. The *Itinerarium* proved a popular work, and was frequently reprinted over the next 70 years.

MERIDIES.

Iesus Christus magnus ille Beller opontes, omnium malorum occisor ascendens Pegasum, hoc est, in Asia fontem doctrinæ aperies Solimos vicit, & chimæram interfecit horibile monstrum quod flammas evomens caput & pectus Leonis habuit, ventrem autem Capræ, & caudam Draconis, hoc est, Superavit ac interfecit filius antiquum Draconem Diabolum, sublato peccato morte ac inferno.

1581

'Asia Secunda Pars Terræ in Forma Pegasir'

Heinrich Bünting
From: Bünting's *Itinerarium Sacrae Scripturae*, Darmstadt, 1581.
Woodcut, 280 x 370 mm

One of the more dramatic curiosity maps is Bünting's map of Asia, depicted in the form of Pegasus, the winged horse of Greek mythology. He sprang from the body of the Gorgon Medusa when Perseus cut her head off. He was tamed by Bellerophon with the assistance of the goddess Athena, and featured in a number of Bellerophon's exploits, most particularly when Bellerophon provoked the anger of the gods by trying to ride Pegasus up to Heaven.

Pegasus' head is represented by Turkey and his wings Tartary; the forelegs are Arabia and the saddle blanket Persia; the right hind leg is India and the left the Malay Peninsula.

It is interesting that despite the *Itinerarium* being about the Bible, the symbolism of classical mythology was still considered appropriate for this map.

1583

'Universe Europe maritime eiusq navigationus descriptio. Generale Paschaerte van Europa…'

Lucas Jansz. Waghenaer
From: Waghenaer's *Spieghel der Zeevaerdt, vande nauigatie der Westersche Zee*, Leiden, 1584.
Copper engraving, 400 x 555 mm

Lucas Jansz. Waghenaer was a Dutch sea-pilot based in the thriving fishing port of Enkhuisen. In about 1579 he retired from the sea, and became chief excise collector for the port. It was about this time that he began work on his great pilot book of the waters of northern Europe, the *Spieghel der Zeevaerdt*…

The first volume was published in 1584, and the second in 1585. In total the *Spieghel* contained 46 charts: 45 detailed coastal charts, preceded by this fine portolano chart of Western Europe, dated 1583, although the chart may actually have been ready as early as 1579 or 1580.

The *Spieghel* was a lavish and prestigious production; although a functional navigational tool, the fine engraving would have made the book an expensive purchase for a seaman, and most examples were probably consulted only in noble and merchant libraries. Certainly the preparation of the *Spieghel* placed a heavy burden on Waghenaer's purse; indeed, to ease his financial pressures he embezzled money from the excise revenues he received. Surprisingly, although detected and dismissed in 1582, the incident does not seem to have harmed his standing – his finances were another matter however – and by dint of his contacts Waghenaer was able to see the *Spieghel* thorough the press, thus securing his financial future.

1583

'Chinae, olim Sinarum
regionis, nova descriptio.
auctore Ludovico Georgio'

Abraham Ortelius
From: Ortelius' *Theatrum Orbis
Terrarum*, Antwerp, 1584 onwards.
Copperplate engraving,
370 x 470 mm

The first map of China to appear in a
European atlas was this copperplate
engraving by Ortelius. Based on a manuscript
map by Jorge de Barbuda, also known as
Ludovicus Georgius, it remained the standard
view of China for nearly a century.

Oriented with north to the right, there are
cartouches for the title, scale and privilege;
while within the map are elephants, Tartar
tents and and even some land-yachts. The
Great Wall of China is shown prominently,
but much of the interior, including the
network of waterways, is pure conjecture.
Japan, which is rather mis-shapen, has an
extra landmass to the east, although its
further reaches are hidden by the
scale cartouche.

The Philippines appear, but with little
accuracy or detail; they were not even named
until *circa* 1588, when a revised edition of the
map – its second state – was published.

At about the same time this map was being
published, the Jesuit missionaries began to
arrive in China. As part of their work, they
gathered more accurate information about
the country, its customs, its science and so on,
but it was only in 1655 that Johannes Blaeu
published the first atlas of China,
based on the maps of one of their number,
Martino Martini.

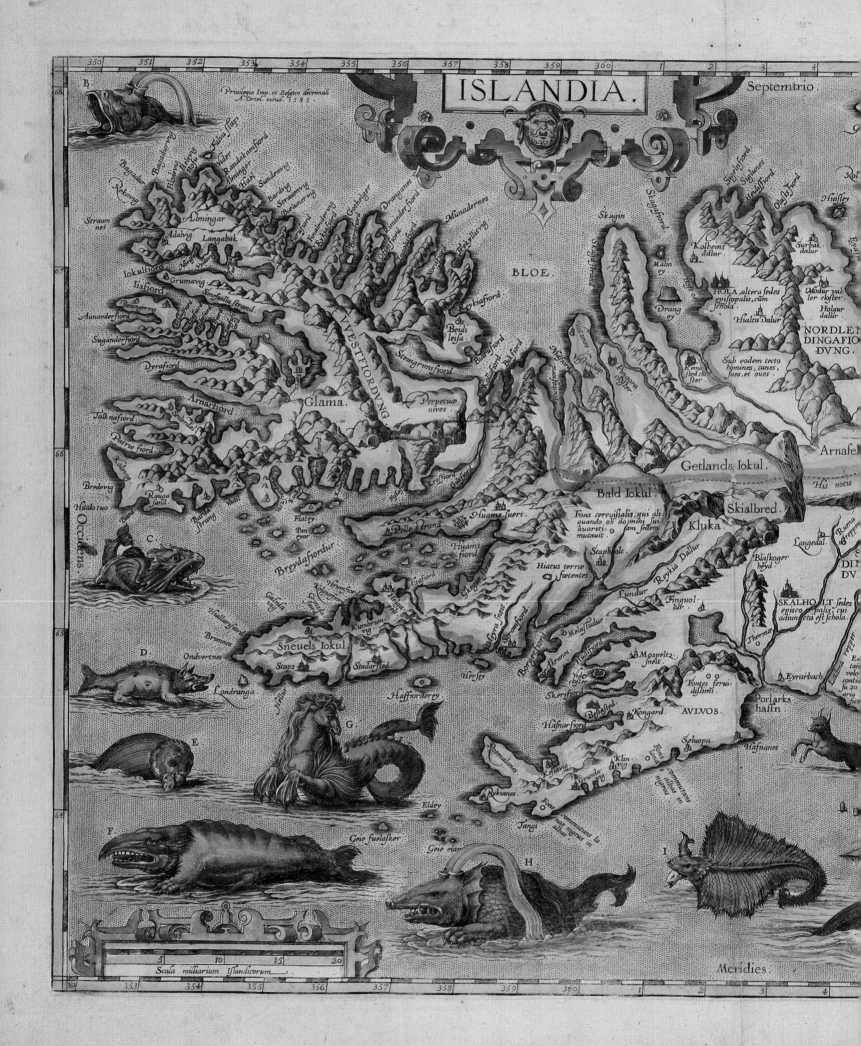

ISLANDIA.

Septemtrio.

Praeuilegio Imp. et Belgico decennali
A. Ortel. excud. 1585

Meridies.

Scala milliarium Islandicorum.

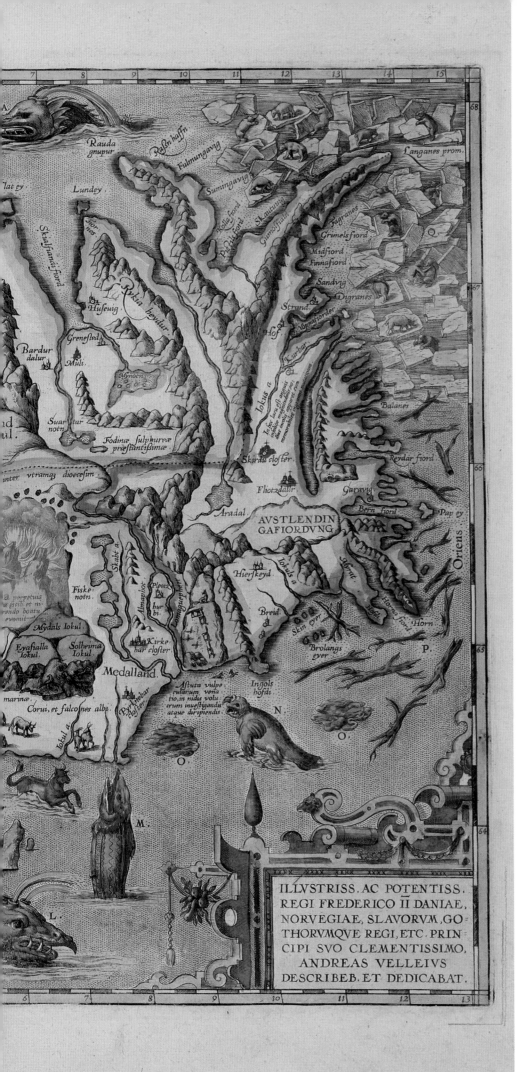

'Islandia'

Abraham Ortelius
From: Ortelius' *Theatrum Orbis
Terrarum*, Antwerp, 1587 onwards.
Copper engraving 390 x 490 mm

One of the more outlandish, and most sought-after of Ortelius' maps is this engraving of Iceland. Apart from the depiction of Hekla, the island's most active volcano, there are 13 sea monsters, many taken from the 'Carta Marina', a map of Scandinavia by Olaus Magnus published in 1539. Each is marked with a letter, referring to a key on the reverse. Rough translations of some of the more entertaining descriptions read:

A is a fish, commonly called NAHVAL. If anyone eats of this fish, he will die immediately. It has a tooth in the front part of its head standing out seven cubits [over 3 m or 11 ft]. Some have sold it as the Unicorn's horn. It is thought to be a good antidote and powerful medicine against poison.

G. HROSHUALUR, that is to say as much as Sea horse, with manes hanging down from its neck like a horse. It often causes great hurt and scare to fishermen.

H. The largest kind of Whale, which seldom shows itself. It is more like a small island than like a fish. It cannot follow or chase smaller fish because of its huge size and the weight of its body, yet it preys on many, which it catches by natural cunning and subtlety which it applies to get its food.

L. STEIPEREIDUR, a most gentle and tame kind of whale, which for the defence of fishermen fights against other kinds of whales. It is forbidden by Proclamation that any man should kill or hurt this kind of Whale. It has a length of at least 100 cubits [50 m or 160 ft].

M. STAUKUL. The Dutch call it Springual. It has been observed to stand for a whole day long upright on its tail. It derives its name from its leaping or skipping. It is a very dangerous enemy of seamen and fishermen, and greedily goes after human flesh.

There is also a description of the polar ice:

Q. Huge and marvellously big heaps of ice, brought here by the tide from the frozen sea, making loud and terrible noises. Some pieces are often as high as forty cubits [20 m or 65 ft]. On some of these, white bears sit together, watching the innocent fish play about in exercise.

1589

'Maris Pacifici, (quod vulgò Mar del Zur) cum regionibus circumiacentibus…'

Abraham Ortelius
From: Ortelius' *Theatrum Orbis Terrarum*, Antwerp, 1589 onwards. Copper engraving 345 x 495 mm

The first map of the Pacific Ocean was primarily based on information from the voyage of Ferdinand Magellan. Setting out with five ships in 1519, he successfully passed through the Straits of Magellan in South America, entering the Pacific, the first time this had been done from the east. He then crossed the ocean, only to get killed in the Philippines. His crew continued west, and in 1522, the sole surviving ship, the *Victoria*, became the first to successfully circumnavigate the world. This is commemorated with a large vignette of the ship, with couplets, in the southern Pacific.

It is interesting that California is shown as a peninsula, predating the misconception that it was an island by 25 years. Magellan's route through the straits that bear his name is marked, with Tierra del Fuego, the southernmost part of South America, shown as part of the huge 'Terra Australis', or the Great Southern Continent. It was not until 1617 that Cape Horn was discovered to be an island, with a vast waterway to the south, and 1820 before anyone went the extra 650 km (400 miles) to Antarctica.

Further north are a huge island of New Guinea and an unrecognizable Japan; Ortelius published a far more accurate map of Japan in 1592, supplied by Luis Teixeira, a Portuguese cartographer.

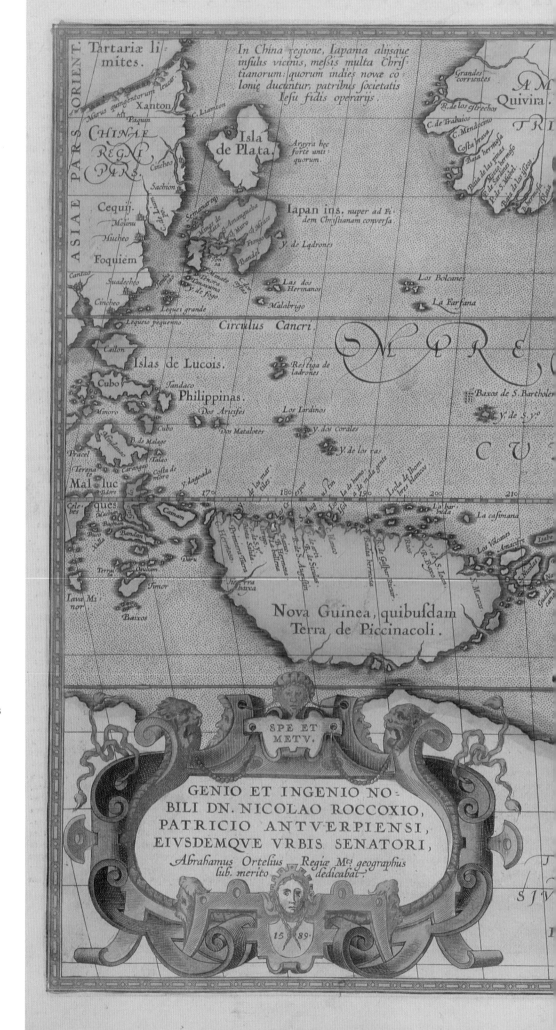

MARIS PACIFICI,

(quod vulgò Mar del Zur)
cum regionibus circumiacentibus, insulisque in eodem
passim sparsis, novissima descriptio.

SEPTEMTRIO

SEPTEM=

OR PARS.

Florida.

MARIS ATLANTICI,

SIVE MAR DEL NORT

Bermuda

Cali=
formia.

Mar Ver=
mejo

Noua Hispania

Messico.

Cuba   Spagnola   PARS.

CIFI=

QVOD   VVLGO

Jamaica   S. Ioan

La Trinidad

Rocca partida

Cartagena

Caribana.

Y. de Cocos

Quito.

Y. de Galopagos

230   240   250   260   270   28   29   300   310   320   330

Circulus Aequinoctialis.

AMERICAE

NOMI=NANT

MERIDIONA=

Peru.

LIOR PARS.

Charcas.

Los Tuberones

S. Petri

C. de Fortuna

Chili.

MAR

DEL

Prima ego velivolis ambivi cursibus Orbem,
Magellane novo te duce ducta freto.
Ambivi, meritoq; vocor VICTORIA: sunt mi
Vela, alæ; precium, gloria, pugna, mare.

ZVR.

Patagones.

AVSTRALIS,

GELLANICA, NON=

Archipe
lagus in
sularum.

Mar
del Nort.

DETECTA.

Cum privilegijs Imp. & Reg. Maiestatum,
nec non Cancellariæ Brabantiæ, ad decennium.

Fretum Magella
nicum

MERIDIES.

Tierra del Fuego.

1590

'Tabula Geographica,
in qua omnes Regiones,
Urbes, Oppida, et Loca
Describuntur, quorum
mentio sit in Actis et
Epistolis Apostolorum,
et Apocalypsi…'

Petrus Plancius
From: [a Dutch Bible,
Amsterdam, 1590].
Copper engraving, 290 x 370 mm

After the beginning of the Protestant
Reformation, it became important for the
new reformed religion to have Bibles for the
use of their congregation and for
encouraging converts, reflecting their stance
on the biblical texts. The Protestant
reformers emphasized the literal sense of the
scriptures, and wanted to encourage an
understanding of the historical context of
biblical events. Consequently, a suite of maps
was frequently felt to be an important part of
the biblical story, and many editions of the
Protestant Bibles contained maps, some
single maps of the Holy Land, or of the
Exodus, extending up to a set of maps
including: the Garden of Eden, the Exodus, a
map of Canaan marking the tribes, the Holy
Land, a plan of Jerusalem and a map of the
travels of the Apostles.

In 1590, Petrus Plancius, a theologian and
also the leading cartographer in the Dutch
Republic, drew a series of such maps for a
Dutch Bible, including this fine map designed
to illustrate the Acts of the Apostles, and the
Books of Letters, with 15 biblical vignettes
surrounding the map.

Plancius's maps, this one engraved by
Baptista van Deutecum, are considered the
finest of all Bible maps.

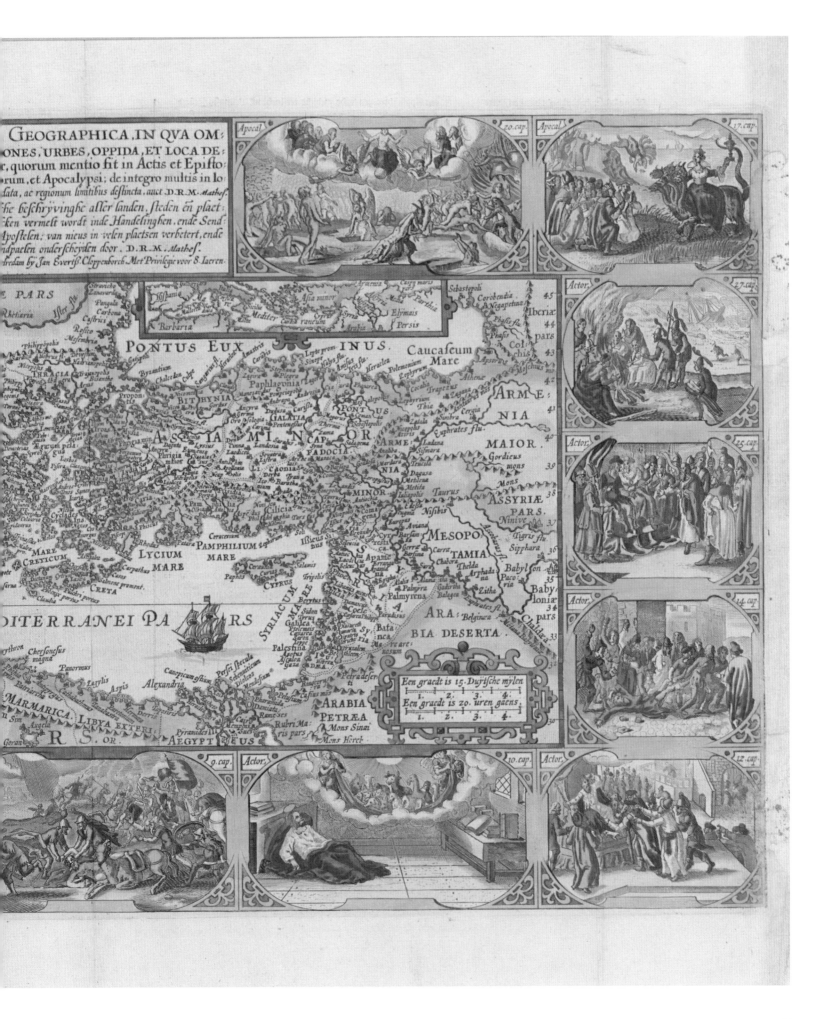

47

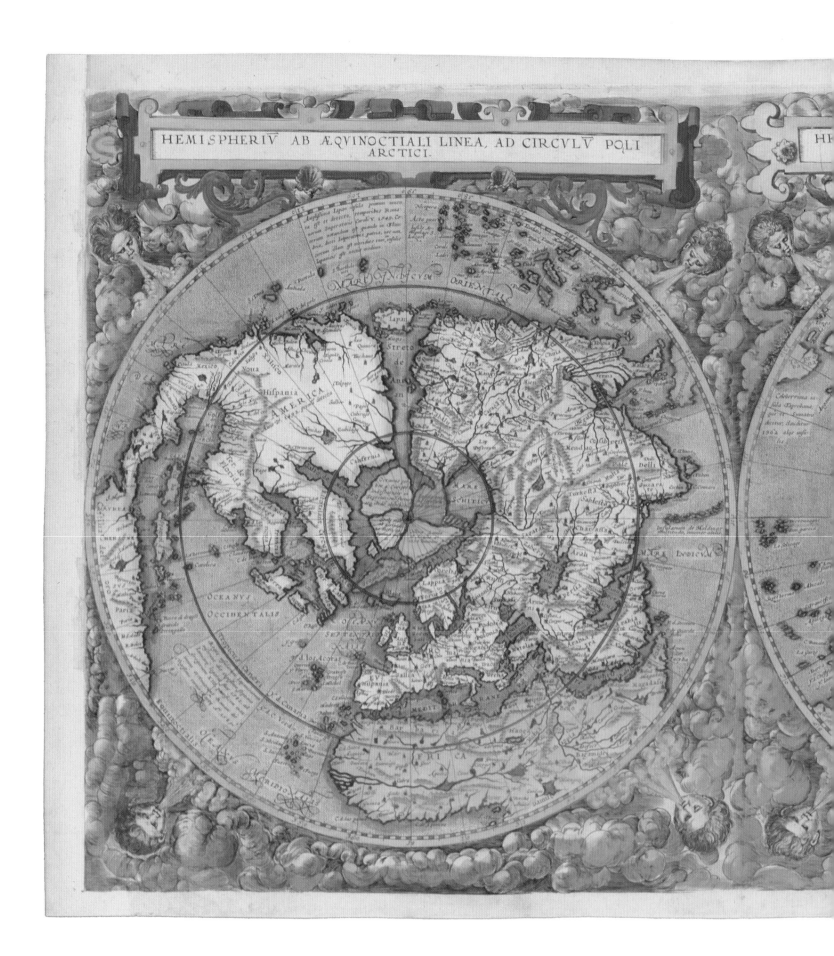

IV AB ÆQVINOCTIALI LINEA, AD CIRCVLV POLI Ā: TARCTICI.

1593

'Hemispheriu Ab Aequinoctali Linea, Ad Circulu Poli Arctici… Ad Circulu Poli A[n]tarctici'

Cornelis de Jode
From: de Jode's *Speculum Orbis Terræ*, Antwerp, 1593.
Copper engraving, 320 x 520 mm

De Jode's fine double-hemisphere world map is unusual for showing the world from the perspective of the poles rather than the equator. A notable feature of the map, in the north, is the depiction of the Arctic favoured by Mercator, although one of the islands is joined to Asia, while Japan is shown closer to California than Asia. In the Southern hemisphere there is a large Terra Australis, divided from South America by the Straits of Magellan.

Gerard de Jode, father of Cornelis, had attempted to produce an atlas to compete with the *Theatrum* of Abraham Ortelius. However, unlike the good relations between Gerard Mercator and Ortelius there appears to have been some bad blood between de Jode and Ortelius, and the latter is known to have used his influence to delay the publication of the *Speculum*. When the atlas appeared in 1578 it was not a success, as the *Theatrum* had already established a dominant market position.

Gerard de Jode's widow and son Cornelis published the second, posthumous edition of the atlas, in which this map appeared, with a number of new maps by the father and son inserted. It was also to be the last edition. It seems not to have been successful and, after Cornelis' death in 1600, the plates were bought by Jan Baptist Vrients, then the owner of the Ortelius plates, merely to stop their reissue and they never reappeared.

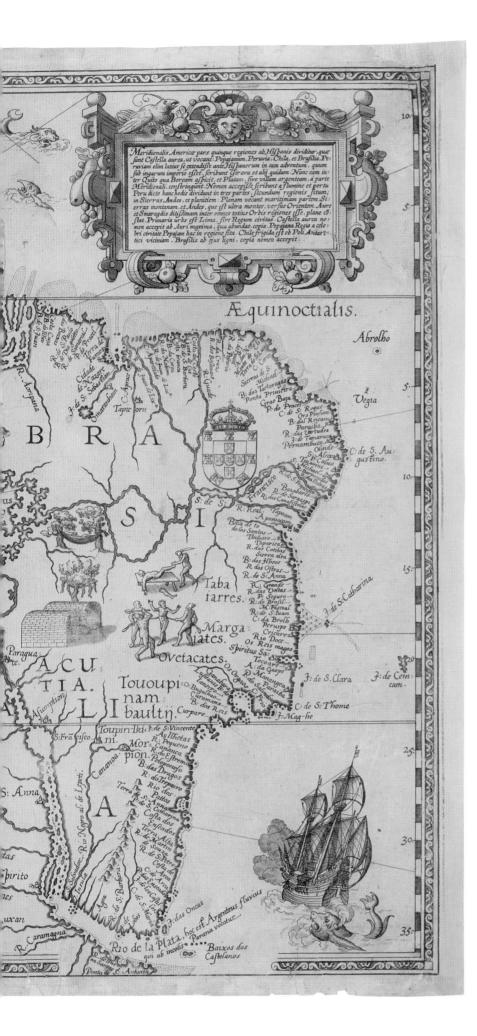

c. 1595

'Meridionalis Americae pars quinque regiones ab Hispanis dividitur…'

Petrus Plancius
Separate publication, [Cornelis Claesz, Amsterdam, 1594].
Copper engraving, 395 x 555 mm

Petrus Plancius was the leading Dutch geographer and cartographer active at the end of the sixteenth century, a status recognized by his appointment as Cartographer to the Dutch East India Company.

In that role Plancius had access to the assembled cartographic materials of the Dutch Republic, much of it in manuscript; then, through his association with Cornelis Claesz, the leading cartographic publisher in Amsterdam, was able to see many of his maps into print. Unfortunately, the majority of Plancius's maps were sold separately, and have had a very high mortality rate, hence their rarity today.

This important map of northern South America is indicative of the high quality of Plancius's output; the engraving, by Jan van Deutecum, is also of a high standard. Typical also of contemporary tastes is the reluctance to leave blank areas within the map, whether on land or sea, and almost every inch of the map has been used. For the interior of South America, where geographical knowledge was extremely limited, Plancius has included many drawings of South American natives, cannibal scenes, and a fine plan of Cusco, albeit composed to a European preconception of what the city should look like.

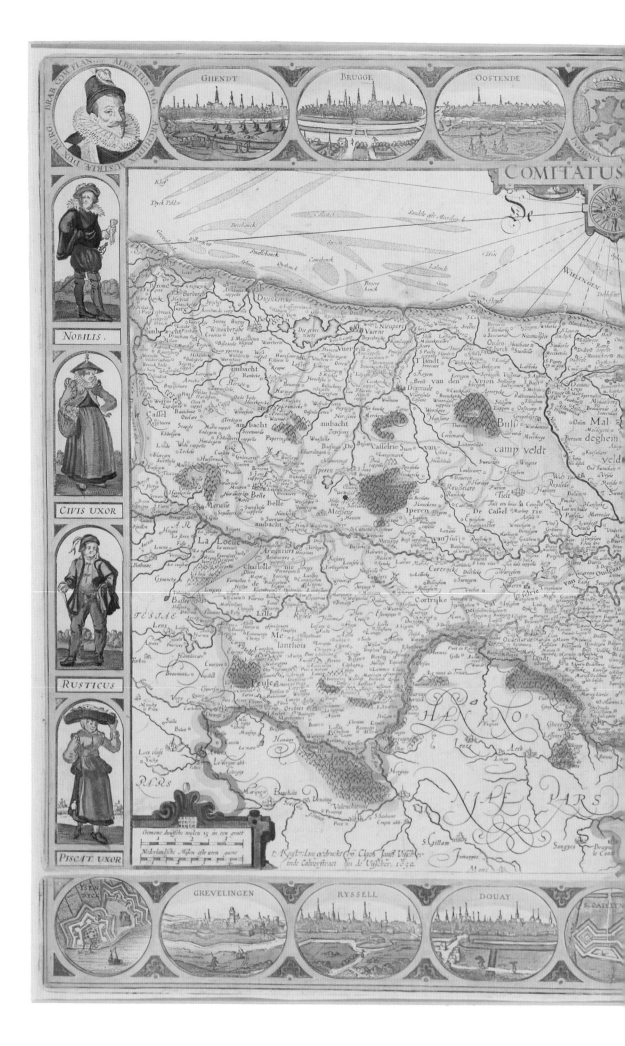

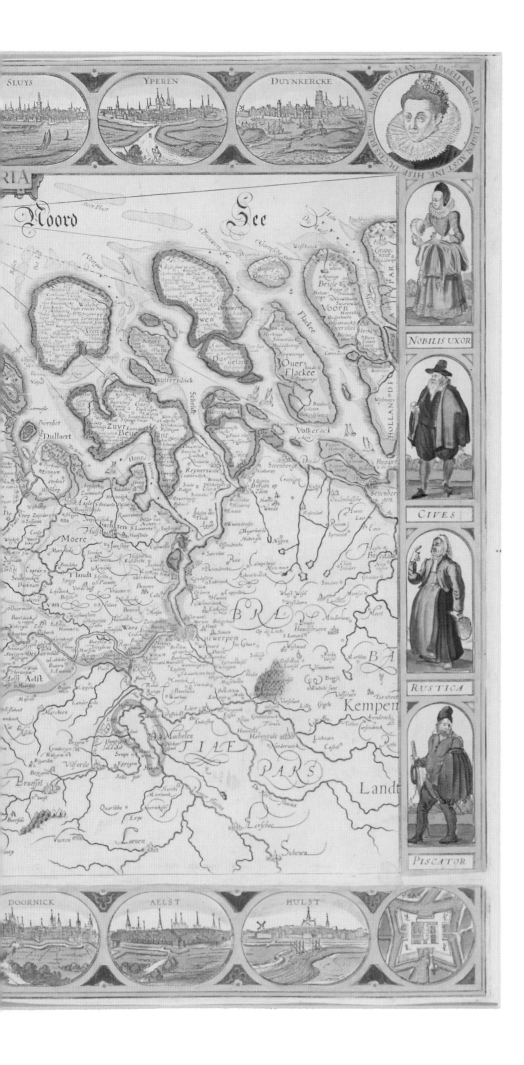

c. 1595

'Comitatus Flandria'

Arnold & Hendrick Florenz.
van Langren
Separate publication,
Claes Jansz. Visscher, 1634.
Copper engraving, 410 x 560 mm

The seventeenth century was a golden age in Dutch cartography. The fight for independence from Spain and the new wealth flowing into Amsterdam from the voyages of discovery mounted by Dutch mariners proved a powerful stimulus to mapmaking.

A particular feature of Dutch maps in the early part of the century was the panelled borders, so-called '*cartes à figures*', from the sides panels of costume figures frequently encountered. Rival publishers vied with each other to make their maps not only more accurate and up-to-date, but more elaborate and more aesthetically appealing, and these *cartes à figures* are visually amongst the finest maps ever made.

Claes Jansz. Visscher was one of the leading proponents of this genre, publishing maps of the world, the four continents, any of the countries of Europe and the provinces of the Low Countries with panelled borders. This map of Flanders was first published by Arnold and Hendrick Florenz. van Langren, *circa* 1595. After his acquisition of the plate, Visscher had the map re-engraved, replacing the outlying geographical detail with the side panels, which include finely etched views of the principal Flanders cities, including Ghent, Bruges, Ostend and Dunkirk.

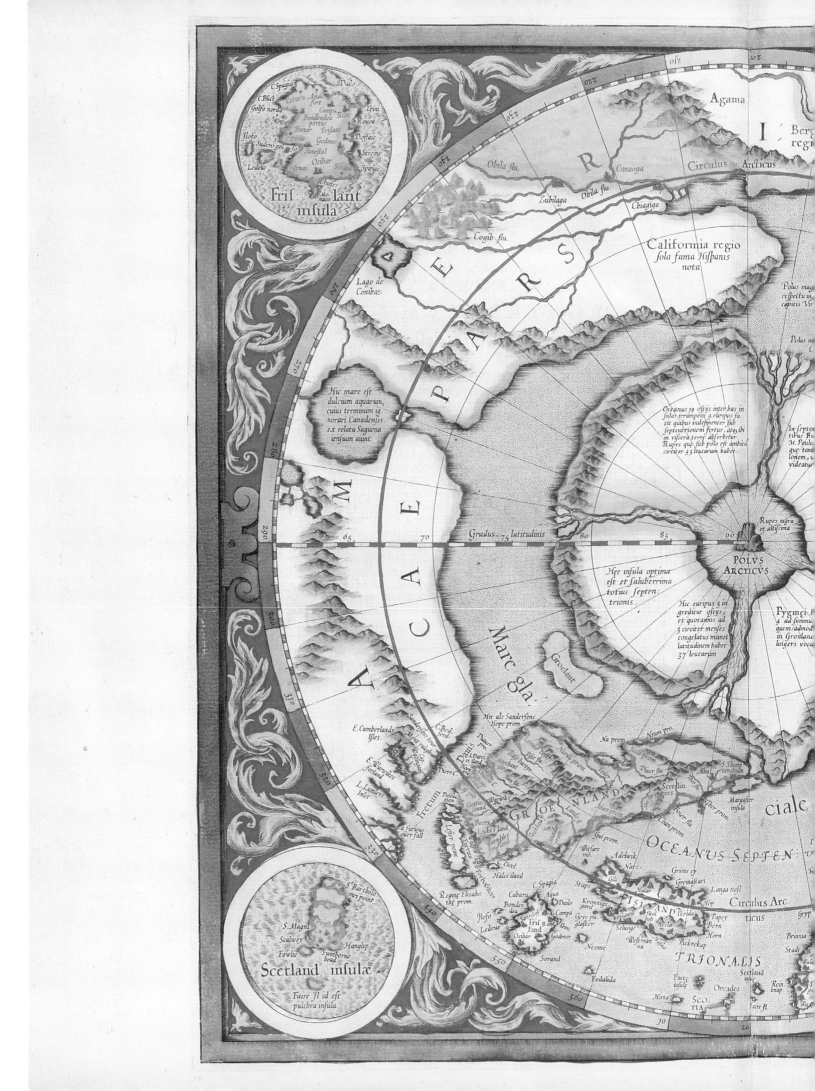

Frisi lant insula

C. Spagia · Joya · Dials
C. Black · Cabaru Andr fort
Golfo norda · Campa · Ibini
Bondendea Rufo · Rouca
Banar · Frislant
Hofo · Derla · Godmec · Doffais
Sudero gol · Jo · Streine
Sanestol · Ocibar · Spirige
Leleue · Vrnai
Antfes
Mo naco

Agama

I, Berg regio

Obila flu. · Canaoga · Circulus Arcticus

Zubilaga · Obila flu. · Chiagiga

P A R S

California regio sola fama Hispanis nota

Cogit flu.

Lago de Conibas.

Hic mare est dulcium aquarum, cuius terminum ig norari Canadenses ex relatu Saguena iensium aiunt

Polus mag respectu in capitis Vir

Polus m C

Oceanus 19 ostys inter has in sulas vrrumpen 4 euripus fa cit quibus indesinenter sub septentrionem fertur, atq, ibi in viscera terre absorbetur Rupes que sub polo est ambitu circiter 33 leucarum habet.

In septen tribus Fr M. Paulu que tan lonem, v videatur

Gradus latitudinis   65   70   75   80   85   90   Rupes nigra et altissima

POLVS ARCTICVS

Hec insula optima est et saluberrima totus septen trionis.

Hic euripus 3 in greditur ostys, et quorannis ad 3 circiter menses congelatus manet latitudinem habet 37 leucarum

Pygmei h 4 ad summu quem admod in Gronlane lingers voca

Groclant

Mare glai.

E. Cumberlands Isles

E. Warwikes Forland

L. Lumlry Inlet

Hit als Sandersons Hope prom

C. Red ford

Na prom

Nrum pro.

Diuer flu.

S. Thom tenebru

Albat

Screlin gers

Margastr insula

Thier prom.

ciale

Freium Desol lion

a furious ouer fall

Lefter Franc

GROE NLAND

Gui prom.

Whitsare mo.

Adelwik

OCEANVS SEPTEN

Regine Elisabe the prom.

Grims ey

Gremastari

Langa ness

Hor

Circulus Arc ticus

C. Spagia

Staps

Gils

Valar

Skal

Perlida

Papey Bern

Gryp

Brama

Stadt

ISLAND

Cabaru

Bonden dea

Ledeue

Duilo

Campa

Frisl land

Godmec

Naua

Kronnigs gard

Geye pu glasker

Seluoge

Westman na

Hecla

Pickrekap

Neome

TRIONALIS

Sorand

Fodaluda

Farre insule

Scetland insule

Orcades

Rein enap

Hirta

SCO TIA

Faire fl.

Scetland insulæ

S. Bartholo mei point

S. Magni

Scalwey

Hanglip

Fowlie

Swinborne head

Faire fl id est pulchra insula

1595

'Septentrionalium Terrarum descriptio.'

Gerard Mercator
From: Mercator's *Atlas*,
Amsterdam, 1606 onwards.
Copper engraving, 365 x 390 mm

Mercator produced the first separate printed map of the Arctic Circle, with the North Pole surrounded by four large islands. At the centre of the pole is a giant whirlpool fed by four rivers, the whirpool sucking the oceans of the earth to the pole and then into an abyss, from where the water would re-emerge as the many rivers of the world, starting the cycle again.

Mercator has marked two poles: as well as the geographic North Pole in the centre of the map, there is also the magnetic North Pole shown as another rocky island, near the Straits of Anian, between America and Asia. When that area was explored more reliably nearly two centuries later, this became the Bering Straits.

Mercator has included the latest voyages in search of the northwest and northeast passages, marking the discoveries of Martin Frobisher and John Davis around Greenland. Within the roundels of the decorative borders are maps of the Shetlands, Faeroes and the mythical island of Frisland.

This second state (post-1606) improves the outline of Nova Zembla, making it one island, and has one of the polar islands receding to allow the inclusion of Spitsbergen.

OCEANUS

ATLANTI·CUS

28 Palma Gomera Tenerifa
S. Clara Lancerote
Mossa Albite Damarri de Non
Nun

Ferro Canaria Forte Ventura
I. Canariæ ol: Fortunatæ

26 C. de Bojador
Pedrezras
Terra Alta
G. Micdaos
B. dos Ruinos
Lafoetr
Sête montes
G. dos Cavallos

Suana Humefen
Cholera
Monfero
Marragueno
Surna
Delto
Vedalon
B. Secaca
Teßet

Ifran
Goaden

ZAN·HAGA.

Tropicus Cancri

Tegunt

Tequed
R. de Ouro
Tene Baje
P.º de Sintra
Terra Daroa
As Montes
A. de S. Cyprian
C. das Barbas
C. Carvoeiro
S. de Santa
C. Blanco
Pedrenoiras
I. Couros
Arguin
Ilhas Daroa
R. de S. Iuan
P.º de Tofia
G. de S. Anna
Turna
Praya Ruyna
Meda
C. Darea
Resguato do Cido
Armarote
C. Tarem
Palmar
Palma seca
R. Senega

Gualata

GUALATA

Gandia

ARGU·IN.
Hebedefex
Hoden.
Hoden

Fulli
FULLI.

Caßali

AFRI·GENE·HOA.
Caragoli
CARA·GOLI.
Tocror.

I. de Cabo
I. do Sal
I. de Bona vista
S. Thiago
I. de Mayo
Verde

I. de Cabo Verde

Genehoa

Tombotu

C. Verde
C. los Maßes

R. de Guadomel
Berenicht
Palmeirinha
R. Acac da barra
As dras Palmeiras
As ostras
De Duque

Budumel ver
As esta outracorte
R. de Jalofes
Jambor
Cahul
Guao

GANBIA
Ducade de Caßan

Niger fluvius

Tambi
Punce
Saluse

Cutumbo

BANGA

MANDINGA.

CARAGO·LES.
Mandinga
Gago

CÆ PARS

MELLI.
Guinola
SOUSOS

SIERRA LIONA

MALAGUETA

Cacers Anguines
GUI

Uxoo
Kabanda
Labore

Coriffene de Alphante grade

Famba

ASSA

DOMA

C. das Palmas
Cabo das Palmas ftin des limites da
costa da Malagueta porta Efquada
E balifa dos da Mina.

Costa dos Alaws

C. 3. Pontas

Demens Avnin

Communes Guincitarum choreæ quibus summo pere delectatur, hoc modo fiunt, in brachys et cruribus quam plurimos habe
nubes, quorum plerisq; tintinnabulis muniti sunt, varium ex metu edêtes tinnitum. Instrumenta quibus canũt sunt pelues, tym-
cariæ, quædam nostrati testudinis similia factæ cycharæ quarum chordæ ex certis arũdinibus, aut setis caudæ Elephãtinæ
cidæ est. Bim plerunque saltant, alterno pede terram quatientes, diversis gestibus histrionicis intermixtis, Inviti

MILIARIA GERMANICA quorum 15. uni gradui respondent.
10. 20. 30. 40. 50. 60. 70. 80. 90. 100.
HISPANICÆ LEUCÆ 17½ uni gradui competentia
10. 20. 30. 40. 50. 60. 70. 80. 90. 100. 110. 120.

Æquinoctialis

Linea

Baptista Doetechomius sculpsit

Hugo Allardt Ex

'Effigies ampli Regni auriferi Guineae in Africa siti … delineata per S. Rovelascum, et politioribus lineamentis figurata per Ludovicum Texeram…'

Petrus Plancius
Separate publication,
Huytch Allard, Amsterdam, *c*.1650.
Copper engraving, 465 x 610 mm

Plancius's map of West Africa is a particularly striking example of his cartographic work, edited from the materials of S. Rovelasco and Luis Teixeira. Rovelasco is otherwise unknown, while Teixeira was Official Cartographer to the Portuguese Crown.

This map was originally published by Cornelis Claesz, *circa* 1602, in the same year that Claesz published Pieter de Marees' *Beschryvinghe Ende Historische Verhael Van Het Gout Konincrijk Van Guinea*, the description of the Gold Coast of Guinea mentioned at the end of the title.

Maps were not merely geographical tools – they were also tools of government – but there is also a growing trend to regard maps as tools of subliminal propaganda, for example in emphasizing the qualities of the Crown (see p.36, for example).

Maps also played an important part in sponsoring overseas trade, with their images of the wealth of the regions outside Europe, and the potential gains to speculators who financed expeditions to these regions. Plancius's map highlights the great, seemingly prosperous 'cities' of West Africa, with its gold mines (marked by crosses), and contrasts that with – to European eyes – the unsophisticated lifestyle of the natives as depicted in the two large vignettes.

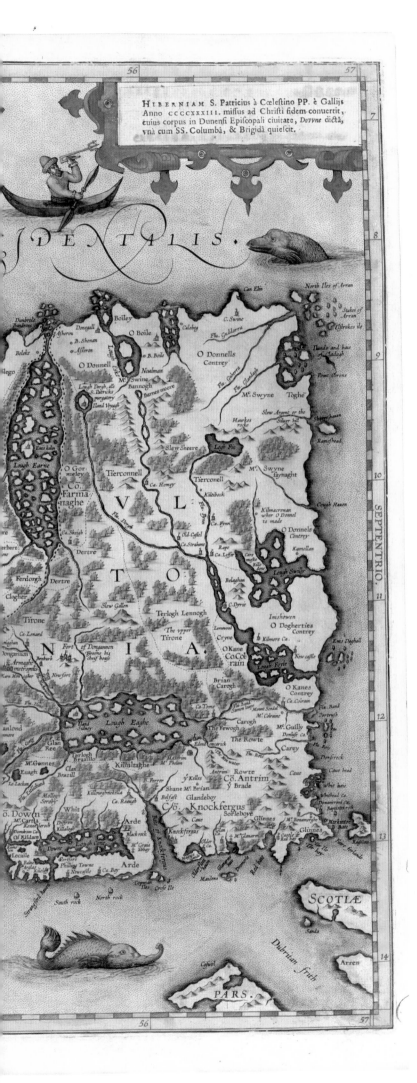

1606

'Irlandiæ Accvrata Descriptio'

Baptista Boazio
From later editions of Ortelius'
Theatrum Orbis Terrarum, as
published by Johannes Baptista
Vrients, Amsterdam, 1606.
Copper engraving, 440 x 580 mm

After the death of Ortelius in 1598 the printing plates for the *Theatrum* were bought by Vrients, who added new surveys that were needed to replace old ones, including the map of Ireland.

Boazio was an Italian mapmaker-surveyor employed by Robert Devereux, Earl of Essex, Lord Lieutenant of Ireland and favourite of Elizabeth I, during the campaign against the rebel Hugh O'Neill, the Earl of Tyrone. An up-to-date map of the country was essential for management of the situation, which Boazio was commissioned to complete, and in 1599 John Sudbury published a version engraved by Elstrach. Despite the seriousness of the work Boazio couldn't help indulging himself: at least two fictitious details appear – *Baptiste's Rock* (off the Antrim Coast) and *Elstrake's Isle* (south-west of Tyrconnell).

Vrients had the map copied for the *Theatrum*. By the time his version appeared in 1603 Elizabeth had died, and so the arms of James I appear in the top right cartouche. Because the plate was wider than the standard size of the *Theatrum*, the map appears with the usual fold down the centre and two more folds near the lateral edges. These extra folds make it hard to find the map in good condition.

1606

'Germania…'

Willem Janszoon Blaeu
From Blaeu's *Atlas Appendix*,
Amsterdam, *c.* 1630.
Copper engraving, 410 x 570 mm

As a companion to his map of the world,
Blaeu also prepared a *carte à figures* map of
'Germania', *circa* 1606, the first map of the
region with the panels of town views.

At this time, the term 'Germania'
represented the Holy Roman Empire. In
the centre of the upper border is a portrait
of the Emperor Ferdinand II. The empire
was an elective monarchy, with the emperor
chosen by an electoral college composed of
clergy and nobles. Blaeu's map is flanked on
the left by three ecclesiastical electors: the
archbishops of Mainz, Cologne and Trier.
On the right-hand panel are three lay
electors: the Count Palatine of the Rhine, the
Duke of Saxony and the Margrave of
Brandenburg.

The upper border contains delicately
engraved vignette views of principal cities:
Basle, Nuremberg, Prague and Cologne
among them.

The map was originally issued separately,
before being incorporated into Blaeu's early
terrestrial atlases, but the additional borders
made the plate height unwieldy and it was
replaced in the atlas, in 1634, by a new map.

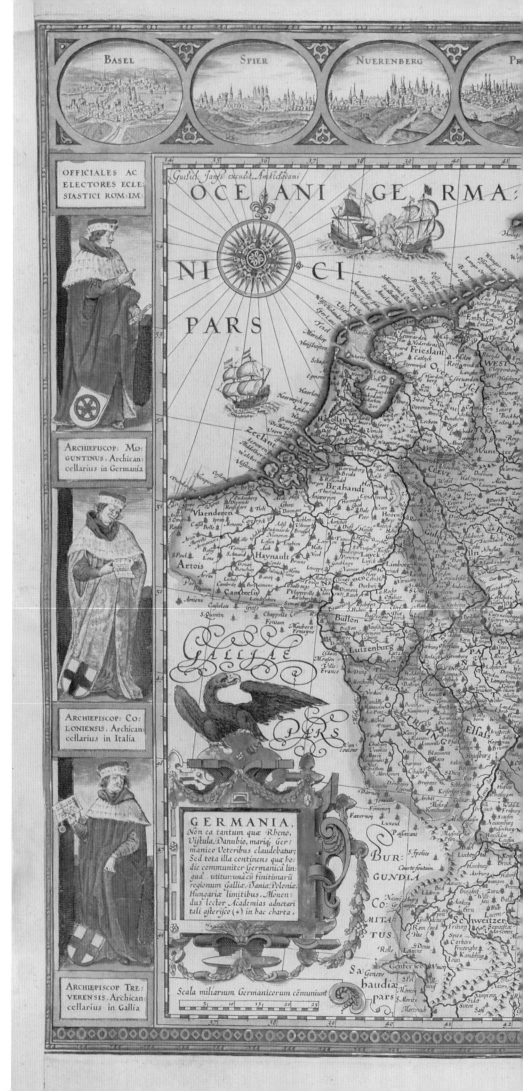

SINUS

CODANUS

HOL

SATIA

MARIS Bornholm in par BAL TICI PARS

Oost ZEE

Bergen Rugen Putbus

POMEREN

BRANDENBURCH

Lunen borg

Braunswet

Meyden burg

Anhalt

SAX

Durrin gen

HESSEN

MEISSEN

Franckenlandt

BOHEM

PFALZ

Neuren berg

BAYEREN

Schwabe

Oosten ryck

Stier marck

Carinthia

TIRO

ITALIÆ PARS

Marca Trevisana

PRUSSIA

MAZOVIÆ PARS

POLONIA

SILESIA

SI LE

Merheren

HUNGARIA

Croatia

BOSNIÆ PARS · Servia pars

OFFICIALES AC
ELECTORES SE:
CULARES ROM: IM:

COMES
PALATINUS
Dapifer

DUX
SAXONIÆ
portiter ensis

MARCHIO
BRANDENBURGEN:
Camerarius

TURCICI IMPERII IMAGO.

1606

'Turcici Imperii Imago.'

Jodocus Hondius Sr.
From the Mercator–Hondius *Atlas*,
Amsterdam, 1606 onwards.
Copper engraving, 360 x 485 mm

The Turkish Empire, covering Greece and
the Balkans, Arabia and much of North
Africa is depicted in this copper engraving.
The portrait above the title is Mehmed II
(1451–81), whose capture of Constantinople in
1453 brought to an end the Byzantine Empire.
As the city controlled the entrance to the
Black Sea it was a bitter loss to Christendom.

The fall of Constantinople also severed the
main overland trade link between Europe and
Asia, which had an unexpected result. The
West now had to turn to ships to create new
trade routes. Attempting to sail around this
enemy in the Middle East, Portuguese
navigator Bartolomeu Dias rounded the Cape
of Good Hope in 1488; and attempting to
reach the Indies by going west Columbus
found the New World in 1492.

1606

'Inferioris Germaniæ Provinciarum Nova Descriptio'

Jan Baptist Vrients
From a posthumous edition of
Ortelius's *Theatrum Orbis Terrarum*,
Amsterdam, 1608.
Copper engraving, 410 x 550 mm

The death of Ortelius in 1598 did not diminish the demand for his atlas. In 1602 Vrients bought the copperplates and continued to publish the atlas, expanding it by adding a small number of new maps to replace the older, outdated ones. In 1612 he sold the plates to the Moretus brothers. That year marked the last edition of the *Theatrum*, although there were later attempts to revive the atlas.

This map of the Low Countries is a most decorative map, orientated with north to the right, with cartouches for the title, scale and key, a compass rose and a vignette sea battle. As this map only appears in the later editions of the *Theatrum* it is comparitively rare for an Ortelius map. This is compounded by the size of the map: as it was larger than the usual Ortelius maps it was often trimmed by careless binders straightening the edges of the book.

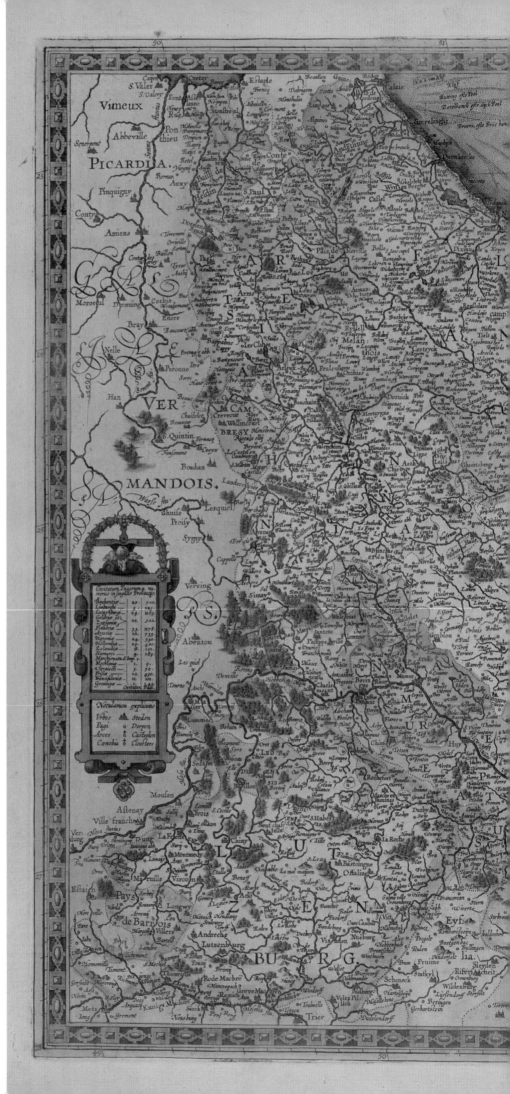

THE COUNTIE PALLATINE
OF LANCASTER DESCRIBED AND
DIVIDED INTO HUNDREDS 1610

PART OF CUMBER SANDE

PART OF WESTMORELAND

PART OF PAR

BLESSED ARE THE PEACE-MAKERS

HENRY VI

HENRY VII

The portraitures of all those kings sprunge fro y royall families of Lancaster and Yorke which with variable successe, got, and enyoyed y Crowne and kingdom. This first syde of his mapp of Lancashire, sheweth them of Lancaster, and the other styles them of the house of York

HENRY V

HENRY IIII

Edmond Crouchbak.E.   Iohn of Gant.D.

NORTH
IRISH
WEST   EAST
SOUTH
SEA

THE BRIGANTES

66

'The Countie Pallatine of Lancaster Described and Divided into Hundreds 1610'

John Speed
From: Speed's *Theatre of the Empire of Great Britaine…*, London, 1612. Copper engraving, 380 x 510 mm

John Speed's *Theatre* is the most famous of the English county atlases. Speed himself was a historian, not a surveyor: the maps are derived from other sources, usually Christopher Saxton or John Norden, but with town plans and other informative details added.

Work started on the atlas possibly as early as 1599, when Speed went into partnership with John Sudbury and George Humble, two publishers. In about 1604 the first manuscript map was ready, and a map of Chester engraved by William Rogers, perhaps the only English engraver competent enough to engrave the series. However Rogers' death meant that the publishers had to look abroad for an engraver, and the manuscripts were sent to Amsterdam for Flemish engraver Jodocus Hondius Sr. to engrave. The finished plates were then sent back to London to be printed by Sudbury and Humble, with the first edition of the atlas appearing in 1612, although the general title is dated 1611.

As befits his historical interests, Speed's Lancashire commemorates the War of the Roses, an intermittent civil war fought between the Yorkist and Lancastrian branches of the Plantagenet family. The Yorkists used the white rose as their emblem, the Lancastrians a red rose, hence the general term for these civil wars. On the left are portraits of the Lancastrian kings, Henry IV through to Henry VII; on the right are the Yorkists Edward IV, Edward V, Richard III and his daughter Elizabeth. It was her marriage to Henry VII that brought the Wars of the Roses to a close, and cemented the English monarchy around the Tudor family.

1611

'Novissima, et accuratissima
Leonis Belgici…'

Claes Jansz. Visscher
Separate publication,
[Amsterdam, 1611].
Copper engraving, 470 x 575mm

The 'Leo Belgicus' is probably the most famous, and among the most elaborate, of all cartographic curiosities. The 'Leo' served as a national icon for the nascent Dutch Republic, so it is hardly surprising that not only did the maps encapsulate the hopes, aspirations and fears of their designers, but also had lavished on them all the care and attention of the best of the Dutch map-engravers.

The first 'Leo' was designed by the Austrian Michael von Eitzing in about 1579, and engraved by the Dutchman Frans Hogenberg for Eitzing's *De Leone Belgico* published in Cologne, 1583. There were many subsequent copies of the image, made over a period of nearly 250 years, although the finest examples appeared in between 1583 and 1648, when the Dutch were engaged in a war of independence against Spain.

In about 1611 Visscher designed and published a new Leo type, with the Lion sitting facing right. This version published during the Twelve Year Truce has a rather more peaceful aspect, with the background scene emphasizing returning prosperity brought about by the truce, while the knight in the foreground rests, although both he and the lion are armed, ready for any attack. With its panels of delicately engraved city views, and the upper panel of the arms of the provinces, this is perhaps the most pleasing of all the Leo images.

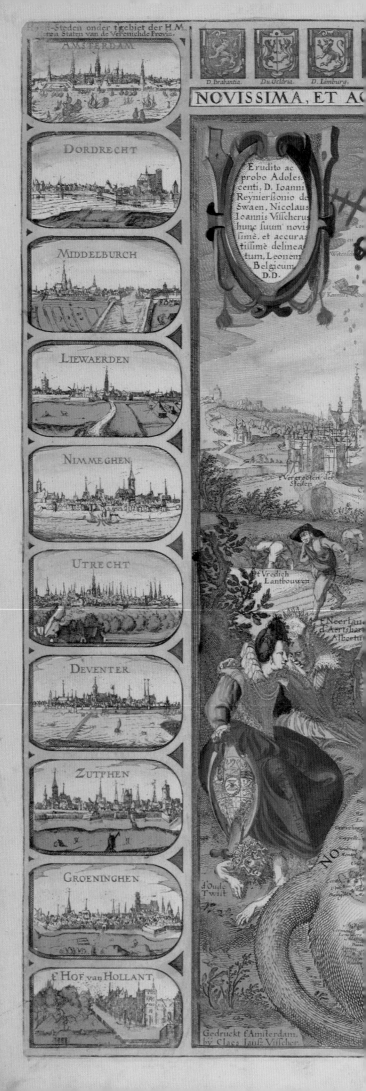

1625

'The North part of America
Conteyning Newfoundland,
new England, Virginia,
Florida, new Spaine,
and Nova Francia…'

Henry Briggs
From: Samuel Purchas *Hakluytus
Posthumus or Purchas his Pilgrimes*,
London, 1625.
Copper engraving, 290 x 350 mm

Briggs's map of North America is one of
the most important early English maps of the
region, incorporating a considerable amount
of new information for the eastern seaboard
regions currently being settled by the English,
with the Plymouth and 'James citie'
(Jamestown) settlements shown.

   The map was probably first published *circa*
1622, when Briggs, one of the great English
mathematicians of his day, contributed a six-
page essay 'A Treatise of the North-West
Passage to the south sea through the
continent of Virginia and by Fretum Hudson'
to Edward Waterhouse's *A Declaration of the
state of the Colony and affaires in Virginia*.
However, the earliest appearance of the
map is in Purchas's collection of travel
accounts of 1625.

   However, Briggs's map is more famous for
its mistake: it is believed to be the first printed
map to depict California as an island, with
text in the map noting: 'California sometymes
supposed to be a part of ye westerne
continent, but scince by a Spanish Charte
taken by ye Hollanders it is found to be a
goodly Ilande'. The misconception was of
remarkable longevity, appearing on printed
maps from 1622 to at least as late as 1806
although, by then, the mistake was
long disproved.

1626

'Africæ, described, the manners of their Habits, and buildinge: newly done into English...'

John Speed
From: *Speed's Prospect of the Most Famous Parts of the World...*,
London 1627.
Copper engraving, 390 x 510 mm

The map of Africa in Speed's atlas of the world was the first map of Africa published by an Englishman (although Speed still had to turn to a Dutch engraver, Abraham Goos, to produce it). England couldn't yet match the sophistication of the Dutch engravers, so the manuscripts were sent to Amsterdam to be engraved, with the heavy copper plates shipped back to be printed.

While the shape of Africa is easily recognizable, the interior is still a mixture of fact and invention. Some of the rivers of western Africa had already been explored, but the source of the Nile remained undiscovered for over three centuries. Here the river originates in twin lakes in the Mountains of the Moon, a concept dating back to the old Ptolemaic maps of the Roman era. Like his contemporaries Speed had added several animals to fill the gaps in his knowledge.

Speed's maps are renowned for their decoration. Along the top of the map are eight city prospects: Tangiers, Ceuta (the Pillar of Hercules opposite Gibraltar), Algiers, Tunis, Alexandria, Cairo, Mozambique and Gran Canaria. Down the sides are eight costume vignettes: a Moroccan, Senegalian, Guinean, Congolese, Egyptian, Abyssinian, Mozambiquian and Madagascan.

On the verso of the map is the atlas text, 'The Description of Africa', containing a mixture of fact and amusing myth, written by Speed.

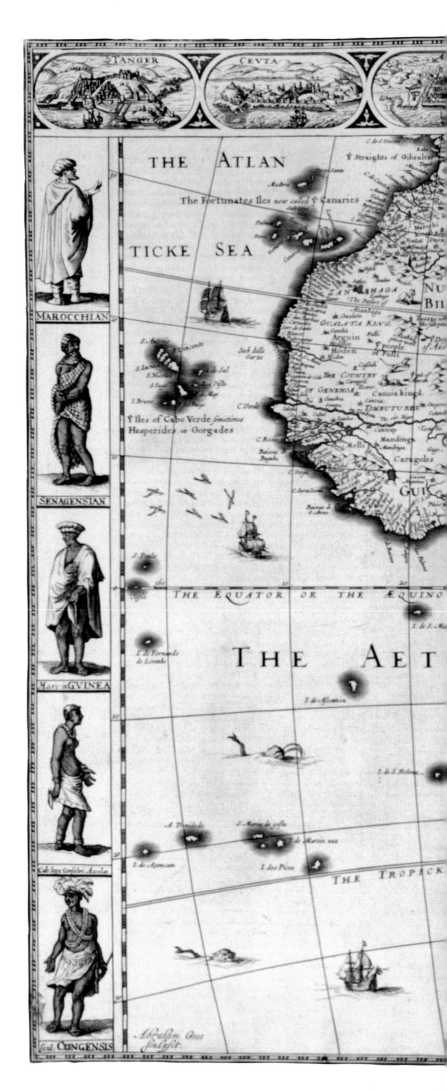

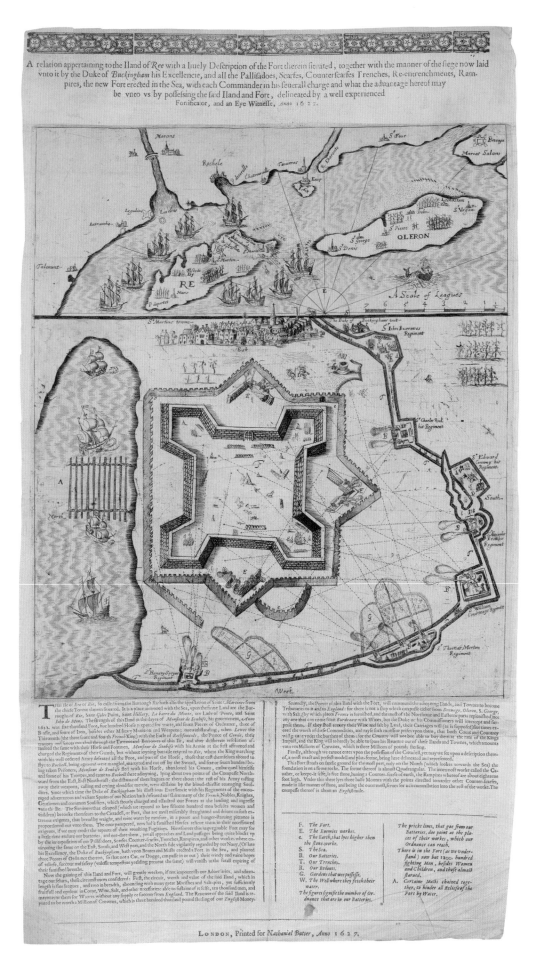

Untitled map of the islands of 'Re' and 'Oleron'/Untitled map of St Martins Fort

Nathaniel Butter
Separate publication,
London, 1627.
Engraving, widest: 430 x 360 mm;
with text: 680 x 365 mm

A rare broadsheet engraving, Nathaniel Butter's map was published to depict the siege of St Martins Fort, on the Isle de Rhé, by English forces commanded by the Duke of Buckingham, the favourite of Charles I. The king despatched English forces to the region in support of the Protestant Huguenots of La Rochelle, who were under siege by the French Army of Louis XIII, directed by Cardinal Richelieu.

It was these events that formed the background to Alexandre Dumas's famous novel *The Three Musketeers*.

Buckingham commanded an expedition of 80 ships and 6,000 men that arrived off the Isle of Rhé, which controlled the approaches to La Rochelle, on 10 July 1627. English troops laid siege to the fortress of St Martin. By the end of September, the defenders of St Martin were close to starvation when a French convoy fought its way through the English blockade to re-supply the fort.

With the weather deteriorating, and French reinforcements on the way, Buckingham was forced to risk all on a frontal assault, which was repulsed with such heavy losses for the English that the siege was abandoned. The English made a second, half-hearted attempt to help La Rochelle the following year, but Buckingham's murder put an end to enthusiasm for the attempt, and the citizens of La Rochelle were left to their fate.

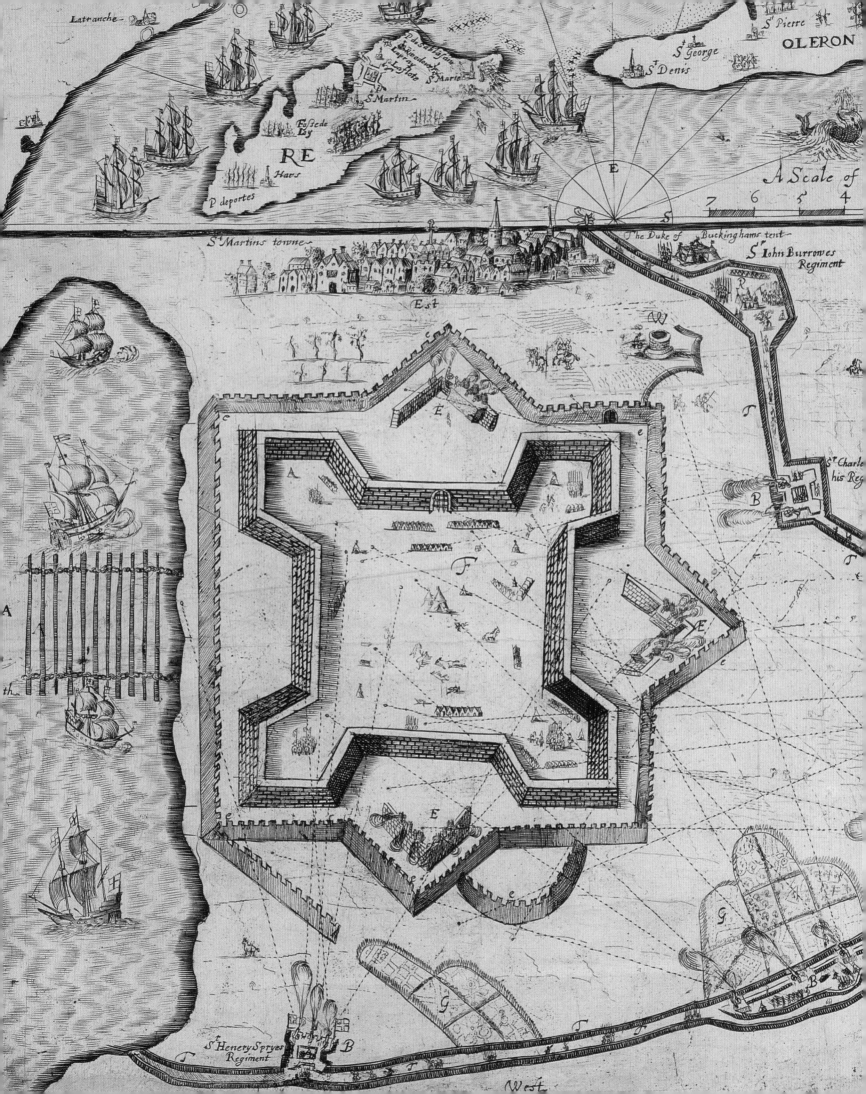

Latranche

OLERON

S Pierre

S George

S Denis

RE

Fosse de Loy

S Martin

Du sel il y sait
Riuedou le
Lapra S Marie

S Martin

Hays

P deportes

E

A Scale of

7   6   5   4

S Martins towne

Est

The Duke of Buckinghams tent

S Iohn Burrowes
Regiment

E

W

A

B

F

S Charle
his Re

B

E

E

e

G

G

S Henery Sptyes
Regiment

B

West

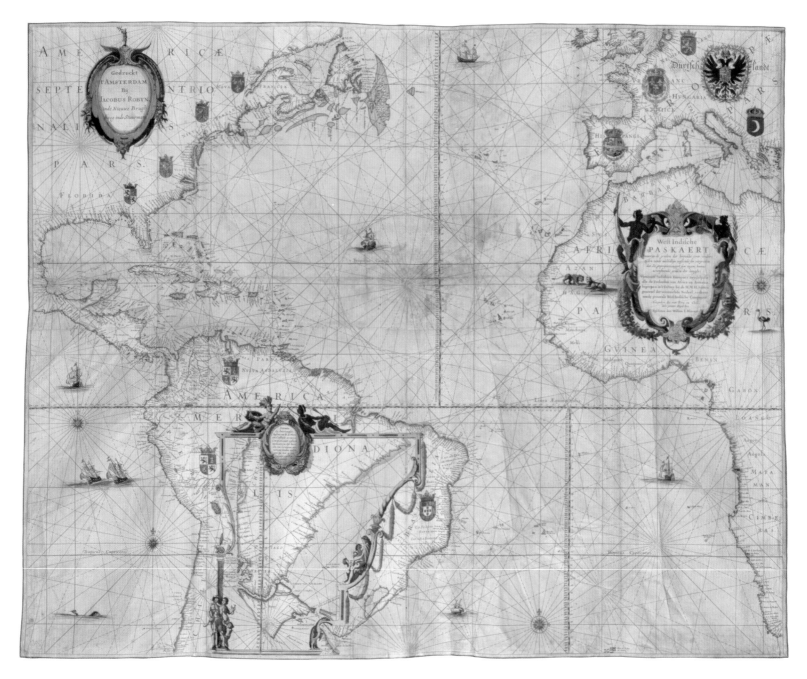

c. 1630

'West-Indische
Paskaert …'

Willem Janszoon Blaeu
Separate publication, Jacob
Robijn, Amsterdam, *c.* 1674.
Copper engraving, 780 x 980 mm

Apart from being an active and successful commercial publisher, Willem Blaeu was also Official Cartographer to the Dutch East India Company, appointed in 1633, in succession to his pupil Hessel Gerritsz.

This was Blaeu's second wall-map of the North Atlantic, but the first prepared on Mercator's projection. The benefit for mariners of Mercator's projection was that it preserves angles between locations on the two-dimensional map surface, meaning compass bearings, and sailing tracks, could be drawn as straight lines onto such charts, making route finding easier than on plane charts.

Indeed, this chart is the first printed chart of North American waters on this projection and, by inference from the title, it was commissioned by the Dutch West India Company to cover the area granted to the company by charter in 1621. However, in order not to contract the scale too much, the southern tip of South America had to be shown as an inset, rather than contiguous with the main map.

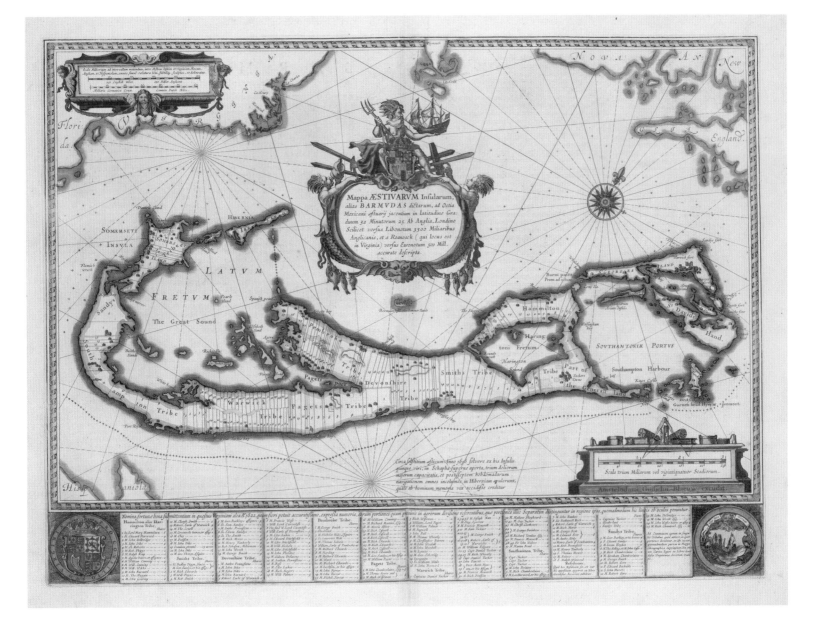

1630

'Mappa Æstivarum
Insularum, alias
Barmudas dictarum…'

Willem Janszoon Blaeu
From: Blaeu's *Atlas Novus*,
Amsterdam, 1645.
Copper engraving, 400 x 530 mm

Bermuda is believed to have been discovered by accident in 1505 by a Spaniard, Juan de Bermudez. However because it was so small the group of islands remained uninhabited until an English expedition of 1609. In 1615 the Bermuda Company was founded to invest and profit from the new colony, and Richard Norwood was sent to survey the islands, using a canoe to travel around. In 1617 he divided Bermuda into firstly large parishes and then 25-acre (10-hectare) strips of shares, to be sold to settlers, as depicted on this map.

His map of the island was published in 1622, but no surviving example is known today. A derivative appeared in Speed's world atlas, the *Prospect of the Most Famous Parts of the World*, and this is believed to be the source for the several continental copies.

One of the most amusing cartographical mistakes developed from Norwood's map. To show the position of Bermuda in relation to the mainland, the outline of North America is shown, with New England on the right and Florida on the left, with a small depiction of Bermuda just under the cartouche. Later cartographers, including Herman Moll, George Louis Le Rouge and Antonio Zatta (as late as 1778) copied the main map, leaving out the outline of North America but retaining the miniature version of Bermuda as extra islands. The mistake could be explained by the use of two names for the islands, the 'Summer Islands' or 'Bermuda'.

1631

'Edenburck in Schottl.'

Daniel Meisner
From: Meisner's *Sciographia Cosmica*, Paulus Furst, Nuremberg, 1638.
Copper engraving, 100 x 150 mm

David Meisner's plan of Edinburgh is the fourth separate printed plan of that city, copied from the Braun and Hogenberg plan/view published in 1572. The view is taken from a vantage point to the south, with the castle at top left.

However, Meisner's plan, and indeed all the plans in his book, include unusual, and rather inexplicable decorative elements and mottos. A cavalier-like figure stands to the right, with swords hanging in mid-air in his line of sight. Above is a quote from Virgil, 'Vim Suscitat Ira', and below, more lines of verse in Latin and German.
Neither the figure nor the text appear to have any connection with Edinburgh.

Meisner's book of town plans originally appeared in 1623 with only 52 plates. Between 1624 and 1626 it was reissued with 416, and again between 1638 and 1642 with a new title, *Sciographia*, containing 800 plates.

c. 1633

'the Cittie of London'

Cornelis Danckerts (I)
Separate publication,
[Anonymous, London, 1640].
Copper engraving 360 x 450 mm;
with text: 510 x 725 mm

Cornelis Danckerts first published this rare broadsheet plan of London around 1633 in Amsterdam. An interesting feature is that the title, imprint and toponymy are all in English, without the apparent bastardization normally associated with foreign piracies, suggesting that Danckerts was working directly from an English original. It is a strong possibility that Danckerts was commissioned to engrave the plan for a London map- or print-seller, particularly as later states were printed in London.

This, and another in the British Library, are the only two recorded examples of this

state, complete with the accompanying letterpress text. The text refers to Charles I as reigning monarch, and suggests a date of about 1640, while Howgego suggests 1645, perhaps too late because of the Civil War, in which London, and her printers, were aligned with the Roundheads against the Crown.

This is the only original plan of London published during the reign of the early Stuart kings, and the map and text together give an important visual and textual description of Stuart London, as it was before the Great Fire of 1666.

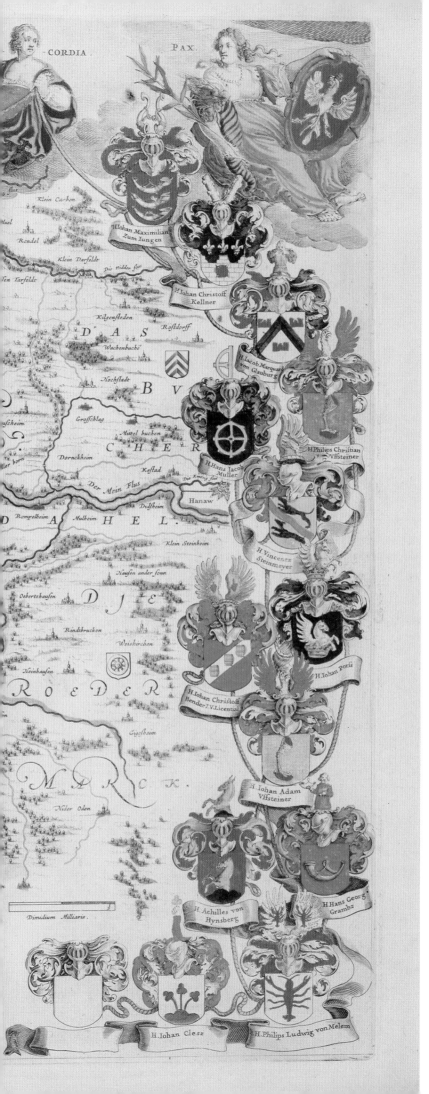

1638

'Novam Hanc Territorii Francofurtensis Tabulam…'

Johannes Blaeu
From: Blaeu's *Novus Atlas*,
Amsterdam, 1638 onwards.
Copper engraving, 455 x 550 mm

One of Blaeu's most beautiful productions is this map of the environs of the German city of Frankfurt-am-Main. The 30 armorials around the map belong to the two mayors and the council of magistrates; the four allegorical figures along the top, all in full colour, personify Counsel, Concordia, Pax and Justitia, appropriate qualities for the ruling council of such an important city.

Founded by the Romans, the city was immensely rich, based on the Frankfurt Stock Exchange. At the time of this map's publication it was also where the monarchs of the Holy Roman Empire of the German Nation were crowned, and host of the most important annual book fair in Europe. Such a city would have been of interest to the Blaeu publishing firm as a potential market: producing such a lavish map of Frankfurt would have made their atlases more desirable to the citizens.

Sed nulla potentia longa est,

A This Paw points out the Caledonian Iarres,
  Sad Harbingers to our intestine Warres,
B The Lion pasant gardant wonders much,
  The Paw should dar presume his Chiefe to touch,
C Strange y from Stooles, at Scotish Prelates hurl'd
  Bellona's dire Alarm's should rouse the World;
D The Lion & y Paw, bent to engage,
  Make Peace at Tweed, so change y Scene & Stage,
E The double headed Eagle wide doth spread
  Her Wings, to fan the Coales y seem'd as dead.

F And makes y Lionesse an Instrument,
  To breake that Peace, and a fourth Parlament,
G The Paw invades y Lion at Tine Flood;
  They fight, make Truce, & stop from shedding Blood,
H The British Notes sound flat, to those more sharp,
  Divisions, Ecch'd from the Irish Harp.
I The Parlament conven'd the Lion try'd
  By Charging Five, The Members to divide
K First Iustice next no Bishops, Priviledge last,
  Cry Multitudes, who to the Houses haste,

L The
  Such
M Twas
  Let u
N Cœles
OP Ted t
Q A bla
R Preds
S The
  By P

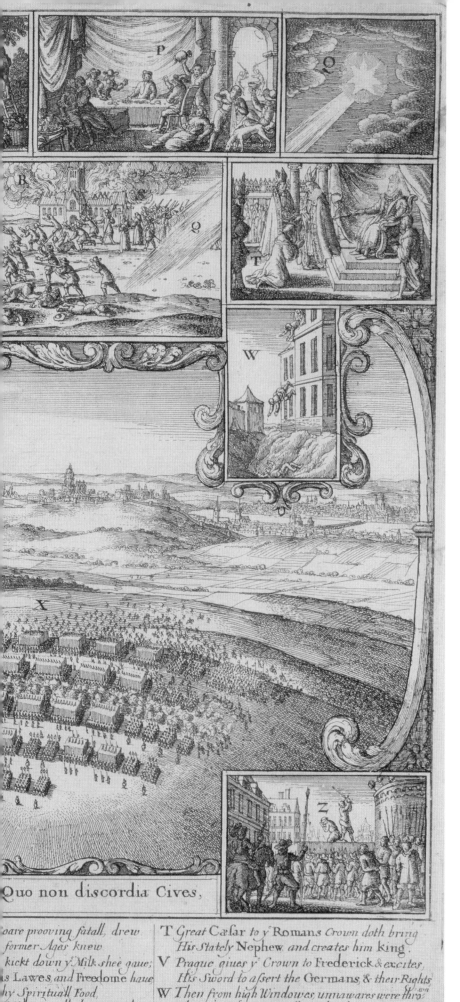

Quo non discordia Cives,

oare prooving fatall, drew
former Agas knew
kickt down y Milk shee gaue;
s Lawes and Freedome haue
hy Spirituall Food,
& Plenty, all that's Good.
y Backsliding showes,
presenteth woes,
them Churches but are stopt
th Aurea Bulla mockt.

T Great Cæsar to y Romans Crown doth bring
His Stately Nephew, and creates him king.
V Prague giues y Crown to Frederick & excites,
His Sword to assert the Germans, & their Rights.
W Then from high Windowes, unawares were thro'
The Emperors Councell ere the Change was known
XY The Blow neer Prague was struck The people ride
Like Iehu out, Warre is sweet before t is try'd
Z What Decollations then? What Blood? What far
Outacted Tragick Scenes ensud that Warre

c. 1643

Untitled map of
the British Isles

Wenceslas Hollar
Separate publication,
[London, 1643].
Copper engraving, 247 x 346 mm

This scarce etching of the British Isles is
attributed to Wenceslas Hollar on stylistic
grounds. It is a general map of the British
Isles with part of the Continent centred on
Prague. The map shows troop formations
across the British Isles, while the Battle of
Prague, 1620, is shown on the mainland.

Around the border of the map are
a series of 17 historical scenes, with
accompanying rhyming couplets along
the lower border, relating to contemporary
political events in England and Europe.

It would seem that Hollar was attempting
to warn of the consequences of political
discord, by contrasting and relating the unrest
and fighting in his native Prague with the
unfolding events of the English Civil War.
Hollar favoured the Royalists cause during the
Civil War and left England in 1644.

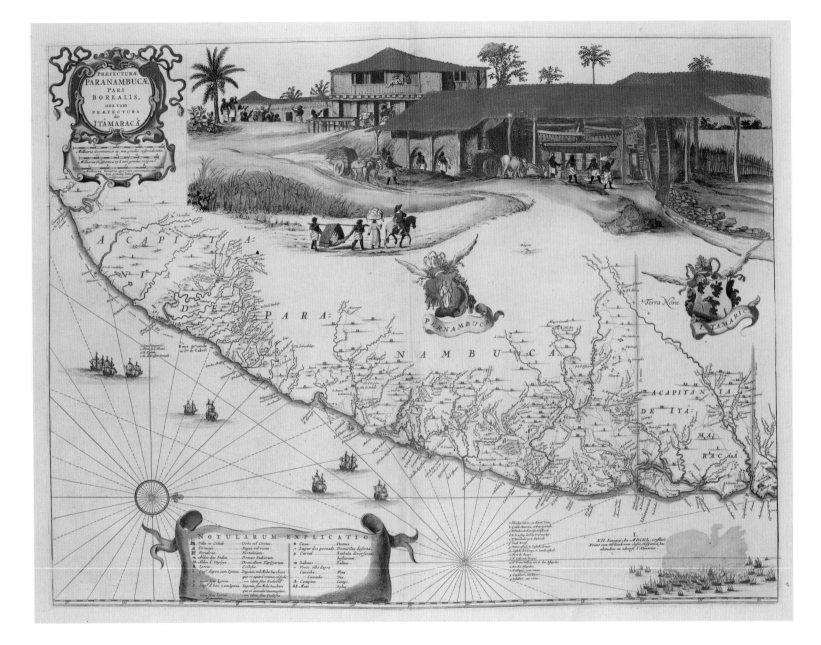

1647

'Præfecturæ Paranambucae
pars Borealis...' [&]
'Præfecturæ de Paraiba,
et Rio Grande'

Johannes Blaeu
From: Blaeu's *Atlas Maior*,
Amsterdam, 1662. Two copper
engravings, each *c.* 420 x 530 mm

The two sheets shown are taken from Blaeu's
nine-sheet wall-map of northwest Brazil,
'Brasilia qua parte paret Belgis', and are
designed to be joined laterally. They celebrate
the Dutch expeditions to Brazil under Johan
Maurits, count of Nassau–Siegen. Their
main objective was to gain control of the
sugar plantations then under Portuguese
control. At the time these were supplying
Europe with 70 per cent of its sugar, a very
valuable asset. This is emphasized by the
large scenes of a sugar mill running across the
top of the two sheets.

The illustrations on the map were drawn
by Frans Post, a capable artist who
accompanied Count Maurits to Brazil. Apart
from being sold as a wall-map, the map sheets
were designed to be complete in themselves,

and appeared as separate sheets in Caspar
Barlaeus' *Rerum Per Octennium In Brasilia…
Historia…*, published by Blaeu in 1647, and in
the *Atlas Maior*, as a suite of maps of Brazil in
the Americas volume.

The Brazilian plantations were too
unhealthy for European settlers, so they were
dependent on slave labour, with such
a high rate of attrition that the African
slave trade boomed. This continued even
after the Portuguese drove the French out
in 1654 and the sugar trade moved to the
Caribbean islands.

Verklaringe
des getals

72 Nieuwe Reguls Poort
73 Pickeur Stall
74 Amstels Brug
75 S Antonis Poort
76 Vleyen burg
77 S Antonis Sluys
78 de Suyder Kerck
79 Ooster marckt
80 Nieuwe Waech
81 Oude Kerck
82 Oudesyts bier Kay
83 de Franse Kerck
84 Oostindisch Huys
85 het Dolhuys
86 't Princen Hoff
87 Wortel marckt
88 des oude Vleeshalle
89 het Spin Huys
90 Illustre Schole
91 Oude mannen huys
92 I Vrouwe gasthuys
93 't Engelse Gasthuys
94 't Minen Gasthuys
95 Verweryen
96 het Stadt Hoff
97 Kluyveniers Doele
98 het Rondeel
99 Turff marckt
100 Grimmenesse sluys
101 de Raemmen
102 Blickeryen
103 de Ossen marckt
104 Vercken marckt
105 Wesoper Veer
106 Muyder en Naerder Veer
107 Lasarus Huys

De Weetering

Niew Haerlemmer Vaert

Haerlemmer Dyck

RIET

LANT

De Kalck

1649

'Amstelodami Celeberrimi Hollandiae Emporii delineatio nova'

Johannes Blaeu
From: Blaeu's *Townbooks of the Netherlands*, Amsterdam, 1649.
Copper engraving, 410 x 540 mm

Johannes Blaeu succeeded his father Willem as head of the Blaeu publishing house, and continued an ambitious publishing programme, establishing the family as the pre-eminent cartographic publishers in Europe.

The history of the Dutch Republic in the first half of the seventeenth century is the revolt to secure independence from Spain. In 1621 the Twelve Year Truce between the rebellious northern provinces and Spain ended, and the armed struggle re-commenced.

When it became clear that the Dutch Republic would secure its independence, Johannes Blaeu began work on his *Townbooks of the Netherlands*, a two-volume work containing, in the first edition, 220 map sheets with plans of the cities of the Low Countries.

The *Townbooks*, and the individual plans, are not only highly regarded for their detail and accuracy, but also as a visual representation, of national pride in the nascent republic. They portray optimism for the future and an expression of the wealth of the republic, exemplified by this fine plan of the Amsterdam, the financial and cultural capital of the Dutch Republic.

1655

'Novi Belgii Novæque
Angliæ nec non partis
Virginiæ Tabula…'

Nicolaas Visscher (**I**)
Separate publication,
Amsterdam, *c.* 1680.
Copper engraving, 460 x 550 mm

In the late eighteenth century an English
historian, Richard Gough, estimated that less
than one in ten maps in circulation were
actually original, the rest being copied from
an existing source, and few would argue
with his statistics. What is interesting,
however, is the way that derivatives could
prove to have a greater influence than the
prototype they copied.

One such instance is Visscher's map of
New England. Geographically, it is based on
Janssonius's map of *circa* 1651. Where
Visscher improved on the original version
was by inserting the inset view of Manhattan,
which is regarded as perhaps the second
or third printed view of New York City.

The view of Manhattan showed a
relatively small and perhaps rather sleepy
community, with the skyline dominated
by the large windmill at left, the church
and the rather primitive dockyard facilities
in the foreground.

Numerous copies of this map were made
by contemporary mapmakers but, with only a
few exceptions, they used Visscher's version
as a model, rather than Janssonius', and in
these different versions, the map remained
in circulation right up to the American
Revolutionary War.

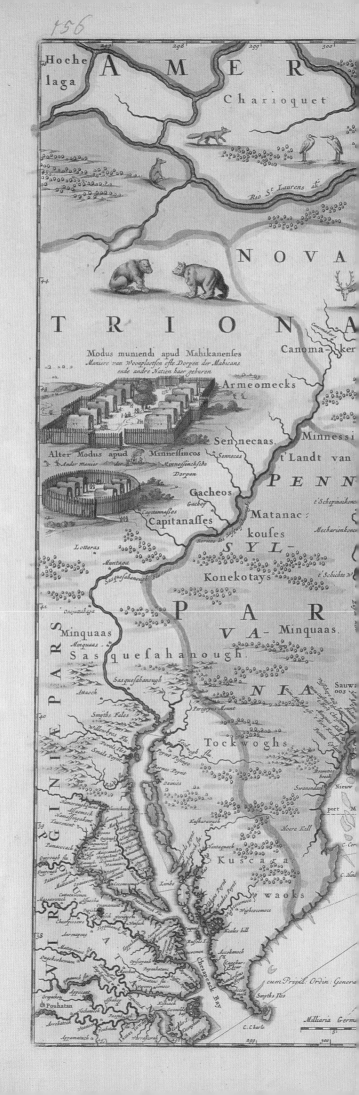

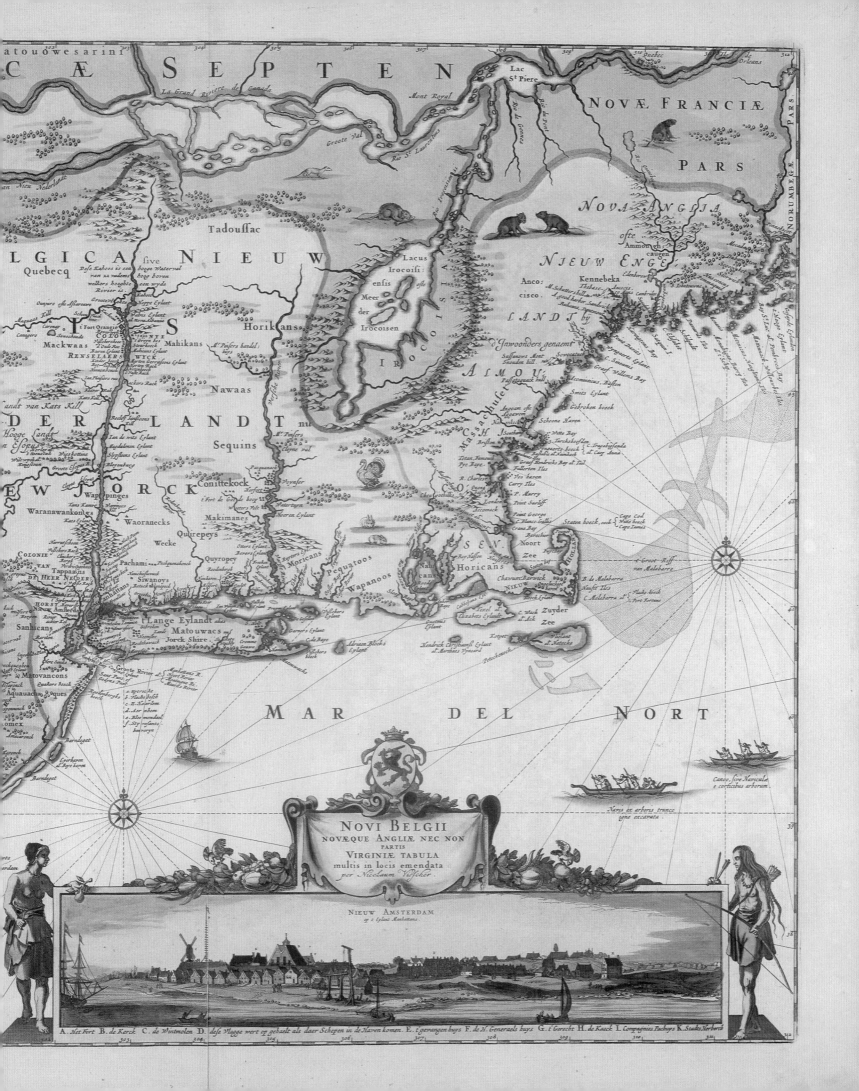

NOVI BELGII
NOVÆQUE ANGLIÆ NEC NON
PARTIS
VIRGINIÆ TABULA
multis in locis emendata
per Nicolaum Visscher.

NIEUW AMSTERDAM
op 't Eylant Manhattans.

A. Met Fort B. de Kerck C. de Wintmolen D. dese Vlagge wert op gehaelt als daer Schepen in de Haven komen. E. t'gevangen huys F. de H. Generaels huys G. t'Gerecht H. de Kaeck I. Compagnies Pachuys K. Stadts Herberch

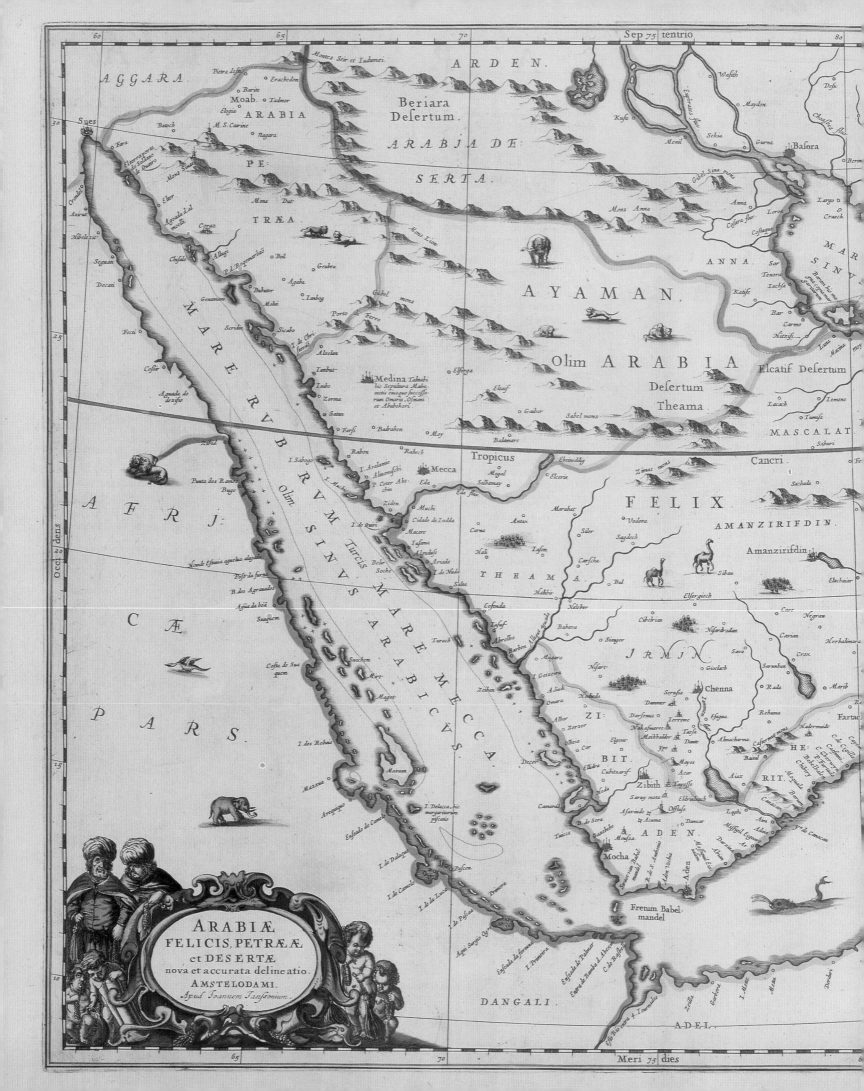

1658

'Arabiæ Felicis, Petrææ et Desertæ nova at accurata delineatio.'

Jan Janssonius
From: Janssonius' *Atlas Novus*,
Amsterdam, 1658
Copper engraving, 440 x 510 mm

Jan Janssonius produced this detailed map of the Arabian peninsula, divided into the three Roman provinces: 'Arabia Felix', 'Arabia Petraea' and 'Arabia Deserta'.

Because of the lack of new information about Arabia, Janssonius has had to rely on Ptolemaic names to give detail to his map. 'Arabia Felix' (a Latin name roughly translating as 'Loyal Arabia') covers most of the peninsula, although quite often the term relates only to the comparatively fertile coastal regions of present-day Asir and Yemen. 'Arabia Petraea' (Stony Arabia) is located in northwestern Arabia, and was a frontier province of imperial Rome.

'Arabia Deserta' (Desert Arabia) in Latin signified the desert interior, populated by nomadic tribes who frequently invaded richer lands. Janssonius has relegated 'Deserta' to quite a small area in the northeast: probably he found this necessary to reconcile the descriptions of the regions with the myriad of rivers he has drawn through the interior, with much of this interior detail imaginary.

1658

'Tabula Magellanica qua Tierræ del Fuego…'

Jan Janssonius
From: [Gerard Valk & Petrus Schenk, Composite world atlas, 1715].
Copper engraving, 420 x 540 mm

In 1520, Magellan's discovery of the straits that bear his name, the first route to be found between the Atlantic and Pacific, caused a sensation. No longer did the spice ships have to pass the unfriendly nations of Asia to reach the Far East. The problem was that in parts the straits are so narrow that constant depth soundings had to be made, done by members of the crew using lines and weights, to ensure the ship did not run aground. Because the route was so slow and tortuous an alternative route was needed.

In 1615 a pair of Dutch explorers, Jacob Le Maire and Willem Schouten, set out from Europe, and continued south past the Magellan Straits. To the south was Tierra del Fuego, the 'Land of Fires' reported by Magellan, which on previous maps had been shown as part of the unknown Great Southern Continent. In 1616 they discovered Cape Horn and Drake's Passage, which separates South America from Antarctica. This route was even worse: most of the year the winds are contrary, the waters turbulent and fraught with icebergs. It never overtook the Straits of Magellan as the preferred route. Fleets of ships attempting the Horn, as Admiral Anson's did in 1741, were beset with terrible headwinds and in that case two of his six ships gave up and returned home. The difficulties of these routes made the vast expense of the Panama Canal much more attractive.

Fifty years after its discovery this map still shows Cape Horn as a single island when it is actually an archipelago.

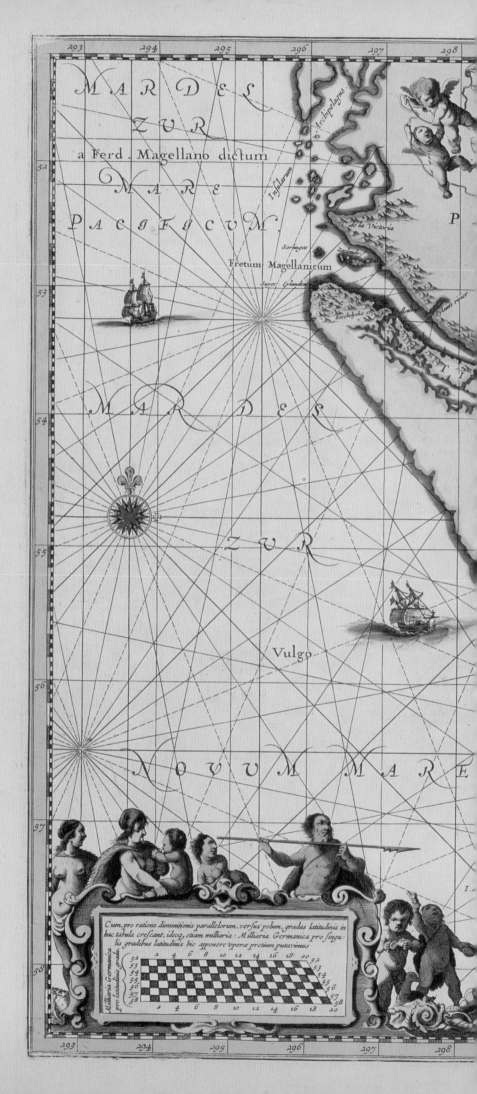

Notarum explicatio

Kruyck   d. Æolus   e. White bay   l. Ongeluckige bay
eylandt   f. Willems bay   g. Ridders bay. R.S.T. Nieuwe Straet
rote wal   h. C. de Naßou   V. Een hooge bergh van
eylandt   i. Gr. Hendr. Fredricks bay   waermen de vorder ge-
k. Onbequame bay   brooken linden can sien

M A R

D E S

Nobilissimo.
Amplissimoque Viro.
D. GVALTHERO de RAET.
IVD. Curiæ Hollandiæ, Zee-
landiæ. West-frisiæque
Senatori eminentissimo.
D.D.D. Ioannes Ianßonius.

B. Gallego

7 Bergen

ONVM

Fretum Magellanicum.

N O R I

IO.

C. de Penas

DEL FVOGO

C. de St Ines

Waygiats

M A G E L L A N I C A.

Verschoors Ree

Mauritius Landt

Staten
Eylandt

Straet van le Mair

De G. Brouwers passage

Valeyns Bay

Nassausche Voerd

A V S T R A E.

I. de Gonçalo

Barnevelts Eylanden

C. Hoorn

TABULA
MAGELLANICA
QUA TIERRÆ DEL FUEGO,
Cum
celeberrimis fretis a F. Magellano
et I. Le Maire detectis
Novißima et accuratißima
descriptio exhibetur.

Amstelodami.
Apud P. SCHENK et G. VALK.
C. Priv.

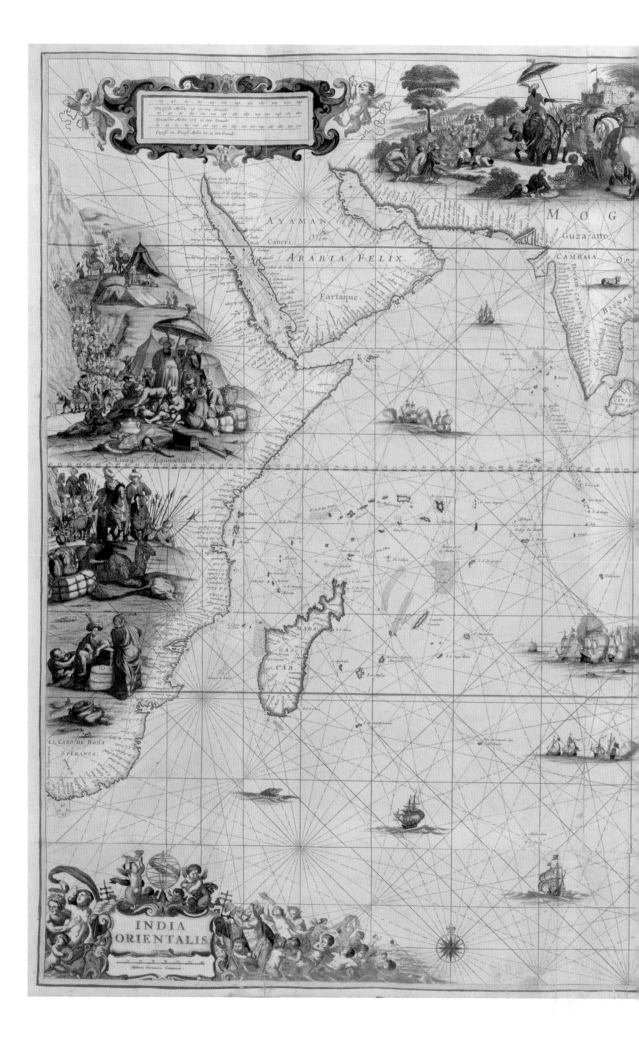

AYAMAN

Cancri. Olim

ARABIA FELIX.

Fartaque.

Linea Equinoctialis

EL CABO DE BONA
SPERANCA.

MOG

Guzaratte.

CAMBAIA

BISNAG

CEYLO

MADA

GAS
CAR.

INDIA
ORIENTALIS

Milliaria Germanica Communia.

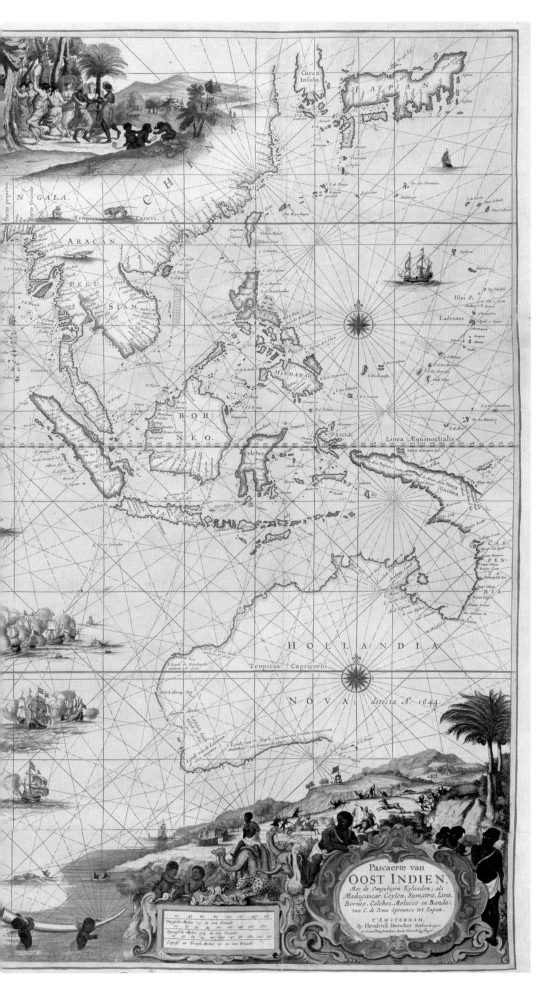

1660

'Pascaerte van Oost Indien …'

Hendrick Doncker
Separate publication,
Amsterdam, *c.* 1660.
Copper engraving, 710 x 905 mm

Hendrick Doncker was one of the most important publishers of maritime materials in Amsterdam in the second half of the seventeenth century, best known for his important series of sea-atlases. Doncker also published a series of wall-maps, which are not so well known on account of their rarity today.

This fine map of the Indian Ocean, East Indies and Australia was prepared, not for shipboard use, but as a wall ornament. The decorative embellishments would have made this an expensive production, with at least as much care lavished on the decorative elements, which emphasize the wealth of the region, as the cartographic element.

Indeed, in the seventeenth and early eighteenth century, Dutch publishers took great pride in the pictorial content of their maps, and this is a particularly good example of the close links between fine art and cartography in Amsterdam at the time, with the finely executed vignette scenes composed by Johannes Leupenius, a pupil of Rembrandt.

1665

'Paskaarte Vertonende alle de Zekusten van Evropa'

Pieter Goos
Wall-map, Amsterdam, 1665.
Copper engraving, printed on
two sheets conjoined,
total 640 x 860 mm

In this particularly decorative sea chart of
Europe, north is oriented towards the right –
a fact denoted by the arrows on the compass
roses – with the text oriented to the west.
While this may be strange to modern eyes,
it was common during this period, for the
simple reason that the map would be readable
without having to turn a heavy tome.

The extents of the map are Spitzbergen,
Novaya Zemla (northern Russia) and
Greenland on the right, and the Azores and
Canaries (off the coast of Africa) on the left.

As a sea chart, the interiors of land have
no detail, so Goos has had to be inventive
with the decoration: north Africa is filled by
the continuation of the chart to the eastern
end of the Mediterranean (although Goos
has managed to squeeze in a couple of
elephants, the classic symbol of Africa); in
western Europe are three large armorials, for
the Spanish, French and Hapsburg
monarchies; in northern Europe are smaller
armorials for the English, Norwegian,
Swedish and Russian; over eastern Europe is
the title cartouche, with the Ottoman arms
appearing in the continuation; and
Greenland has a pair of fur-wrapped natives.
Other decorations include a cartouche for the
publisher's details and no fewer than four sets
of scales, each within a cartouche, one of
which features two polar bears.

The publisher, Pieter Goos (1616–1675),
was an Amsterdam publisher specializing in
sea charts. This chart was influential, copied
by a number of other publishers, including
Frederick de Wit.

c. 1666

'Paskaarte van Nova Granada. en t'Eylandt California…'

Pieter Goos
From: Goos' *De Zee-Atlas ofte Water-Wereld*, Amsterdam, 1666.
Copper engraving, 440 x 540 mm

As described on p. 70, it seems that the Englishman Henry Briggs was responsible for popularizing the myth of California as an island. California's first appearance on printed maps was as a peninsula, but in about 1620 a Carmelite friar, Father Antonio Ascension, drew a map showing California as an island, and despatched a copy back to Spain. *En route*, the ship, and map, was captured by the Dutch. Ascension's map was circulated in Holland, with a copy reaching Briggs in London, thus ensuring wide dissemination of the idea.

If the longevity of the misconception is a surprise, then so too is the enthusiasm with which map- and chart-makers adopted the notion. Pieter Goos's chart is one of two charts apparently published in the same year that are the earliest devoted to California. For a mistaken delineation, Goos was able to show considerable detail; one might have expected a certain uniformity of outline, but some mapmakers showed the northern coastline of California to be flat, as seen on Briggs' map for example, while Goos shows an indented northern coastline, following another English mapmaker, Luke Foxe.

1669

'Nova Totius Americæ sive novi orbis tabula…'

Alexis Hubert Jaillot
Separate publication, Paris, 1669.
Copper engraving, total
dimensions 820 x 1080 mm

Alexis Hubert Jaillot produced a set of maps of the continents of which this fine wall-map of the Americas is one. Published in Paris in 1669, this particular map does not bear his imprint.

In keeping with the tastes of the time, blank areas are heavily decorated, the sea with all manner of ships, battles and fantastic sea monsters, while South America is filled with equally fanciful depictions of native life and rituals.

Around the border of the map are 16 vignettes of costume figures from the Americas, while the lower border comprises 12 finely engraved views of important settlements. Among these are: Pomeiooc in Virginia; Fort Caroline, the French fort in modern South Carolina; St Augustine in Florida, the oldest continuously inhabited settlement in the modern United States; Havana; Mexico City; Rio de Janeiro; and the famed silver mountain, Potosi.

Prominent in the North Atlantic is an elaborate vignette of a king being drawn on a water carriage, by sea-horses. This wall-map is one of the very earliest and most important of Jaillot's maps, and it seems plausible that the figure depicted is the French Dauphin, son of the king, with Jaillot's tribute to him designed to bring him royal favour and patronage. Indeed, Jaillot was subsequently appointed official geographer to the French king.

NOVA AMERICÆ
DESCRIPTIO.

c. 1674

'A Mapp of New Jarsey by John Seller'

John Seller Sr.
Separate publication,
London, c. 1674.
Copper engraving, 430 x 535 mm

The first printed map of the New Jersey colony was published by John Seller, Hydrographer to Charles II. Following the British capture of New York in 1664, Charles granted James, Duke of York extensive tracts of land as a proprietary province; in turn, the Duke of York granted what became New Jersey to two of his loyal supporters, George Carteret and Lord Berkeley.

On 18 March 1673 Berkeley sold his half of New Jersey to the Quakers, with William Penn as one of the trustees, creating the provinces of East and West New Jersey. The Quakers set about colonizing their half.

Both George Carteret, the dedicatee of this map, and William Penn were well aware of the benefits of having good maps of the colonies on which to superimpose settlement grids, partly to make the business of granting lands easier, but also as a promotional tool to encourage would-be settlers to emigrate to the new colony.

Seller's map, with its extensive unmapped areas, must have presented an image of a blank canvas on which the new settler could make a new life, and would have been very important, and influential in the success of the colony.

The map extends northwards to include New York, and Seller has included a version of the Visscher view of New York (p. 88) as an inset in a blank area of the plate, the only English map to include this view.

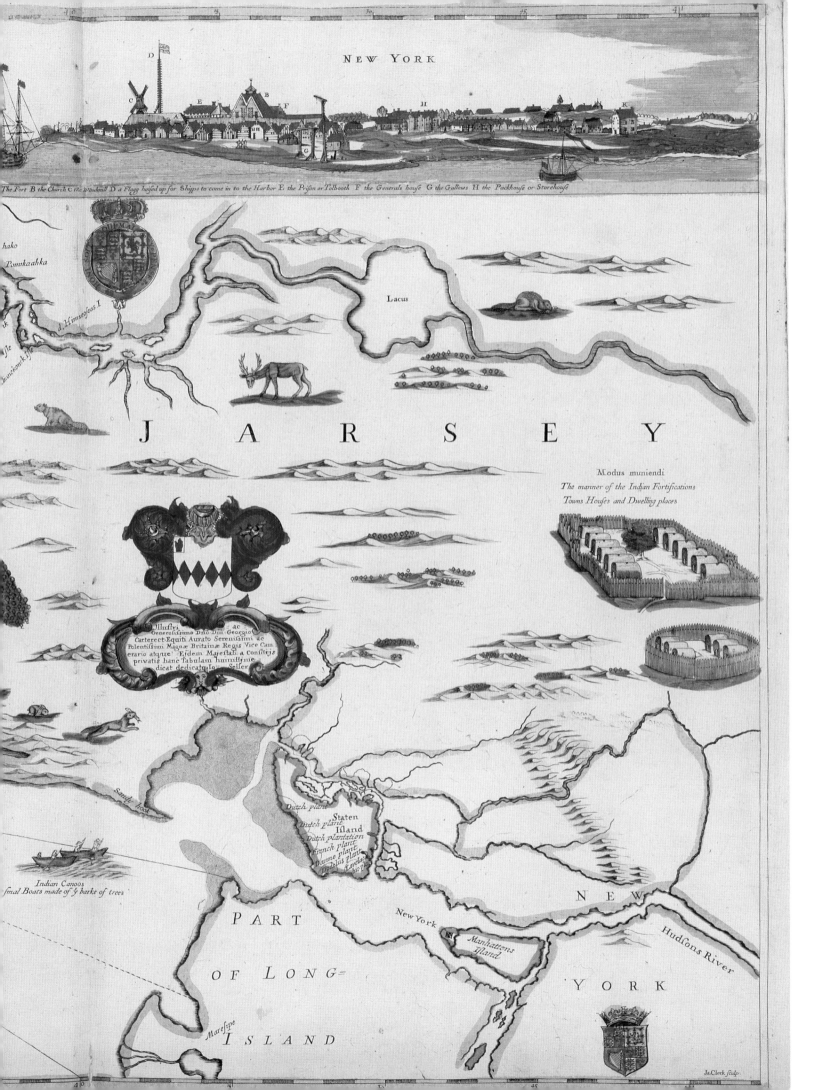

NEW YORK

A the Fort B the Church C the Windmill D a Flagg hoised up for Ships to come in to the Harbor E the Prison or Tolbooth F the Generals house G the Gallows H the Packhouse or Storehouse

hako
Pomrkaahka

d, Himaeyseas I

Lacus

J A R S E Y

Modus muniendi
The manner of the Indian Fortifications
Towns Houses and Dwelling places

Illustri   ac
Generosissimo Dño Dñi Georgio
Carterect Equiti Aurato Serenissimi ac
Potentissimi Magnæ Britaniæ Regis Vice Cam
erario atque   Eisdem Majestati a Consilijs
privatis hanc Tabulam humillime
dicat dedicatq. Io   Seller

Sandy hook

Dutch plant
Dutch plant   Staten
Dutch plantation   Island
French plant
Danne plant
Englis plant

Indian Canoos
smal Boats made of y barke of trees

New York

N E W

P A R T   New York

Hudsons River

Manhattens
Island

O F   L O N G=   Y O R K

Maresspe   I S L A N D

Ja. Clerk sculp.

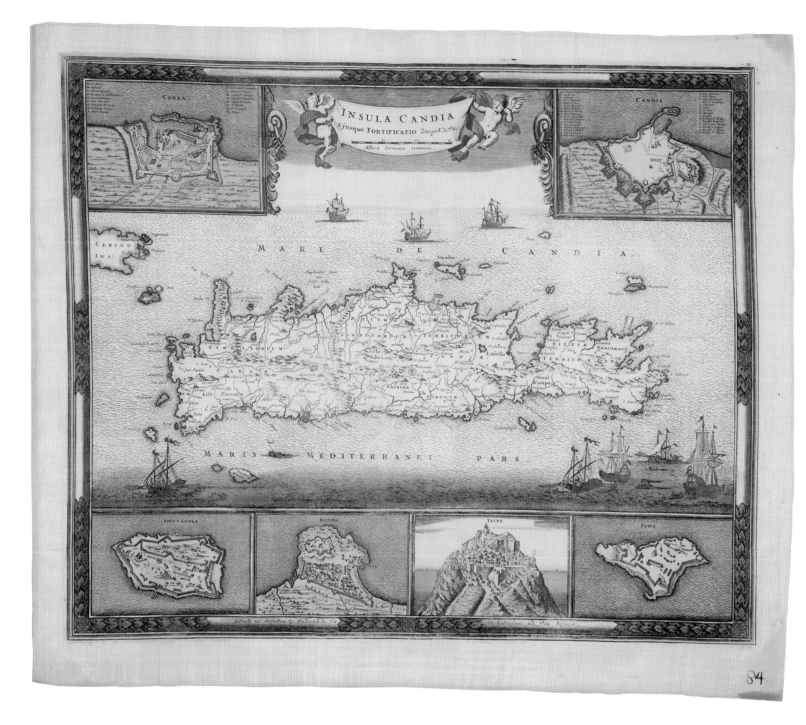

1675

'Insula Candia Ejusque
Fortificatio…'

Frederick de Wit
From: de Wit Composite atlases,
Amsterdam, *c.* 1675.
Copper engraving, 465 x 555 mm

Frederick de Wit's is one of the most
decorative maps of Crete, based on the
map by Sébastian de Pontault Beaulieu, a
French military engineer who had mapped
the fortifications of many Mediterranean
islands. His map of Crete was published in
1674, only five years after Crete had fallen
to the Turks after an epic 24 year siege.
The seas around the island are filled with

galleons and galleys representing this
dramatic struggle.

Above the map the title is on a banner
held aloft by putti, and the corners have plans
of the fortfications of Canea and Candia
(Heraklion). Under the map are four more
plans of other Venetian strongholds in the
region, all of which also fell to the Turks.

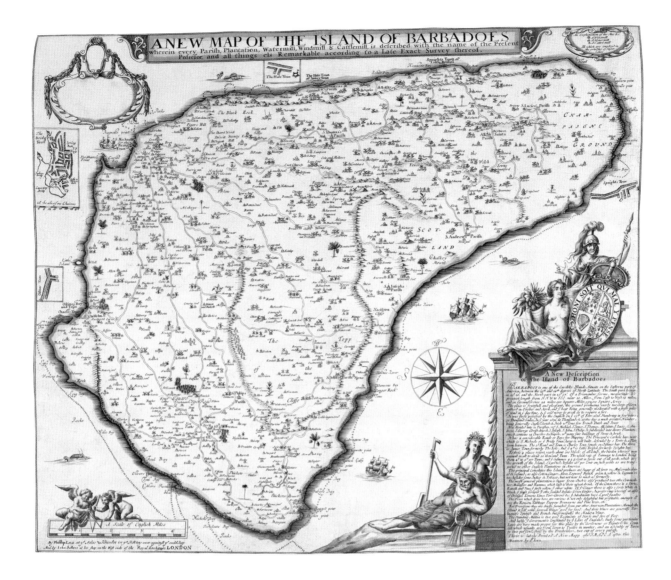

1675

'A New Map of the Island of Barbadoes wherein every Parish, Plantation, Watermill, Windmill & Cattlemill, is described with the name of the Present Possesor'

Richard Forde
Broadsheet publication,
Philip Lea & John Seller Sr.,
London, *c.* 1685
Copper engraving, 480 x 560 mm

Forde's map of Barbados, first published circa 1675–6 and re-issued to about 1750, is at once one of the most important and most unusual of all English maps of the colonial era.

Management of England's colonial possessions was entrusted to the office of the Committee of the Lords of Trade and Plantations in London. Governing such far-flung possessions in the days before telephone and satellite necessitated a good geographical understanding of each colony, and the Lords of Trade were active in soliciting new and up-to-date maps of their charge from each governor. The Governor of Barbados, Sir Jonathan Atkins, was lax in this regard, and was forced to refer the Lords to a map of the island compiled by and printed for a surveyor working in private practice on the island.

The cartographer, Richard Forde, was a

Quaker and had settled in Barbados in 1680 where he had lived in Bridgetown with his wife, child and two slaves. The Quaker religion has stongly held beliefs in, for example, pacifism. Despite the extra utility (and therefore sales), Forde's faith prevented him from including any of the several forts, artillery batteries or other military locations on the island, which would have been desired by the Governor, the island Assembly and the Lords of Trade.

Where the map is important, both in the history of Barbados, and of the wider American colonies, is that it is the first published economic map of any of England's possessions in the New World, and an extremely important record of the Barbadian sugar plantations, and their ownership, before the devastating hurricane of August 1675.

c. 1676

The 52 Counties of England and Wales, geographically described in a pack of cards

Robert Morden
Set of playing card maps.
Engravings,
each card *c.* 95 x 55 mm

Among the most popular types of playing cards were those with maps on. Quite by chance, it happens that, under the old county divisions of the sixteenth and seventeenth century, England and Wales were divided into 52 counties, a county for every card in a standard pack.

As a consequence, there are several series of packs of playing cards based on the English and Welsh counties, the first drawn by one W.B. (possibly William Bowes) and published in 1590. Perhaps the most popular, and most successful, set was published by Robert Morden in 1676, with later printings into the mid-part of the eighteenth century. Morden divided England and Wales into four regions, each forming one suit, the suit marks stencilled onto each card.

The cards were both recreational and educational, each forming a brief introduction to the geography of each county. Surprisingly, the cards are also significant as being the first series of maps of the English counties to show the major roads throughout England.

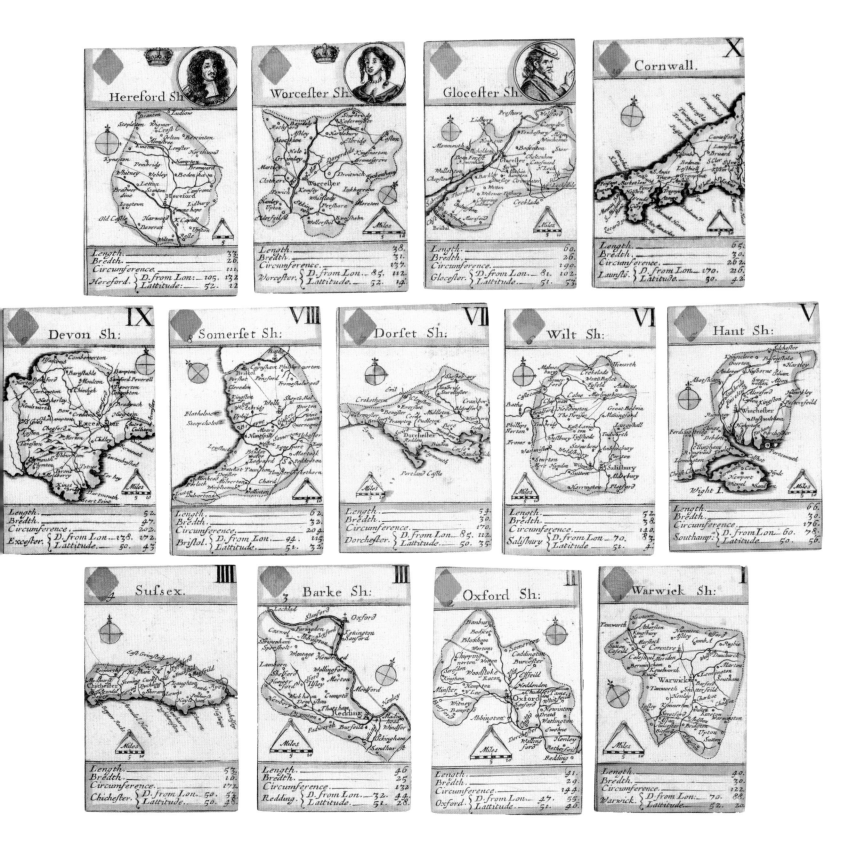

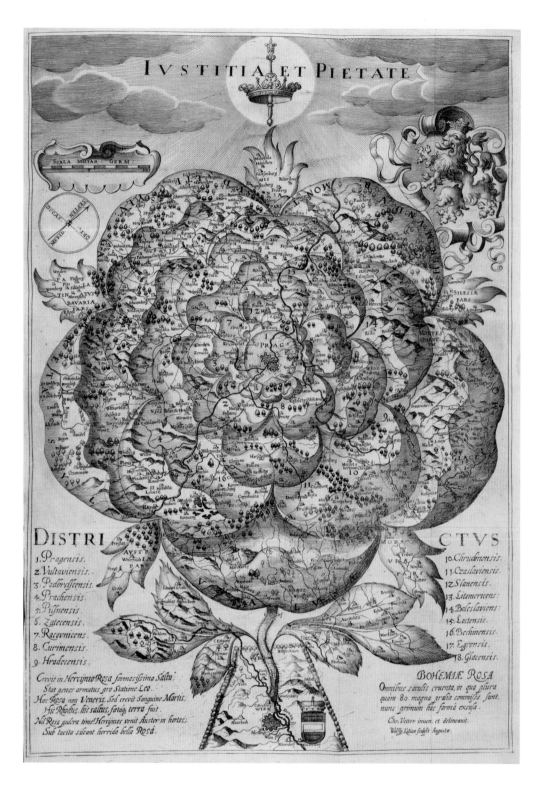

1677

'Bohemiæ rosa omnibus sæculis cruenta…'

Christoph Vetter
From: Bohuslav Babin's *Epitome Historica rerum Bohemicarum*, Augsburg, 1677.
Copper engraving, 395 x 265 mm

Representing countries in allegorical form was a popular form of cartographic expression, particularly where there was a national emblem that could readily be used for the purpose.

This allegorical map of Bohemia, drawn by Christoph Vetter in 1668, shows it in the shape of a rose; the rose was a popular regional symbol, most particularly associated with southern Bohemia. A five petal rose was the emblem of the Rozmberk (Rosenberg) family who ruled the region for over 200 years. The Rozmberks were known as the Masters of the Rose, and the rose was adopted by many towns of the region, with Festivals 'of the Five Petal Rose' continuing to the present day.

At the centre of the rose is the city of Prague, with the root based in Vienna. The five large petals are the provinces of Austria, Bavaria, Moravia, Silesia and Misnia (Meissen). The petals are subdivided into the 18 administrative divisions of Bohemia, including Prague itself.

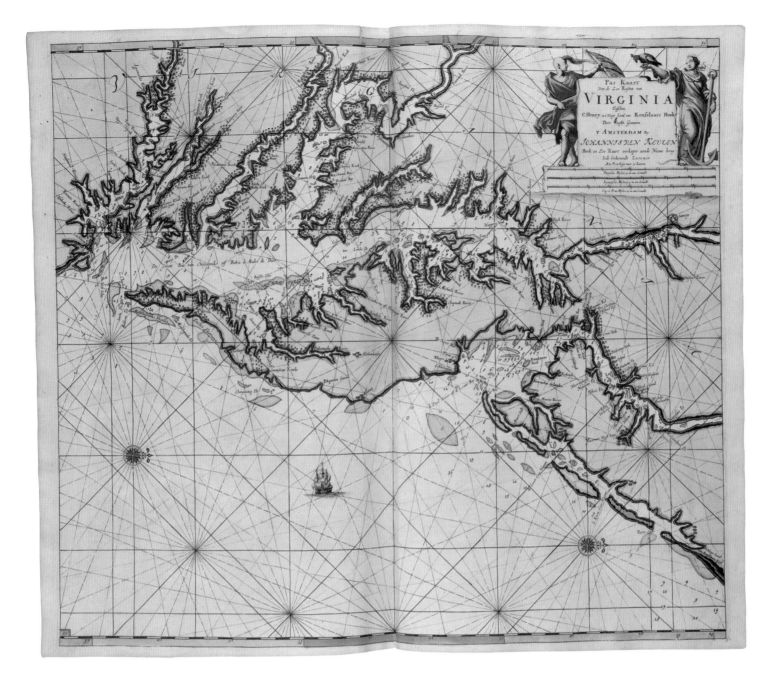

c. 1684

'Pas Kaart van de Zee Kusten van Virginia…'

Johannes van Keulen
From: van Keulen's *Zee-Fakkel…*,
vol. IV, Amsterdam, *c.* 1684.
Copper engraving, 510 x 580 mm

The van Keulen family were the leading private firm of chart-makers and publishers in Amsterdam from the 1690s to the 1790s, under the guidance of successive members of the family.

In the 1680s Gerard van Keulen, founder of the firm, commenced on his *Zee-Fakkel*, a multi-volume sea-atlas, with each volume devoted to one of the regions of the World. Volume IV, devoted to North America and the West Indies, was the most important Dutch publication on the region.

However, and perhaps surprisingly, this fine chart of the Chesapeake and Delaware Bays, with the coast between, was actually based on an English terrestrial map – Augustine Herrman's landmark four-sheet survey of the Virginia colony, published in 1673. The direct influence of the Herrman map extended well into the eighteenth century, but was even outlasted by this chart, which was reprinted, apparently without material geographical change, up to about 1790, long after it had been superseded by better charts.

1689

'Isola di Malta, olim Melita…'

Vincenzo Maria Coronelli
From: Coronelli's *Atlante Veneto*,
Venice, 1691.
Copper engraving 460 x 615 mm

Malta and Gozo are engraved in Coronelli's unique style in this large and decorative map. Surrounding the islands are 62 engraved armorials of the Grand Masters of the Knights of Malta.

The Knights of Malta were originally founded as the Knights Hospitallers, a quasi-military order helping pilgrims in the Holy Land. Forced to leave after the failure of the Crusades, the order moved from island to island in the Mediterranean, before arriving in Malta in 1530. There they established their base, and from here they campaigned against the Barbary Pirates, earning the wrath of the Ottoman Sultan. In 1565, the Sultan sent a force of some 40,000 men to capture Malta, but the order managed to hold out until relief came. When the replacement city was built it was named Valetta after the Grand Master who conducted the defence, Jean de la Valette.

After that the Knights of Malta stayed there, secure until the French Revolution. In 1798 the French fleet sailing for Napoleon's conquest of Egypt asked for shelter in Valetta then turned on its host. Losing the island caused a diaspora and diminishing of the order, although it still exists today.

LONDINI ANGLIÆ REGNI METROPOLIS NOVISSIMA & A

THE RIVER THAMES

Places of Southwark

1. St Mary Overs
2. St Olaves
3. St Thomas's
4. St Georges
5. St Magdalens
6. The Old Abby
7. Winchester house
8. The Kings Bench
9. The Marshalsea
10. The Bear garden

SOUTHWARK

St George's Field.

LAMBETH

The Road to Uxbridge

St James's

LONDON

t'Amsterdam by
IOANNES DE RAM.
Conft en Caart verkooper op den Dam.
Met Privilegie van de E. Heeren Staaten
van Holland en Westfriesland.

Names of Places Contain'd in this Mapp.

1690

'Londini Angliae Regni
Metropolis Novissima
& Accuratissima Autore
Ioanne de Ram'

Johannes de Ram
Separate publication,
Amsterdam, *c.* 1690.
Copper engraving, 495 x 580 mm

Johannes de Ram produced a fine map of
London as it was 25 years after the Great Fire
of 1666, with a prospect underneath showing
the many churches built under the
supervision of Sir Christopher Wren. The
architect's most famous creation, St Paul's
Cathedral, sits in the middle, despite it not
being completed for another 20 years. Top
right is a 148-point key containing 'Names
of Places Contain'd in this Mapp'.

One name not in the key but on the map
itself is 'Cuckold's Point', on the south side
of the Thames near Deptford. The site was
marked with a pair of horns (the sign of a
husband with an unfaithful wife, and also a
candidate for the origin of the infamous
English 'V-Sign') mounted on a pole to
commemorate the Horn Fair held at
Charlton. Legend has it that King John
gave the fair as a concession to a miller whose
wife he had seduced after a hunting trip. At
Cuckold's Point was a gibbet where the
bodies of river pirates were hung where all
Thames traffic could see them.

However, it is not the rebirth of London
that is the salient feature of the map: it is a
celebration of the success of the Glorious
Revolution of 1688, which saw the unpopular
King James II fleeing the country having
upset the Protestant populace with his
Catholic policies. Invited to rule in his place
were James's daughter Mary and her Dutch
husband, William of Orange. Their portraits
adorn the map; oranges dominate the
garlands around them and the putti under the
map. Their accession to the throne decided
the future of England as a protestant country.

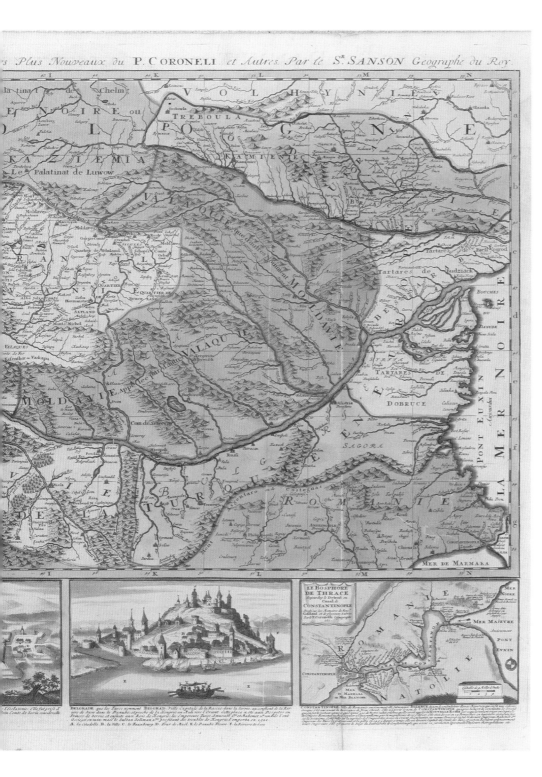

'Le Cours du Danube depuis sa Source jusqu'a ses Embouchures…'

Alexis Hubert Jaillot
From: Jaillot's *Atlas Nouveau*, Amsterdam, 1692[–1693].
Copper engraving, three sheets conjoined, total 595 x 1120 mm

Alexis Hubert Jaillot's large and decorative map of the Danube was derived from Vincenzo Maria Coronelli's map published by Nolin in Paris in 1688. The fine baroque title features medallion portraits of Pope Innocent XII, the Holy Roman Emperor, and the kings of Poland, Hungary and Bavaria. Underneath are five prospects of fortress towns from the region and a chart of the Bosphorus.

The map commemorates the Christian alliance assembled to resist the Ottoman advance northwards through the Balkans, a threat for much of the sixteenth and seventeenth centuries. Having captured Constantinople in 1453, the soft underbelly of Europe was exposed and the Turks sought to advance northwards with the intention of capturing Vienna – because of the city's strategic control of the Danube waterway.

However, the last Turkish attempt was foiled in the Battle of Vienna, fought on 14 July 1683, when the Christian allies destroyed the Ottoman army. The subsequent Treaty of Karlowitz handed Hungary and Transylvania to the victorious Austrians.

1700

'Les Deux Poles Arcticque
ou Septentrionale,
et Antarcticque ou
Meridionale...'

Pierre Mortier
Amsterdam, *c.*1700
Copper engraving, 440 x 530 mm

Centred on the North and South Poles, this
double-hemisphere world map is not the
typical 'Old and New' projection. This
unusual plan, omitting the equatorial third of
the world, highlights how little was known
about the polar extremes. In the cusps are two
smaller spheres, centred on Paris.

    Based on a map of 1657 by the Frenchman
Nicolas Sanson, whom Mortier credits in the
title, the geographer of the main spheres has
not been updated to 1700: on the left
Australia is still depicted as part of the great
southern continent, and on the right
Greenland is still connected to the Arctic
regions. The two smaller spheres are far
more accurate.

    Mortier has filled the corners with the
most elaborate allegorical vignettes, copied
from the Visscher/Berchem map of 1658, as
if in an attempt to draw attention away from
the antiquity of the map. Not only do they
depict the four seasons, but also (clockwise
from top left) the Rape of Persephone (Fire),
Zeus in his chariot drawn by eagles (Air),
Demeter and the harvest (Earth), and
Poseidon in his chariot (Water).

    As one of the centrepiece maps of the
atlas, much attention was paid to the
colouring, making this a stunning example of
the golden age of cartography.

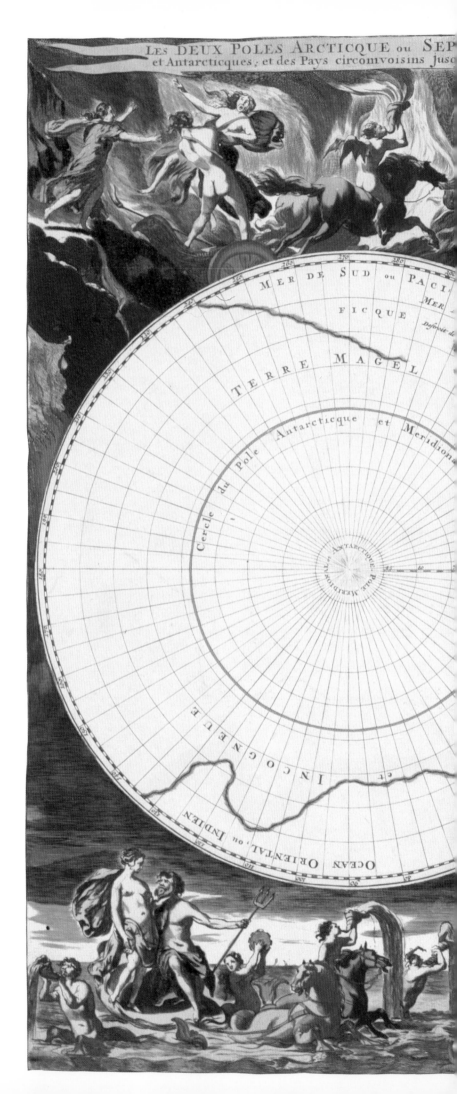

du Globe Terrestre en   Planisphere dont la ville de Paris est le Centre.

AMERIQUE

ASIE

AFRIQUE

AMERIQUE

MER DE NORT

OCEAN ATLANTIQUE

MER MAGELLANIQUE ou ETHIO

MER DU NORT

OCEAN PACIFICQUE

NOUVEL CE

SEP TENTRIONALE

TENTRIONALE

no

ou

TERRE DE YESO

CANADA

AMERIQ

Groenland

POLE SEPTENTRIONAL ou ARCTIQUE

Cercle Arctique

MER GLACIALE

MER DU CANADA

ISLANDE

MER DE FRANCE

BRIT TANI

GRAND OCEAN

SEPTENTRIONAL GLACIAL et

SCYTHIQUE et TARTARE

MER DE TARTARIE

Pole

MER DE

EUROPE

Sep Nova Zemla

MER DE MOSCOVIE

RUSSIE BLANCHE ou

SIBERIE

POLO GNE

MOSCOVIE

TARTARIE DES

USBEX

TURQ

ZAGATHAI

MER NOIRE

MER CASPIENNE

OCEAN MERIDIONAL ou ETHI

PARTIE DE L'AMERIQUE

du Globe Terrestre en   Planisphere ou les Antipodes de Paris servent de Centre

1700

'L'Africa …'

Paolo Petrini
Separate publication,
Venice, 1700.
Copper engraving, 945 x 1145 mm

Perhaps more than any other continent, with the possible exception of South America, the mapping of Africa lagged behind the others. For much of the 'discovery' and 'exploration' period of European overseas expansion, the European powers were content to coast the shores of Africa, establishing trading posts along the littoral, but relying on the tribes of the coast to bring trade goods from the interior.

Petrini's four-sheet wall-map of Africa gives a good overall outline of the continent, but much of the interior detail is imaginary or legendary, rather than based on first-hand observation; however, in keeping with the new mood of scientific reasoning being applied to cartography in the early eighteenth century, Petrini has omitted many of the dramatic images used by earlier mapmakers to fill the interior.

The two prominent lakes in southern Africa depicted as the source of the Nile, Lakes Zaire and Zaflan, are sometimes said to be proof of early European knowledge of Lakes Victoria and Tanganyika, with the 'Mountains of the Moon' the Ruwenzori Range, but this seems to be an example of cartographic legend bearing a coincidental resemblance to actuality rather than a sign of any knowledge of the region, which was not properly explored until the late nineteenth century.

GLOBES, SPH[...]
Mathematical *Books and* [...]
Sea & Land: *with many other* [...]
Gold, Silver, Steel, Brass, Ivory, & [...]
Sea Plats, *Charts & Prints*. Sold *at i[...]*
Charing Cross *& against y Royal Exch*[...]
By Tho. Tuttell. Mathematical [...]
To the Kings most Excellent [...]
WHERE ARE *Taught all Parts of t*[...]
Tho: Tuttell *Ingenieur de sa. M*[...]
pour les INSTRUMENTS MAT[...]
Armes du Roy *et Globes a* [...]
sa Botique *vis a vis la Bou*[...]
CORNHILLaLON[...]

Tuttell fecit

Tuttell fecit

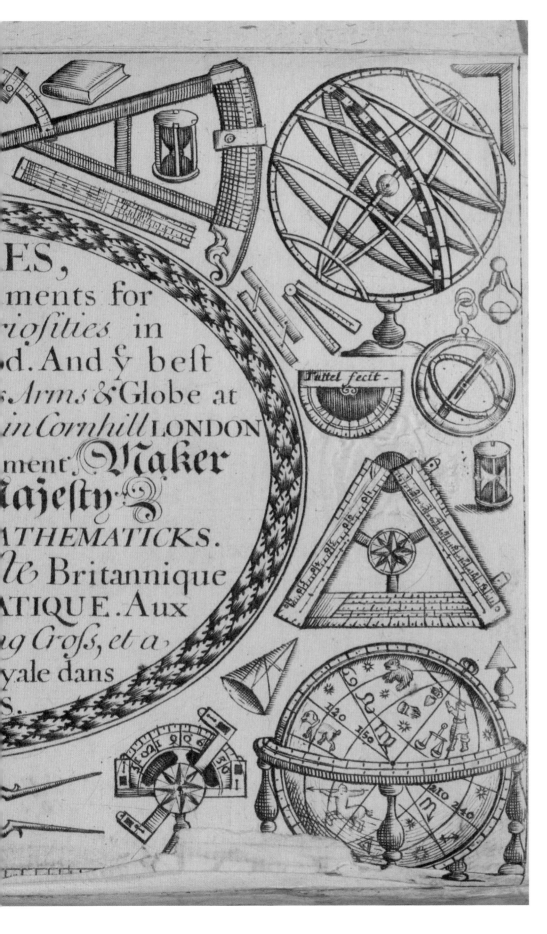

1700

Untitled pair of trade cards

Thomas Tuttell
Separate publications,
London, *c.* 1700.
Copper engravings,
200 x 155 mm & 175 x 285 mm

In the seventeenth and early eighteenth centuries, there were few opportunities for mapmakers and publishers to advertise their wares. What newspapers there were tended to have relatively small circulations, and were largely text only.

Consequently, tradesmen of all types looked to other means to advertise their shops and wares. A common method was elaborate trade cards, such as this pair engraved for Thomas Tuttell. Tuttell was appointed Mathematical Instrument Maker to William III in 1700, and later the same year appointed Hydrographer to the King.

These cards show a wide range of instruments, including sundials, mathematical instruments, cross- and back-staffs, Gunter's Rules and so on. Tuttell also dabbled as a globe-maker, and two examples can be seen on the larger trade card. From a cartographic viewpoint, the central vignette (overleaf) is particularly interesting as giving an unusually detailed delineation of a surveyor and assistants at work.

(see also overleaf) ↓

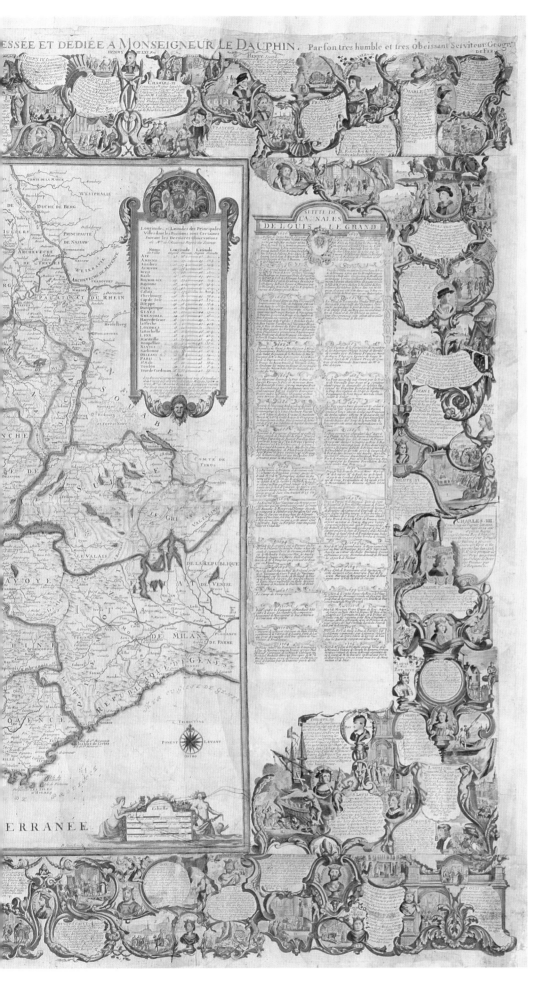

1705

'La France dans toute son Étendue…'

Nicolas de Fer
Separate publication, Jacques-François Bernard, Paris, 1722.
Copper engraving, 1030 x 1540 mm

France is shown in this rare four-sheet wall-map, engraved in 1705 by P. Starckman for Nicolas de Fer. This example was published by Jacques-François Bernard, de Fer's son-in-law and successor, in 1722.

Around the map is an extensive pictorial surround with the second title, 'La France Triomphante sous le Règne de Louis Quinze…', and depicting scenes from the history of France, with portraits of the various kings. Two large panels of text relate the life and the reign of Louis XIV, a time of extensive foreign wars.

Nicolas de Fer was Geographer to the French King. Royal patronage, and accompanying salary and other benefits, was often an important source of income for mapmakers. In return, the monarchs and other patrons expected the mapmaker to glorify their achievements. Here de Fer emphasizes the conquests made, and victories gained, in the reign of Louis XIV. While Louis' campaigns were generally successful, the costs of the near continuous wars all but bankrupted the French economy, and were met with rising disquiet within France.

VENI
VIDI
VICI

LAWINGEN

DALLINGEN

Hausen

The Camp of the Enemy two Nights before the Battle

Schertzheim

Altheim

Steinheim

Atorselnheim

Theisenhofen

HOCHSTET

A PROSPECT of

A. The Duke of MARLBOROUGH, giving a Note to Colonel Park. B. Prince EUGENE of Savoy. C. The Prince of Anhalt Dessau.
H. Nuns Mill. I. The Village of Bleinheim. K. The Center or Main Battalia of the French. L. The Village of Lutzingen. M. The Village of Sonderen

Lautzingen

Sonderen

Bleinheim

Kesler
schenbach

Unterklan

Scheinbach

Bergbaulion

Wolperstette

Wood

and

Hill

of

Goudre

Schreiningen

Daysheim

Münster

Ippershoven

Praasfat

The Camp of the Confederate the Right before the Battle

A most Exact and Accurate
PLAN
of the Several Attacks at the Famous
BATTLE of BLEINHEIM
And of the Incampments of both Armies
Before & after the Battle
The whole Survey'd upon the Spot, by the
Quarter-Master General, Assisted
by the best English Ingeneers
and Corrected & Approved
by all the Generals.

LONDON

Sold by DAVID MORTIER
Book Map, and Print Seller
in the Strand at ye Sign of
Erasmus's Head near the Savoy

EXPLANATION
of the
References in this Plan

A. The Confederate Army Marching in Nine Columns from their Camp at
B. The Camp of the French & Bavarians just before the Battle.
C. The Dispositions made by the Confederates for the Attack.
D. The four Mills which the Enemy set on Fire, together with the
Bergheim, Weiler, Unterklau, and a Farm-House.
E. The Enemies Batteries
F. Batteries of the Confederates
G. Twenty Battalions design'd for the Attack of the Village of Bl
H. Fifteen Squadrons which were to Support them.
I. The Rest of the Battalions who after having pass'd the Rivulet to Atta
K. The Place where some of our Cavalry pass'd the Rivulet
L. The Places where the Rest of the Left Wing pass'd the said River
M. The Farm in which they drew up after having pass'd the Rivulet
N. Three Battalions brought up by former the Cavalry, who where in t
Enemy from the Village of Oberklau, and afterwards drew up where
O. Ten Battalions attempting to pass the Rivulet over against Oberkla
of them that pass'd at first were almost intirely cut in Pieces
P. The Place where the Right Wing pass'd the Rivulet, and was Drew F
Q. The Right Wing drawn up after having pass'd the Fourth Time
R. The Cavalry of our Left Wing, drawn up after having Forced
the Enemy, and intirely cut of two Brigades of their Infantry, that w
by their Horses
S. The Place where the Enemies Cavalry rallied.
T. Archleight where Part of the Enemies Cavalry (upon the Appr
charge them) broke, and ran down in the greatest Disorder toward
Danube, and some along the Meadows toward: Meihetet In
Tallard was taken Prisoner at the Mill of Sonderen mark'd
U. The Remainder of the Right Wing of the Enemies Cavalry radd
on Motion to attack them, they faced about and march'd off, b
Squadrons pursuing them towards Morselingen.
V. The Rest of our Cavalry halted at V to observe the Motion
Enemy, which by this Time was drawn up beyond the Morgan
During this Halt at V, the Elector of Bavaria was perceiv'd
his Retreat from the Village of Lutzingen, upon which Order
General Vengnick, who follow'd the Enemy towards Morselingen
and march to join them which halted at V.
X. The Place where our Army drew up, and lay on their Arms that
Y. The Place where the Enemy drew up, and continued till within the
March'd off towards Dillingen & Lawingen.
Z. The Duke of MARLBOROUGH Quarters that Night.
& Part of our Infantry Surrounding the Village of Bleinheim
Battalion, and 12. Squadrons of Dragoons, where made Pr

Horse }
Infantry } of the Conf
Horse }
Foot } of the En

A Scale of 1000 Geometrical Paces

ORDER of BATTLE of the CONFEDERATE ARMY as they March'd up to the ENEMY, the 13th Aug 1704. N.S.

The Duke of MARLBOROUGH, Cap: Gen: of the Queen of Great Brittain's Forces.   Prince EUGENE of Savoy, Field Marshall of the Emperor
His Highness the Duke of WIRTEMBERG

CHURCHILL   P: of ANHALT   d. Essan   P: of HANNOVER   Count de la TOUR, Gen: of the Horse   Prince of BAREITH
Prince of HESSE Gen:l of ye Horse   Ingolsby   HORN   Scholten   Prince DOURLAGH   Violets, County Post: Prince LSORKNEY   Marquis de CESANI
Emerald: Prince of HESSE Gen:l of ye Horse   Lord CUTS.   Rantzau   Count Fugger   TILLIERS Pr: of Hesse Homburgh Wittinghoff   Lue, Rantzau, Poland   Bibra   Count CARAFF
Tind Gen: LUMLEY, Hompesch D. of Wirtemberg   Erbagh, Weyslin   St Paul Fink Natzmer   Bateman   Greiswald   Brockdorff   WEBB Kuffen Sachsen Borgsfee Son Rotschild
Emerald: Gen: WOOD, Aurea Schaulenbourgh   Tergston: ROW: Halsen Walron Asdenbergh: Walck   Fort   Dragoons   Dragoons   Foot   Dragoons
Brigadier: Gen: ROSS   BALDWIN

Horse   Dragoon   Foot   Dragoons   Horse   Dragoons   Horse

Corp of Res.

First } LINE 75
Friend }
Corp of Reserve 16

18

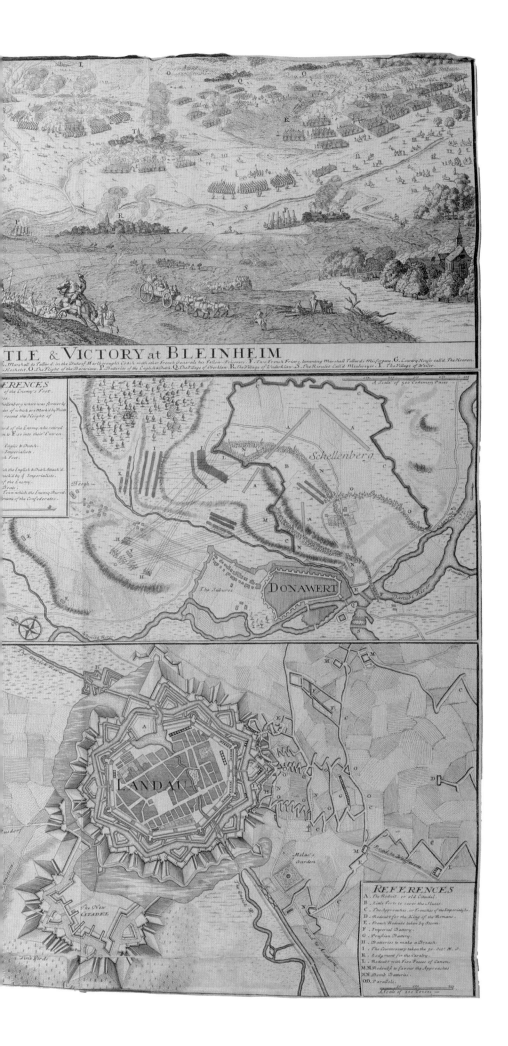

TLE & VICTORY at BLEINHEIM

REFERENCES

DONAWERT

Schellenberg

LANDAU

REFERENCES

c. 1705

'A most Exact and Accurate
Plan of the Several Attacks
at the Famous Battle
of Blenheim…'

David Mortier
Separate publication,
London, c. 1705.
Copper engraving, 590 x 815 mm

The Battle of Blenheim was a major
engagement of the War of the Spanish
Succession fought on 13 August 1704, at
the village of Blenheim, near Höchstädt in
Bavaria. A joint Franco-Bavarian force was
threatening Vienna. John Churchill, Duke
of Marlborough, was dispatched from the
Netherlands with the English army to link
up with the Austrian general, Prince Eugene
of Savoy. Once their forces were united,
Marlborough gave battle to the Franco-
Bavarian Army.

   The battle of Blenheim was a great
tactical victory for Marlborough. For the
first time in two generations the French had
suffered a crushing, total, defeat. The allies
conquered Bavaria and Vienna was saved.
The territorial ambitions of Louis XIV
beyond the Rhine were checked, and France
was placed on the defensive. Overnight the
Duke of Marlborough became a national
hero, and Blenheim Palace was built for him
as a gift from a grateful nation.

   In London rival publishers vied with each
other to be first to publish a plan of the battle
to capitalize on public interest. This plan,
with its detailed view of the battle, was
published by David Mortier, a Dutch
publisher resident in London, and is probably
the finest contemporary plan of the battle
published in England.

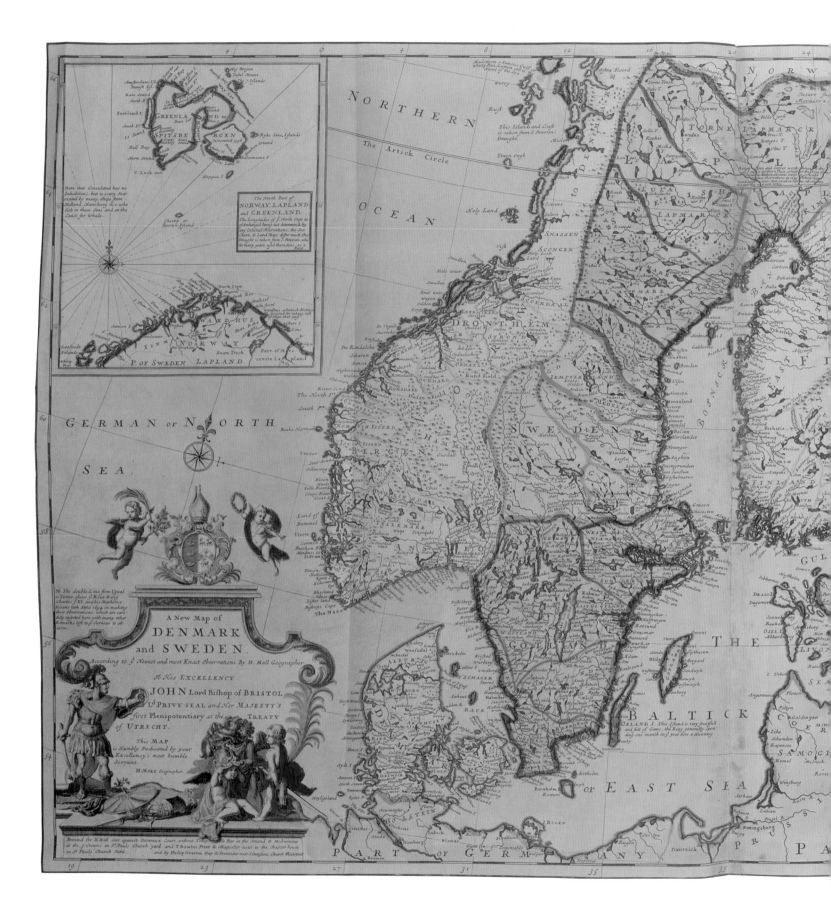

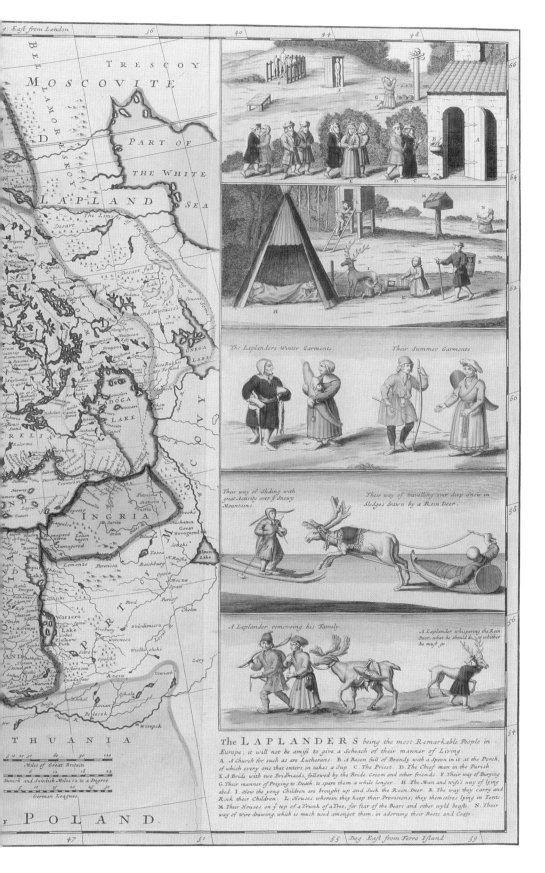

'A New Map of Denmark and Sweden…'

Herman Moll
From Moll's *World Described*,
London, *c.* 1719.
Copper engraving, 610 x 1015 mm

Herman Moll produced a fine map of Scandinavia from one of the largest English atlases of the period. The map has an inset map of the northern reaches of the mainland and Spitsbergen. Down the right side are five vignettes depicting the lifestyles of the Laplanders, who Moll describes as 'the most remarkable people in Europe'; these scenes show a very early representation of skiing, their use of sledges drawn by reindeer, and 'A Laplander whispering the Reindeer, what he should do, or whither he must go'.

Such a publication was a large and expensive production, impossible for one publisher to bear. The publication line here lists four different London map-sellers, who shared the publication costs, and the financial risks.

At this time it was not yet possible to make a sheet of paper large enough for maps this size, so the maps were printed on two sheets and joined together. Even with the maps folded in half the bindings would have had to be huge, so usually the maps were folded twice more. These extra folds were weak points, so often these maps are found with cracks or separation along the folds.

1713

'The Roads of England According to Mr. Ogilby's Survey'

George Willdey
Separate publication,
London, *c.* 1713.
Copper engraving, 523 x 528 mm

England and Wales are depicted in this very scarce diagrammatic map, showing the network of roads as surveyed by John Ogilby, radiating out from London. Distances between the towns are marked in miles.

John Ogilby published his *Britannia* in 1675, creating an instant publishing sensation. The *Britannia* was Europe's first printed road atlas, and the first English atlas to a uniform scale, at one inch to a mile. The 'mile' had never been standardized across the country: the mile that Ogilby used, 1,760 yards (1,600 m), became the 'statute mile', the standard unit of measure in England.

Before Ogilby few maps attempted to show roads; after him, no map could be without them. The next year Bassett and Chiswell, publishers of the *Speed county atlas*, added a schematic diagram copied from Ogilby's maps; referring to this piracy, Ogilby complained that Bassett and Chiswell 'have rob'd my book'. Three pirate editions of the *Britannia* were published in the next century, the roads shown by Ogilby were copied onto county maps, and other publishers, like Willdey here, even felt free to use Ogilby's name on their copies.

1715

'A New and Exact Map
of the Dominions of
the King of Great Britain
on ye Continent
of North America…'

Herman Moll
From Moll's *World Described*,
London, 1715.
Copper engraving, 1010 x 610 mm

Moll's two-sheet map of the English
possessions in North America is generally
termed 'The Beaver Map' from the large
inset scene of beavers making a dam, but
the map is an important and influential
compilation of the most important
contemporary materials for the English
colonies of the eastern seaboard.

Moll was an emigrant from Germany, who
established himself as an engraver,
but latterly in his career termed himself
'geographer'. Of relatively humble means,
Moll was anxious to be accepted in eminent
scientific circles, and so adopted the interests
of these individuals, which he represented
through his maps. Thus he became an ardent
proponent of English empire in the
Americas; the 'Beaver Map' is as much about
promoting colonial expansion, and
encouraging the commercial exploitation
of the region, as providing a geographical
picture of the region, employing subliminal
imagery to portray the perceived wealth
available to the new settler or the merchant
willing to trade with the American colonies.

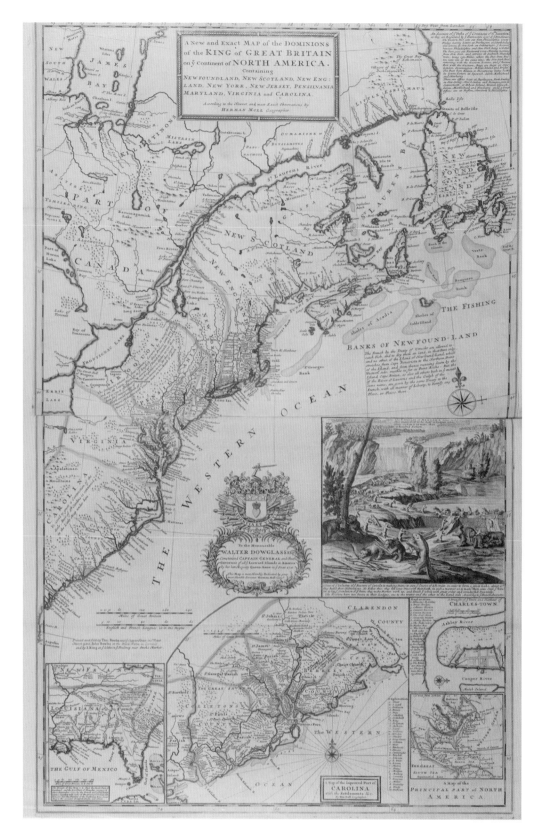

PLANISPHERE
REPRESENTANT TOUT L'ETENDUE DU MONDE.
DANS L'ORDRE QU'ON A   SUIVI DANS CE LIVRE.

1715

'Planisphère représentant Toute l'Étendue du Monde'

Louis Renard
From: Renard's *Atlas de la Navigation et du Commerce*, Amsterdam, 1715. Copper engraving, 430 x 265mm

This is the engraved frontispiece to Renard's sea-atlas, showing the globe being supported on the shoulders of Hercules, who can be recognized by his lion skin and club. As one of the preliminary leaves in an atlas, and one of the first that a potential buyer might see, publishers tended to lavish particular care on engraved title, frontispieces, and the first map, generally a world map, so as to catch the customer's eye.

In one version of the story of his labours, Hercules held up the world while Atlas, who normally had that burden, stole the 'Apples of Hesperides' from his own daughters. However, Hercules then had to trick Atlas into resuming his responsibility.

The projection is unusual, because it shows the whole world in one single hemisphere, rather than the more familiar North Pole projection extending south to the Equator, as one would expect. This, of course, causes much distortion, but not the lateral widening of Australia. Other oddities shown include California as an island, a northwest passage, and a river right through sub-equatorial Africa, linking the Atlantic with the Indian Ocean.

HELVETIAE PAGI seu CANTONES. XIII. OHRT der EIDGENOSSSCHAFT. 1. ZÜRICH. 2. BERN. 3. LUCERN. 4. URI. 5. SCHWEIZ. 6. UNDERWALDEN 7. ZUG 8. GLARUS. 9. BASEL. 10. FREIBURG. 11. SOLOTHUR
1. S. GALLEN ABT. 2. S. GALLEN STATT. 3. PÜNDTEN. 4. WALLIS. 5. MULHAUSEN 6. BIEL. 7. NEÜBURG NEUFCHATEL 8. GENFF GENEVE. 9. BISCHOFF BASEL Tigurinis, Lucernenfibus, Urij, Suitenfibus, Sublylvanis, Tugurensibus, Glaronensibus qu vn Cantones veteres, vn alte Ohrt vulgo vocant
THAL adscitis Abbatiscellanis Tigurini, Bernensibus, Lucernensibus, Urij, Suitenfibus, Subsylvanis, Tugensibus, Glaronensibus, qui VIII Cantonum Veterum nôie veniunt, paret BADEN. Graffsch XII. prim. Canton jurisdiction. agnoscunt Præfecturæ Transalpinæ 1. LAUIS. LUGANO. 2. LUGARus. LOCARNO. 3. MENDRIS. 4. ME
BE. 5. GRANSON. Uriorum, Suitenfium et Subsylvanorum sunt 1. BELLINZONA. 2. RIVIERA. 3. VALLEBREGNIA PALENSERTHAL. Suitorum et Glaronensium GASTER. CASTRARHAETICA. Sui juris sunti. RAPERSCHWEIL. 2. ENGELBERG. 3. GERSAU.

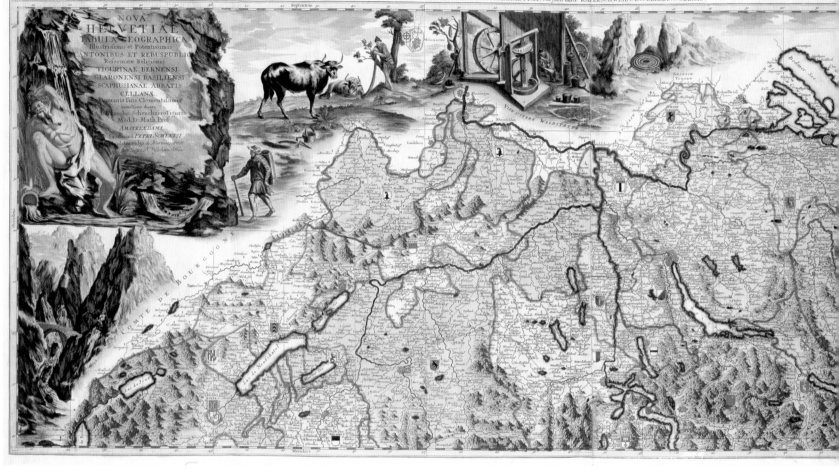

1716

'Nova Helvetiae Tabula Geographica'

Johann Jacob Scheuchzer
Wall-map on four sheets
joined as two,
Pieter Schenk, Amsterdam, *c.* 1716.
Copper engraving, 850 x 1110 mm

Scheuchzer (1672–1733) was a Swiss mathematician, geologist and geographer, living and working in Zurich. From 1706 to 1708 he published his *Beschreibung des Naturgeschichten des Schweitzerlands*, an important description of Swiss mountains, rivers and geology. Much of it was based on the observations that he made as he travelled around Switzerland, in nine separate journeys.

In 1712 Scheuchzer, drawing on experiences from his travels, published his map of Switzerland on four sheets. It is one of the earliest large-scale delineations of Switzerland, perhaps the best map of that country before the nineteenth century and certainly one of the most dramatic, with the finely engraved vignette scenes and views filling every inch of blank space outside the map proper.

There are views of Switzerland's mountain scenery, the waterfalls, Alpine plateaus and even some industrial drawings, which encapsulate not just the geography but also life in Switzerland for an interested observer.

Scheuchzer's map was quickly copied by foreign mapmakers; this example was published in Amsterdam by Pieter Schenk.

Such was the influence of Scheuchzer's map and travel accounts, that it has been suggested that he provided the early impetus for tourism in the Alpine regions as, stimulated by his work, people came from all over Europe to see Switzerland for themselves.

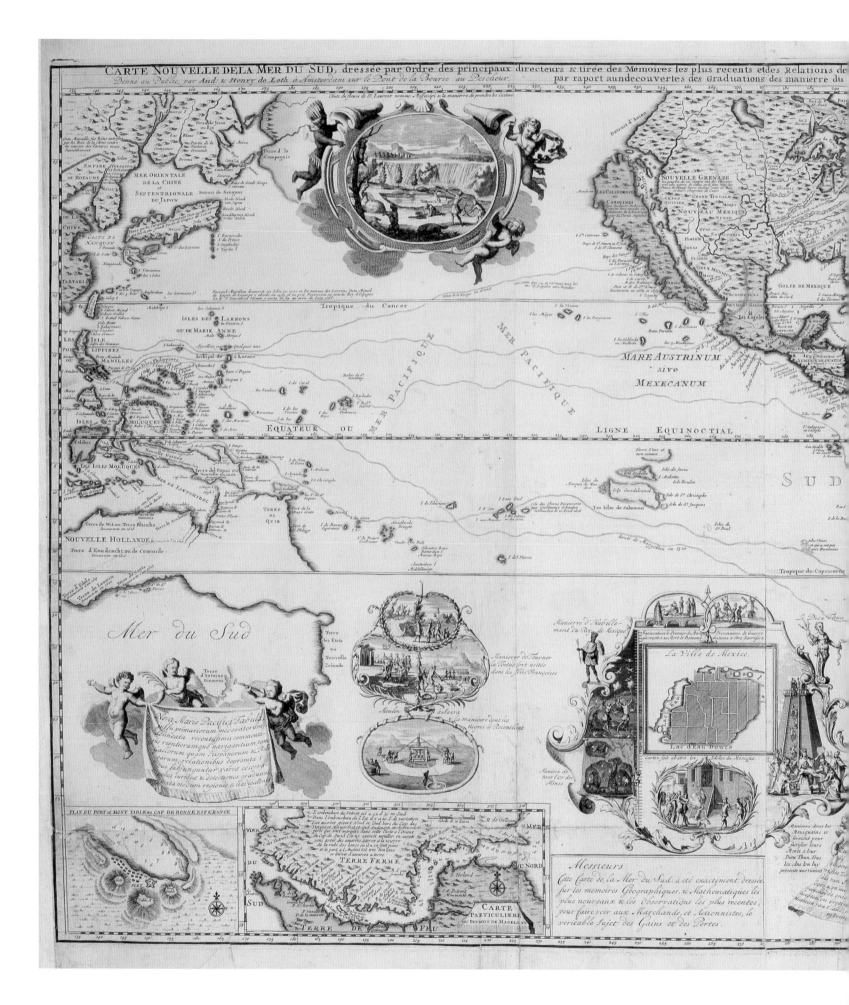

c. 1720

'Carte Nouvelle de la Mer du Sud, ...'

Anders & Hendrick de Leth
Separate publication,
Amsterdam, c. 1720
Copper engraving, 595 x 940 mm

Anders and Hendrick de Leth's wall map of the Americas is one of two very similar maps published within a year or so of each other, each centred on the Americas, with the neighbouring coasts of Europe, Africa and Asia.

Geographically, neither map is very advanced - evidence of limited European penetration into the interior. Both, however, are notable as pictorial encyclopedias of the New World, with every inch of blank space in the map crammed with images portraying the life and customs of the natives of the region. There are also inset maps of important features, as well as two representations of the Cape of Good Hope in Africa.

The de Leth version, which was published separately, is considerably scarcer than the rival map by Henri-Abraham Chatelain.

'A New and Correct Map of
the Roads in England and
Wales. Wherein are Contained
all the Road Waies And the
Principal Cross Roads, with
the Computed Distances'

Henry Overton (I)
Separate publication,
Henry Overton, London, 1726.
Copper engraving, with borders
581 x 1020 mm.

The London map trade in the early eighteenth
century was not considered to be an innovative
period. The emphasis was frequently on a county
atlas, a large plan of London and a large map of
the British Isles and of England and Wales. With
everyone producing similar subjects, using the
same geographical materials, and with the
resultant maps looking very much the same,
publishers sought to out-do each other, and make
their offering more marketable, by working up
the decorative elements.

Henry Overton led the way in this regard; this
fine two-sheet map of England is complete with
the two additional side panels pasted outside the
map border, with one titled 'The Coats of Arms
of all the City's and Shire Towns of every
County in England and Wales, with Some of the
Corporations...' and the other 'An Alphabeticall
Table of all the Cities and Market Towns in
England And Wales shewing their distance from
LONDON and Market days &c...'

The main map is a simple road map of
England and Wales, emphasizing then, as the
importance of the road network fanning out
from London does now, the hub of the system.

An interesting feature of the map is the series
of diagrams at the bottom of the right-hand
column, which acts as a colour guide, illustrating
the standard engraving conventions used to show
the colourist the correct colours for the
armorials, with the shields showing: 'Azure [or]
Bleu', 'Vert [or] Green' 'Sable [or] Black' '
Or [or] Yellow', 'Argent [or] White' and
'Gules [or] Red'.

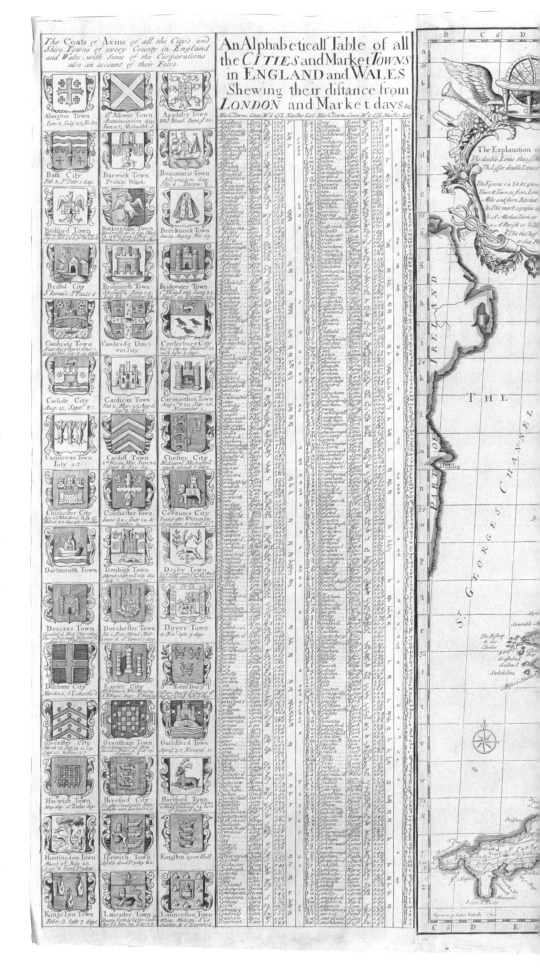

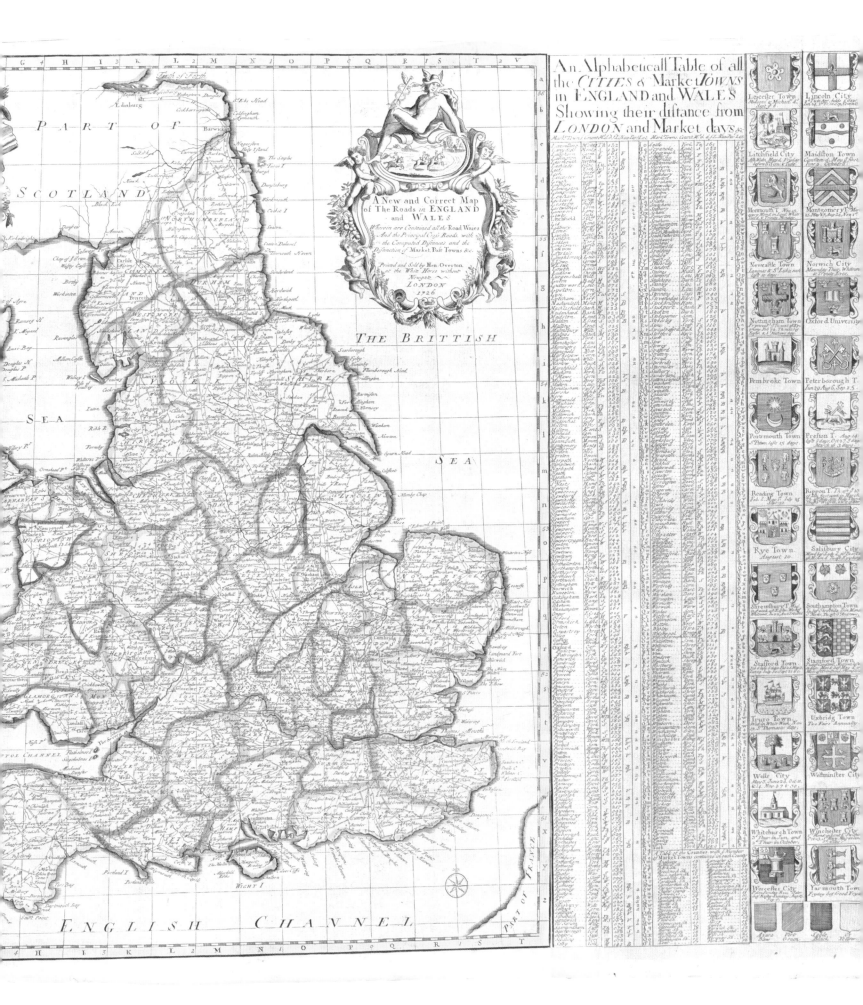

'A New and Correct Mapp of Middlesex, Essex, and Hertfordshire…'

John Warburton, Joseph Bland & Payler Smyth
Separate publication, [London, 1725]. Widest: 972 x 1515 mm; with armorial borders: 1156 x 2175 mm

Prior to the mid-eighteenth century English mapmakers were very much the poor relation in European cartography. The large continental firms, such as the Blaeus and the Hondius-Janssonius family dominated atlas publishing in Europe, while the English market was simply too small to be lucrative.

To overcome their financial difficulties, English mapmakers adopted a variety of means to finance their output. Most frequent was forming loose alliances to finance projects, but a bolder move was to raise the money required to see an ambitious book or map through the press by subscription – offering a discounted price for payment in advance and often offering to incorporate the subscriber's name and/or arms within the publication.

In terms of subscribers signed up, Warburton, Bland and Smyth's six-sheet wall-map of Hertfordshire, Middlesex, and Essex is the most impressive of all English map-publishing projects. The panelled borders include the arms of ten towns or city corporations and 726 individuals. Unfortunately, even with this number of subscribers, each apparently paying 16s. 6d. (82.5 pence in modern terms), the partners would still have lost a considerable amount of money, and this was the last project on which they worked together.

This was unfortunate as Payler Smyth, the surveyor, did a very good job, within the financial constraints the partners faced, at creating a new survey of these three counties.

c. 1725

'A New & Correct Map of Denmark'

George Willdey
Separate publication,
London, 1725.
Copper engraving, 445 x 365 mm

This unusual map of Denmark comes from a series of oval maps published by George Willdey, the London publisher.

Willdey seems to have pioneered the use and construction of large screens adorned with maps: one extant example, in a private collection, has Willdey's world map in the centre, flanked by these oval maps and two celestial hemispheres, all designed in heavy frame-like borders, with inset notes on the region depicted.

Surprisingly, the maps do not bear the name of a publisher; however, three of the group are signed by an engraver Samuel Parker, and presumably all can be attributed to him, while the advertisement on Willdey's world map seems to link those maps to him as a publisher.

The set of maps are very scarce, with no set in a British institution.

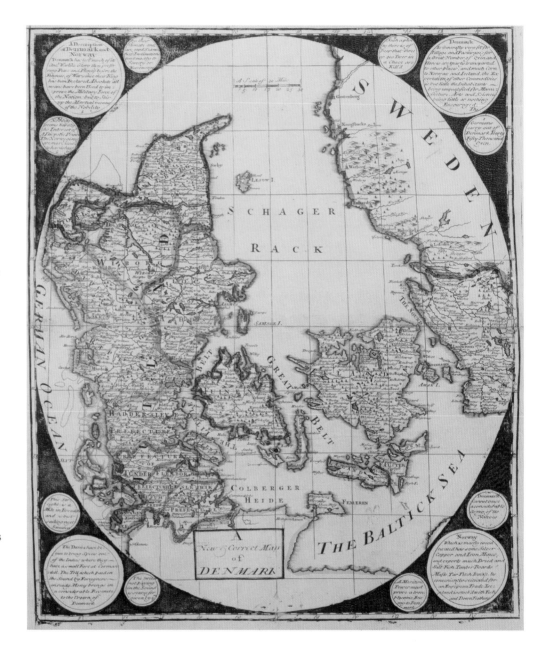

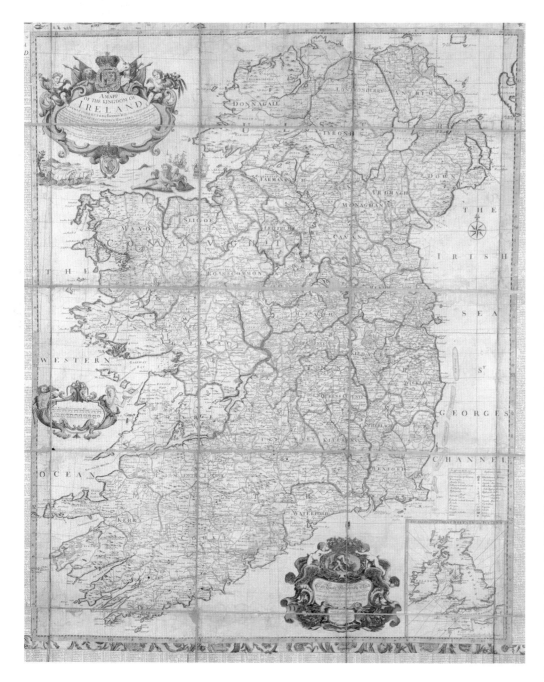

'A Mapp of the Kingdom of Ireland newly Corrected & Improv'd by actual observations...'

Henry Pratt
Separate publication, wall-map, George Grierson, Dublin, *c.* 1728. Copper engraving, 1210 x 60 mm

The Glorious Revolution of 1688 saw the Catholic King James II ousted by the Protestants William, Duke of Orange, and his wife, Mary, James' daughter. The final act of his overthrow was fought out in Ireland, culminating in the Battle of the Boyne, where the pro-James (Jacobite) Catholic forces were roundly defeated. Subsequent English Kings and Queens were frequently faced with rebellions by alliances of disaffected Catholics, notably the Jacobite Risings of 1715, 1719 and the '45, led by Bonnie Prince Charlie, grandson of James II.

To secure their control over Ireland, the English installed garrisons across the island, to enforce English rule. In 1708 Henry Pratt published a wall-map of Ireland, revised and updated to show the latest geographical information, in the manner of any good map of Ireland. But in view of the perceived volatility of the situation, his map also highlights the garrison towns within the plan, and in the side margins there are detailed miniature plans of the principal cities and fortified towns.

The leading bookseller and publisher in Dublin for much of the first half of the eighteenth century was George Grierson. He was also the principal map publisher, though this part of his business was broadly based on pirating the most recent maps and atlases published in England, and recycling them for an Irish audience. Indeed, the version of Pratt's map illustrated here was published by Grierson; other than the presence of Grierson's name in the dedication, the two maps appear indistinguishable.

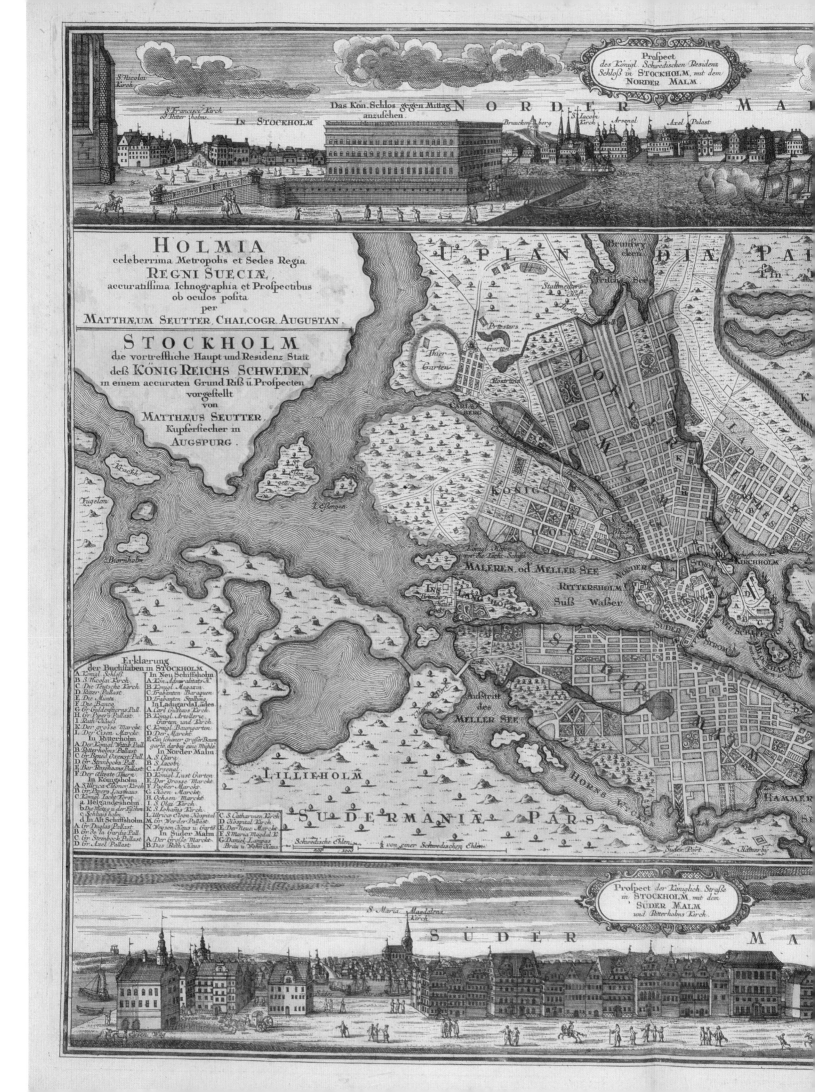

S. Nicolai Kirch

S. Francisci Kirch od Ritter holm

IN STOCKHOLM

Das Kon. Schlos gegen Mittag anzusehen

NORDER MALM

Brunckenberg   S. Jacobi Kirch   Arsenal   Axel Palast

Norder Strom

HOLMIA
celeberrima Metropolis et Sedes Regia
REGNI SUECIÆ,
accuratissima Ichnographia et Prospectibus
ob oculos posita
per
MATTHÆUM SEUTTER, CHALCOGR. AUGUSTAN.

STOCKHOLM
die vortreffliche Haupt und Residenz Statt
deß KÖNIG REICHS SCHWEDEN,
in einem accuraten Grund Riß u. Prospecten
vorgestellt
von
MATTHÆUS SEUTTER
Kupferstecher in
AUGSPURG.

UPLANDIÆ PARS

Stallmeister

Priestus

Garten

Thier Garten

Rosthult

CARLS BERG

KÖNIG HOLM

Knackh

Fugelon

Esfingen

Björnholm

Königl. Flotten von de Jacht Schiffe

MALEREN od MELLER SEE

RITTERSHOLM
Suß Wasser

NORDER STROM

KIRCHHOLM

Brandkyrka   Langholm

Auftritt des
MELLER SEE

LILLIEHOLM

SUDER MALM

HORNS WEG

SUDER STROM

SCHIFFSHOLM

HAMMER

SUDERMANIÆ PARS

Schwedische Ehlen   ⅛ von einer Schwedischer Ehlen
500   1000

Erklärung
der Buchstaben in STOCKHOLM

A. Königl. Schloß
B. S. Nicolai Kirch
C. Die Teutsche Kirch
D. Ritter Pallast
E. Die Müntz
F. Die Banco
G. Gr. Gyldenstierns Pall.
H. Gr. Piper's Pallast
I. Rath Hauß
K. Der grosse Marckt
L. Der Eisen Marckt
In Ritterholm
A. Der Königl. Werk Pall
B. Ritterholms Pallast
C. Gr. Bened. Oxenst. Pall.
D. Gr. Steenbocks Pall.
E. Bar. Bosehaans Pallast
F. Der älteste Thurn
In Kongsholm
A. S. Ulrica Eleanor Kirch
B. Gr. Piper's Lusthaus
C. Königl. Jacht Forst
a. Helgandesholm
b. Die Brücke u. der Fischen
c. Schlauß Holm
d. In Alt Schiffsholm
A. Gr. Duglas Pallast
B. Gr. de la Gardie Pall.
C. Gr. Steenbock Pallast
D. Gr. Axel Pallast

In Neu Schiffsholm
A. Ein Admiralitäts H.
B. Königl. Magazin
C. Trabanten Baraquen
D. Trabanten Stallung
In Ladugarda Lädes
A. Carl Gustavs Kirch
B. Königl. Artollerie,
Garten und Kirch
C. Königl. Baumgarten
D. Der Marckt
E. Ein schöner grosser Baum
garte, darby eine Mühle
In Norder Malm
A. S. Clara
B. S. Jacobi
C. Arsenal
D. Königl. Lust Garten
E. Der Grosse Marckt
F. Packer Marckt
G. Hoen Marckt
H. Ochsen Marckt
I. S. Olai Kirch
K. S. Johanis Kirch
L. Ullrica Cleon. Hospital
M. Gr. Werder Pallast
N. Weysen Hauß u. Gartz
In Suder Malm
A. Der grosse Marckt
B. Das Rath Hauß
C. S. Catharinen Kirch
D. Hospital Kirch
E. Der Neue Marckt
F. S. Maria Magdal. K.
G. Daniel Lampas
Bräu u. Wohn Hauß

S. Maria Magdalena Kirch

SUDER MALM

Ritter Weg

'Holmia celeberrima
Metropolis et Sedes
Regia… Stockholm…'

Matthæus Seutter
From Seutter's *Atlas Novus*,
Augsburg, *c.* 1730.
Copper engraving, 500 x 570 mm

After the success of the Braun and
Hogenberg series of town plans there were
few attempts to publish an updated version
for nearly a century. In the 1660s Janssonius's
townbooks mostly comprised reissues of the
Braun and Hogenberg plates with a few
additional plates; and of Blaeu's more
comprehensive series only Italy and the
Low Countries volumes were completed
before a fire in the printing works all but
bankrupted the firm. Other publishers tended
to issue town plans as individual plates, or as
inclusions in general atlases.

With the emergence of Germany as a
leading centre of European map publishing,
there was fresh impetus for town plans. Both
Johann Baptist Homann in Nuremburg and
Seutter started including them in their atlases,
but standardizing the format: the main map
would show the street plan (unlike the map-
view approach of Braun and Hogenberg),
while there would be at least one prospect of
the city above or below the map.

Here we see Stockholm, at the time the
capital of the Swedish Empire. Seutter has
included two prospects: above is a general
view of the city from the sea, with the King's
Palace centre left; below is the main street of
the city.

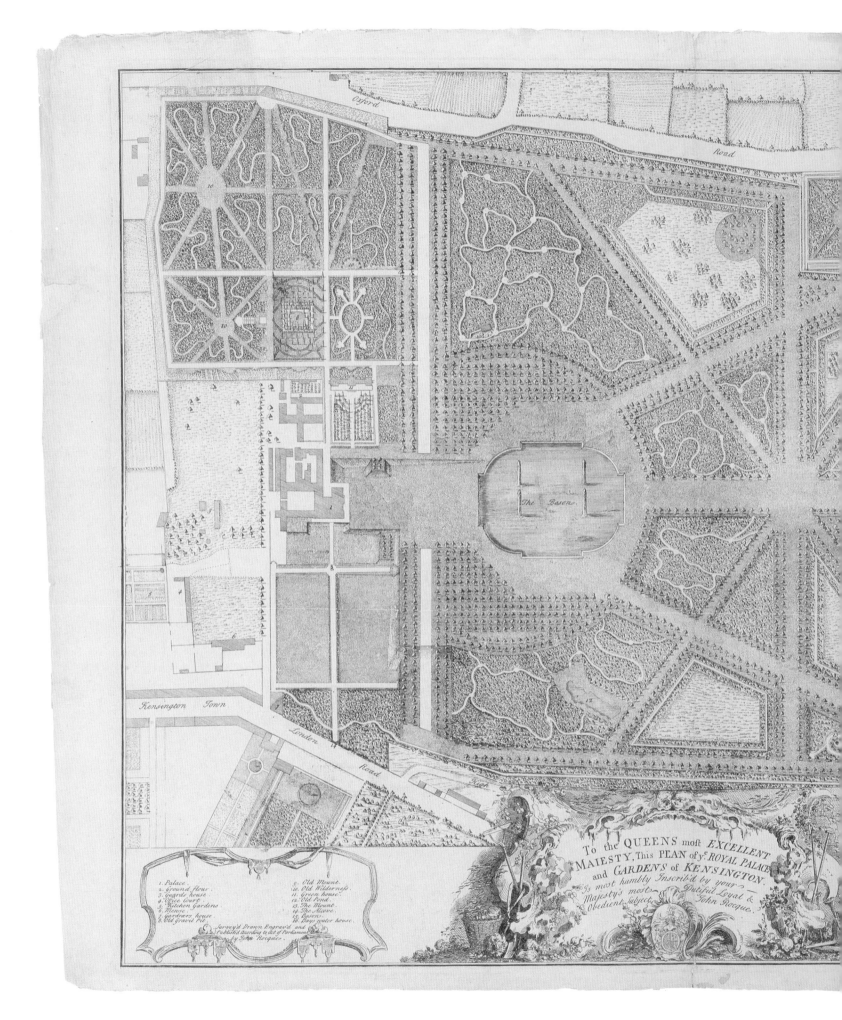

Oxford

Road

Kensington Town

London

Road

Rich

The Bason.

To the QUEENS most EXCELLENT
MAIESTY, This PLAN of yͤ ROYAL PALACE
and GARDENS of KENSINGTON,
Is most humbly Inscrib'd by your
Majesty's most
Obedient Subject
Dutiful Loyal &
John Rocque.

1. Palace.
2. Ground floor.
3. Guards house.
4. Open Court.
5. Kitchen Gardens.
6. Menue.
7. Gardeners house.
8. Old gravel Pit.
9. Old Mount.
10. Old Wilderness.
11. Green house.
12. Old Pond.
13. The Mount.
14. The Alcove.
15. Basons.
16. Days water house.

Survey'd Drawn Engrav'd and
Publish'd according to Act of Parliament
by John Rocque.

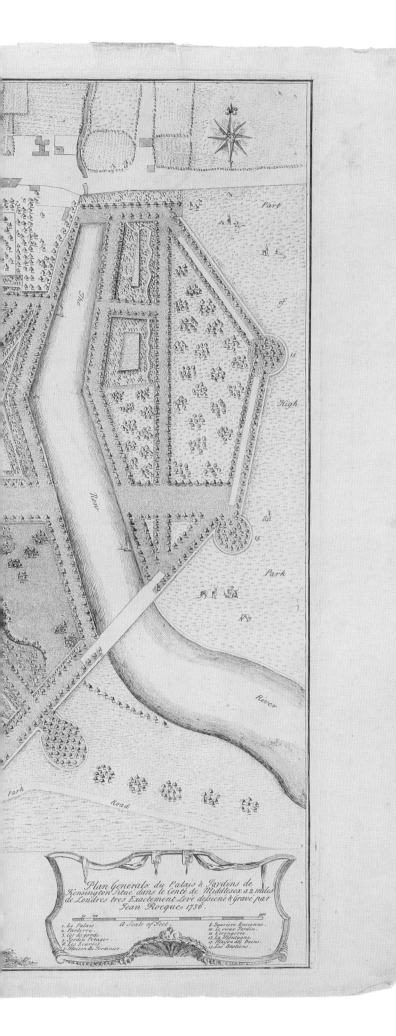

1736

'Plan General du Palais & Jardins de Kensington …'

John Rocque
Separate publication, *c.* 1745.
Copper engraving, 530 x 660 mm

John Rocque, a Huguenot refugee who settled in London, prepared this finely executed plan of Kensington Palace and gardens. Rocque established himself as one of the leading surveyors and mapmakers of his day. His earliest output, from when he started work in 1734 onwards, was a series of fine estate plans, intended to bring him to the attention of the Royal Family and the aristocracy of the British Isles, who might be relied on to patronize his future ventures and to commission him for vanity projects in relation to their own estates.

Although these plans seem to have been successful in establishing his reputation, it would appear that this phase of his career was not financially lucrative, and he turned his attention to surveys that would have more general appeal, such as an important series of plans of principal cities, including London, Bristol, York, Exeter and Dublin, and then large-scale surveys of the English and Irish counties, with those of Shropshire, Berkshire and Surrey of particular merit.

Kensington Palace was adopted as a royal residence in the 1690s by William III (William of Orange) who found the riverside palaces (Whitehall and Hampton Court) very damp, which exacerbated his gout. Kensington Palace was also used by the Hanoverian kings, but they also used Richmond Palace in Kew. Rocque's plan of Richmond Palace was apparently his earliest published work, while Hampton Court and Windsor Castle were also both mapped by Rocque.

1739

'Plan de Paris commencé
l'Année 1734 … sous les
ordres de Messire Michel
Étienne Turgot … achevé
de graver en 1739…'

Louis Bretez
Separate publication, Michel
Etienne Turgot & Louis Bretez,
Paris, 1739. Copper engraving,
2500 x 3200 mm

Louis Bretez's plan of Paris is one of the
outstanding surveys of that city, and indeed of
any city in the eighteenth century. The map,
drawn on a bird's-eye projection, was
commissioned by Michel Etienne Turgot,
Prévot de Marchands in Paris, in 1734. Turgot
was deeply interested in the embellishment of
Paris, particularly in redeveloping and
improving the principal streets of shops.
Bretez, the surveyor and artist, was a
distinguished architectural draughtsman,
fully capable of the task
of producing such an important map.
    The map is most frequently encountered
bound in the separate sheets, but when
encountered joined, as here, allows full
appreciation of this spectacular survey
of Paris.

c. 1740

'Grand Théâtre de la Guerre en Amerique Suivant les Plus Novelles Observations des Espagnols, Anglois, François & Hollandois…'

Reinier and Joshua Ottens
Separate publication,
Amsterdam, *c.* 1740.
Copper engraving, 835 x 1570 mm

The War of Jenkins' Ear between the British and Spanish (see p.155 for a more detailed account of the war) excited a great deal of interest throughout Europe. Ever since news of the riches discovered by the Conquistadores in Mexico and Peru had first filtered back to Europe, other European powers – and their citizens – had developed a fascination for the treasures of the Indies being brought back to Spain.

Both British and Dutch fleets had already had notable successes in capturing Spanish treasure fleets; indeed, Drake captured so much treasure in his circumnavigation he was forced to throw his cannons overboard to make extra room.

The Ottens brothers produced a very detailed map of the West Indies, the largest printed map of the region to date, to show the theatre of war, but have given particular prominence to the routes taken by the annual Spanish bullion fleet's passage back to England, to satisfy the cupidity of their audience, and in the expectation that the British would attempt to attack the fleet at the first opportunity.

(see overleaf) ↓

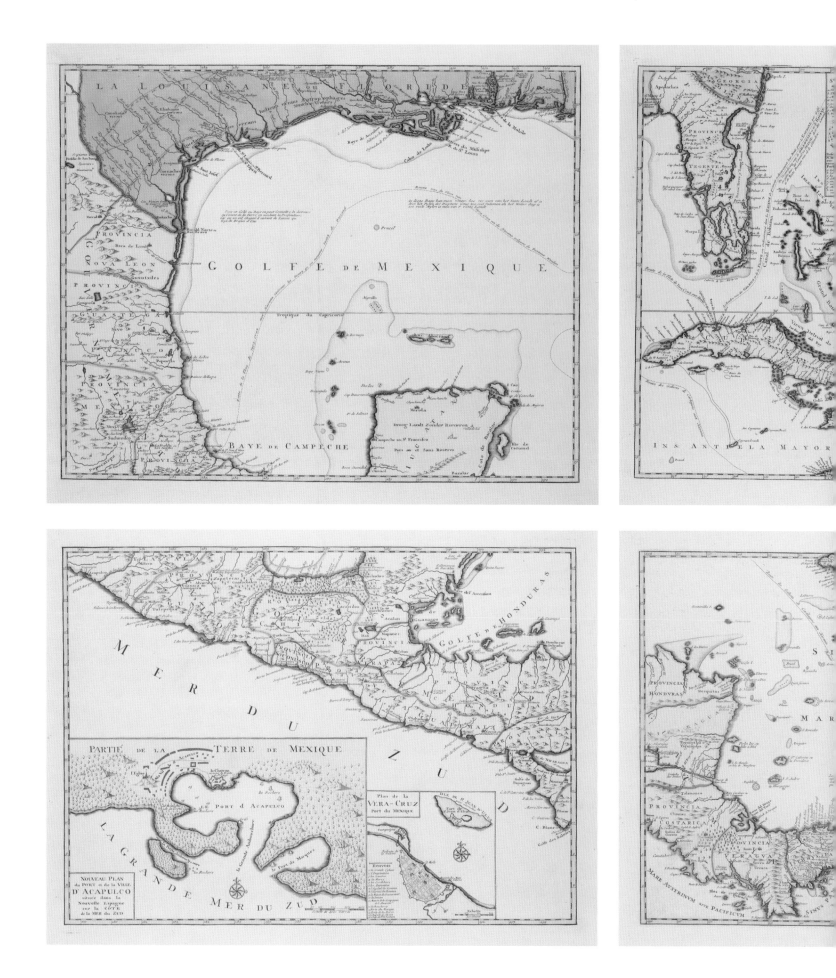

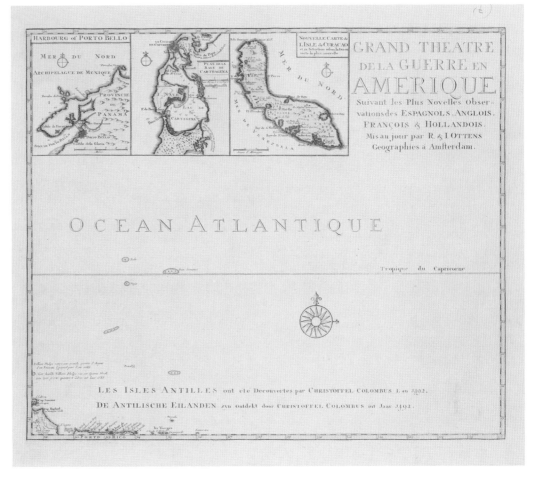

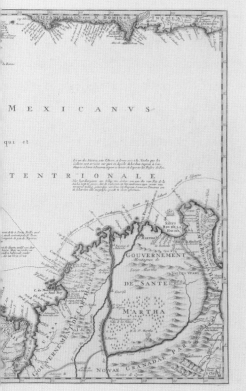

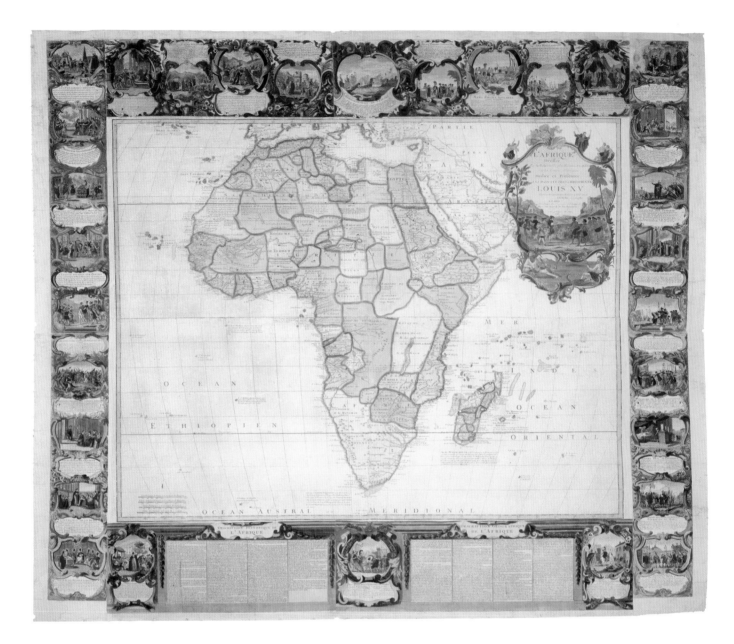

1740

'L'Afrique…'

Jean-Baptiste Nolin Jr.
Separate publication,
Crépy, Paris, *c.* 1760.
Copper engraving,
1290 x 1430 mm

Jean-Baptiste Nolin Jr. was a Parisian mapmaker and publisher, active between about 1717 and 1762, in succession to his father Jean-Baptiste Sr. As mapmakers, the family are not highly regarded; their output was largely derivative but, as commercial publishers, they seem to have been quite successful.

Jean-Baptiste Jr.'s output is notable for a highly decorative set of wall-maps of the four continents, including 'L'Afrique' (this map) and the companion map of America (the next map). The title is set in an elaborate cartouche, and contains a dedication to the French king Louis XV. The symbolic scenes around the cartouche emphasize the evangelical role played by the Catholic Church, but also the importance of slavery – a good supply of cheap, expendable labour was needed to work the plantations in the West Indies.

Around the map are four elaborate borders, including two lengthy panels of text, giving an historical description and a geographical description of the continent. These are illustrated with 30 scenes from the history of Africa; curiously, the scenes have a very European flavour to them, whether to make them familiar to the map's European audience, or through laziness on the part of the designer. Each scene is accompanied by a short description.

Geographically the map is not particularly significant; its function is more as ostentatious and decorative wall display rather than a definitive rendering of contemporary knowledge of the continent. However, the number of later printings of the map suggests that the customers were not unduly concerned by the lack of information and accuracy.

1740

'L'Amerique Dressée Sur
le Relations les Plus Recents
et Rectifées...'

Jean-Baptiste Nolin Jr.
Separate publication, Paris, 1740.
Copper engraving on several
sheets conjoined,
total 1205 x 1400 mm

Published by one of the most ambitious French cartographic families of the period, this is a superb wall-map of the Americas.

As the skills of the engravers and printers improved, so did the competition between the publishers to create memorable maps. Here Nolin has gone for size: the map is printed on four folio sheets, with thirty baroque-bordered vignettes on additional strips. These wall-maps were frightfully expensive, designed for a rich man's library, and not for the schoolroom. Once joined for display they were notoriously difficult to preserve, making examples that were in good condition very hard to find.

In order to capture the luxury market the cartography had to be as up-to-date as possible. Here the shape of South America is complete, having been thoroughly explored by the Spanish (apart from the far reaches of the interior). In the Pacific northwest, however, Nolin has rushed to include a new feature on the American coastline, the 'Mer de l'Ouest', seen here as an unnamed indentation above California. Copied from a manuscript map by Nolin's rival Guillaume Delisle, this mythical inland sea replaced 'California as an island' as the most common American cartographical misconception, lasting up to the voyages of Cook and Vancouver at the latter part of the century.

The decorative vignette scenes include cannibalism, Jesuit missionaries converting the natives, beavers, cannibalism, and Europeans driving off attacks from the natives with rifle fire. Each vignette has an engraved descriptive text, with two larger general descriptions under the map.

A Scale of English Miles.

Furlongs 0   1   3   4

ZIENAGA DE QUENCA,
the Swamp (or Bog) of Quenca.

N.ª S.ª de la Popa

F. S. Lazare

Point Cuno

A Remarkable Rock

Cartagena

Xemani

Playa grande

Zunta   Alcua

Bofques

Isle de
Manga

Jardinillo

Sur-gi-de-ro

or the
Moorings

Boca Grande

Boca Corrada

Fort Manzanill

Castilio grande

TIERRA BOMBA

Tejar
de los
Jesuites

Ceuallo   Albornos

Boxander

La Cruz

El Mamonal

Zuniya

Castillo Chico

Boca Ch

S. Jag

Most humbly Inscribed
To the R.ᵗ Hon.ᵇˡᵉ SIR CHARLES WAGER,
first Lord Commissioner of the Admiralty.
THIS PLAN:
Of the Harbour, Town, and Several Forts, of
CARTAGENA.

In which is Exhibited a Perfect VIEW; of the English Fleet, as they
Anchored all along the Coast, in the Bay, near the Town, and also
after they moved and laid under the Forts of S. Jago, and S. Philipe,
and at the Boca-chica, or Mouth of the Harbour: Likewise of the
English Ships as they moved in different parts in the Harbour, in order
to lay Siege to the Town.

This Plan, I do affirm to be the only true Copy of the Draught, brought over by me, to shew
the different Movements of his Majesty's Fleet, laid before the Regency, & the Lords of the Admiralty.
Will's Coffee House 26ᵗ May 1741.
Will. Laws

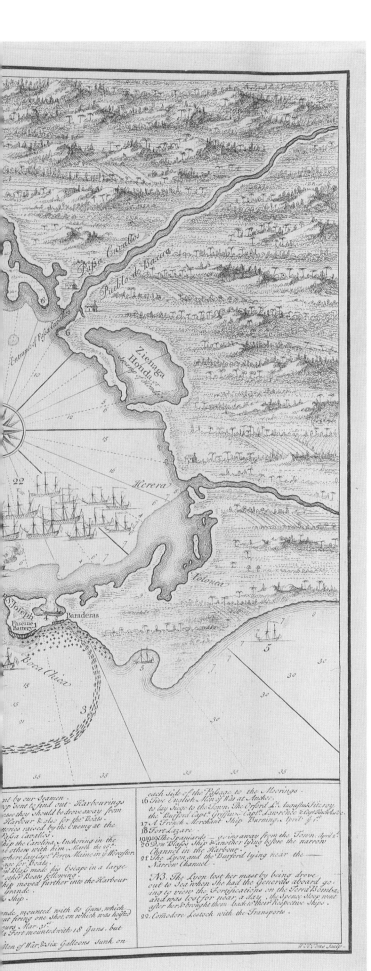

1741

'Most humbly inscribed … this Plan of the Harbour, Town, and Several Forts, of Cartagena… a Perfect View, of the English Fleet, as they Anchored all along the Coast…'

William Laws
Separate publication,
Samuel Harding and William
Henry Toms, London, 1741.
Copper engraving, 440 x 590 mm

William Laws created a detailed plan of the British attack on Cartagena in 1741, an engagement that was part of the conflict often termed the 'War of Jenkins' Ear' (1739–48). This set England against Spain after Captain Robert Jenkins claimed to have had his ear cut off by the Spanish coastguard which proved a *casus belli*. The map is inscribed to the 'Rt Honble Sir Charles Wager, First Lord Commissioner of the Admiralty'.

The attack on Cartagena was commanded by Sir Edward Vernon, who had seized the Spanish town of Porto Bello, in Panama, with just six ships. When he attacked Cartagena, with a force of 186 ships and 23,600 men, there were high hopes of success, as reflected in this plan, but disease and dogged Spanish defence, by a garrison of only about 850 men – compelled Vernon to abandon the siege and try his luck elsewhere.

It in unclear whether Laws was the cartographer responsible for the plan, or simply the messenger who brought the plan back to London but, in a very short space of time several very similar plans were in circulation around the leading London map-publishers.

c. 1741

'A New Mapp of Europe divided into its Principall Kingdoms & Countries…'

Henry Overton (I)
Separate publication,
London, *c.* 1741.
Copper engraving, with borders
1160 x 1350 mm

While many of the European mapmakers offered a wide range of wall-maps as part of their inventory, it was a very different story in England. There were very few wall-maps published in England before the mid-eighteenth century, if one thinks of maps composed of four or more sheets, designed for separate sale. If one were to exclude wall-maps of England and of London, obvious subjects for an English publisher, the total is dramatically reduced.

Even more surprising, perhaps, is the small number of wall-maps that survive. The first wall-map published in England is believed to have been issued by Clement Adams in 1549, with no surviving example today. The next, Anthony Jenkinson's wall-map of Russia, 1562, is known in only a single example, in a Polish university. While it is dangerous to argue from negative evidence, it seems plausible that the survival rate is as much to do with the limited market for such maps, as for the very high mortality rate for wall-maps.

The Overton family, John, Henry (I) and Henry (II) were probably the most ambitious English publishers of wall-maps, if their catalogues are any sort of guide. However, there are few surviving examples of their work, with this fine map of Europe not traced in any of the major British map collections.

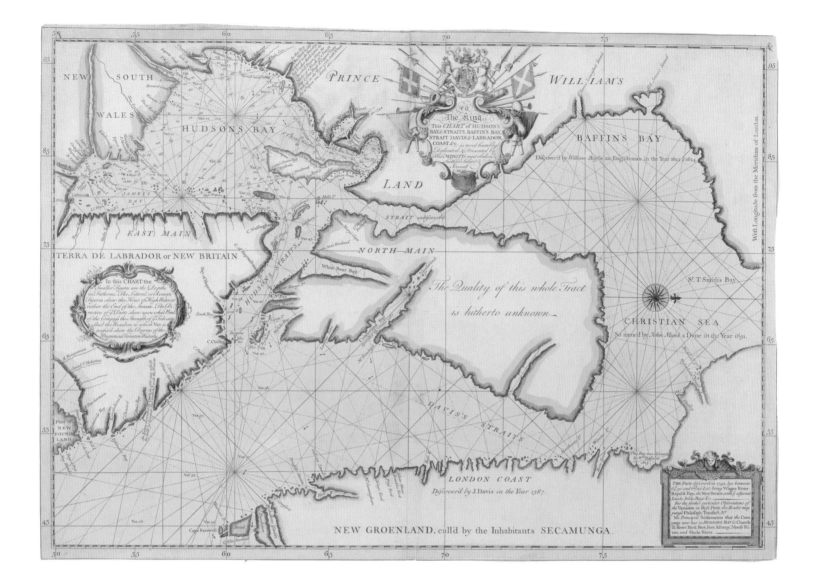

1743

'To The King, this Chart
of Hudson's Bay & Straits,
Baffin's Bay, Strait Davis
& Labrador Coast &c. is most
humbly dedicated
& presented…'

Christopher Middleton
Separate publication,
London, 1743.
Copper engraving, 475 x 670 mm

The earliest voyages to the East Indies and
Far East were made by the Spanish and
Portuguese, who came to dominate the
southerly routes round Africa and Cape
Horn. Naturally, the English and Dutch were
regarded as unwelcome interlopers and, if
caught, could expect little mercy.
Consequently, both countries searched for
a northern route, either round Russia, or
through one of the myriad waterways of
Arctic Canada.

In the 1740s Middleton was hired by
Arthur Dobbs, an ardent believer in a

northwest passage. Middleton led an
expedition to explore Hudson's Bay, in search
of such a passage, but with no success.

On his return, Middleton drew this
remarkably accurate map of Hudson's Bay,
which looks strange to the modern eye, as
it is rotated so that north is at the right.

Dobbs managed to convince himself,
against all the evidence, that Middleton was
deceiving him, and thus began a campaign of
recrimination and vindication, through the
press, by the two men.

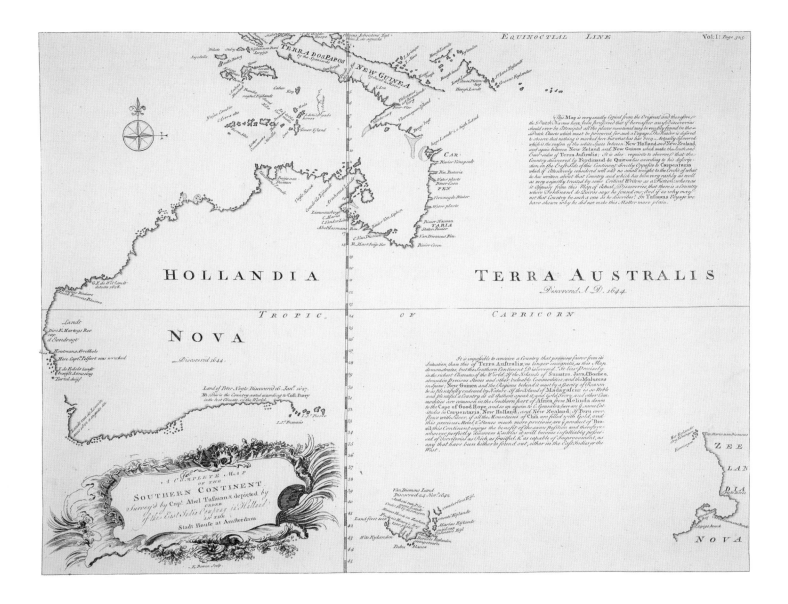

1744

'A Complete Map of the
Southern Continent. Survey'd
by Capt. Abel Tasman
& depicted by Order of the
East India Company in
Holland in the Stadt House at
Amsterdam'

John Harris
From: *Complete Collection of Voyages
and Travels,* second edition.
Copper engraving, 380 x 490 mm

A very early English map of Australia was
produced by John Harris, although copied
from a map by Frenchman, Melchisedech
Thevenot, 1663. Bowen has added the Tropic
of Capricorn and two texts: the upper block
emphasizes that no assumptions have been
made, so white space abounds between New
Guinea and Carpentaria, and between the
mainland, Tasmania and New Zealand; the
lower text starts:

'It is impossible to conceive a Country that
promises fairer from its situation, than this of
Terra Australis; no longer incognita, as this
map demonstrates…'

Although the map states the country was
discovered in 1644, Dutch ships had first
sighted Carpentaria in 1608. However it was
Abel Tasman's voyage of 1644 that gave
Australia a recognizable shape, discovering
both Tasmania and New Zealand. When this
map was published, a century later, very little
had been added: it was in 1770 that Captain
Cook mapped the eastern coastline, but even
he did not discover Tasmania's relationship to
the mainland.

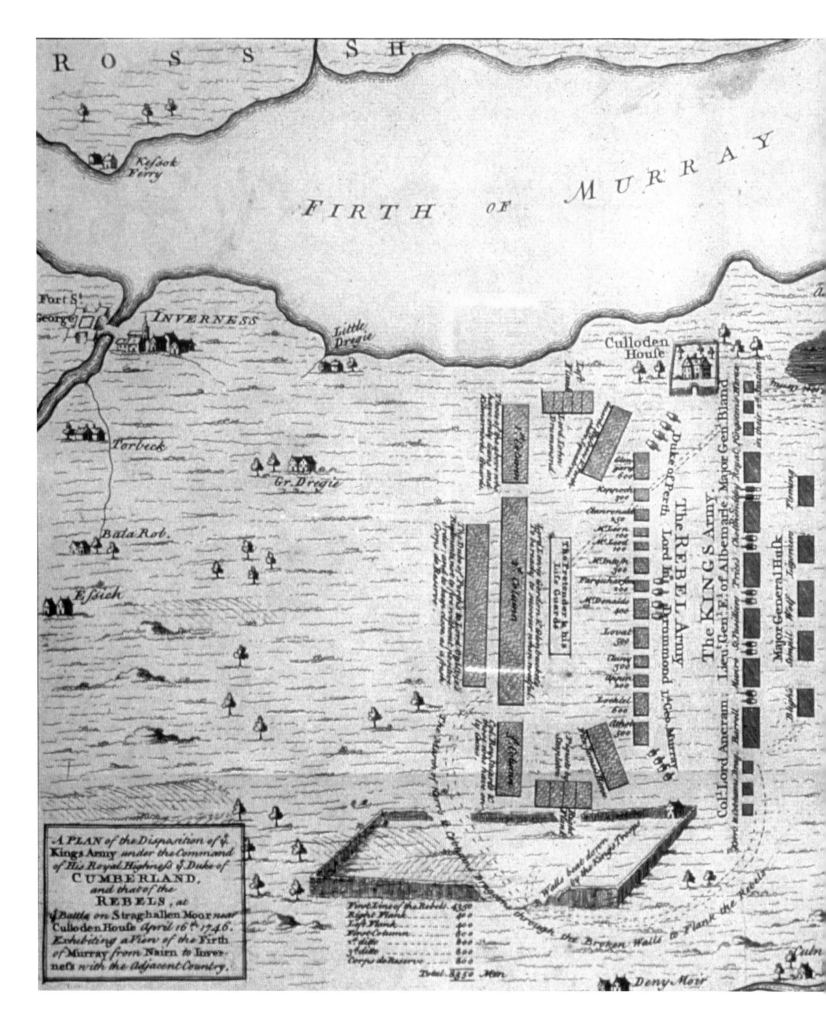

ROSS SH.

FIRTH OF MURRAY

Kessok Ferry

Fort St George

INVERNESS

Little Dregie

Culloden House

Torbeck

Gr. Dregie

Bala Rob.

Essich

Left Flank

The REBEL Army

The KING'S Army

Col. Lord Ancram. Lieu. Gen. E. of Albemarle. Major Gen. Bland

Duke of Perth. Lord High Drummond 1. Geo. Murray

Major General Husk

A PLAN of the Disposition of y. King's Army under the Command of His Royal Highness y. Duke of CUMBERLAND, and that of the REBELS, at y. Battle on Straghallen Moor near Culloden House April 16. 1746. Exhibiting a View of the Firth of Murray from Nairn to Inverness with the Adjacent Country.

Deny. Moir

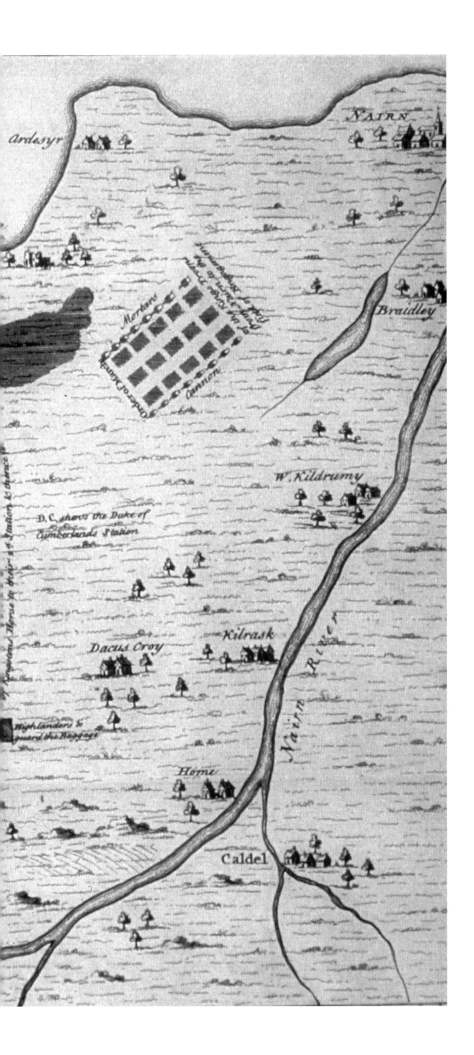

1746

'A Plan of the disposition of ye Kings Army under the Command of His Royal Highness ye Duke of Cumberland, and that of the Rebels, at ye Battle on Straghallen Moor near Culloden House April 16th 1746...'

Separate publication,
Thomas & John Bowles,
London, 1746.
Copper engraving, 240 x 340mm

In 1603 James Stuart, James VI of Scotland, became King James I of England. The Stuart dynasty (the name is a corruption of Steward, the family's status under previous kings of Scotland) did not prove popular kings, with both Charles I and James II being deposed, the latter in the 'Glorious Revolution' of 1688, which saw the succession pass to James's Protestant daughter Mary, and her husband William of Orange, on to Queen Anne, and then the Hanoverian King, George I.

However, the Stuarts were not prepared to relinquish their claim, and in the eighteenth century, their supporters, the Jacobites, mounted three rebellions against the Hanoverians Kings, in 1715, 1719 and 1745–6. Although the Hanoverian dynasty did little to endear themselves to the British people – George I would not even learn English – the risings received little support outside Scotland.

The most serious of the three risings – the '45 – was the crisis point of the Hanoverian dynasty, but Bonnie Prince Charlie was unable to garner sufficient support and the Jacobite dream died, along with very many Scottish clansmen, at the battle of Culloden in 1746, the last battle fought on British soil.

Culloden battle was fought on 16 April 1746, while this detailed plan was published less than a month later, on 13 May, rushed into print to capitalize on widespread relief at the victory.

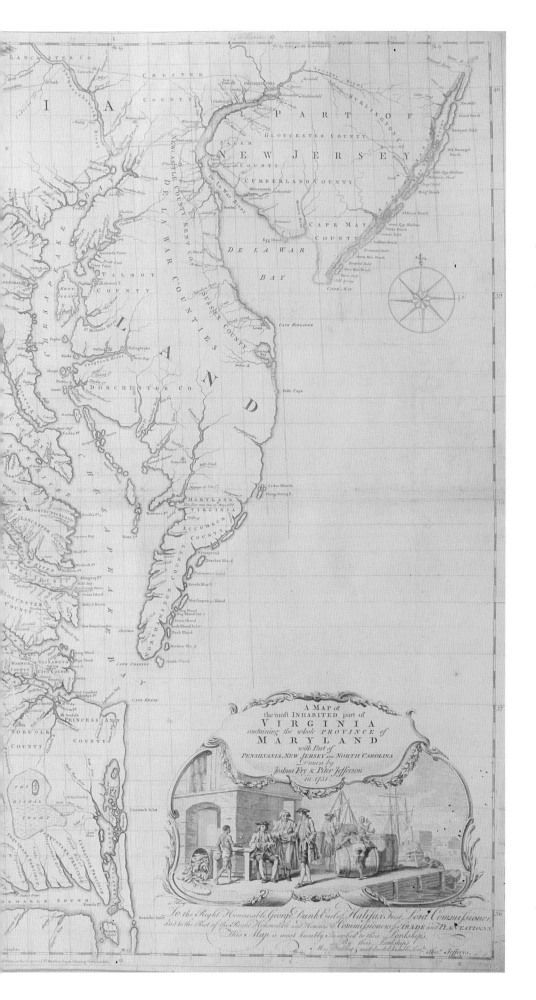

'A Map of the most Inhabited part of Virginia containing the whole Province Of Maryland with Part of Pensilvania, New Jersey and North Carolina…'

Joshua Fry & Peter Jefferson
Separate publication,
Thomas Jefferys Sr., London, c. 1755.
Copper engraving, 775 x 1240 mm

While the British Crown was happy enough to administer the English colonies in America, the government was reluctant to spend unnecessary money on these colonies, and this is particularly evident in the field of cartography. During the colonial period, the British Government invested very little effort, and even less resources, into the mapping of the American colonies. In wartime this effort increased; in peacetime it tailed off. Fortunately, through the thorough training given to engineer officers in the Tower of London (among other places), there were a large number of trained and highly skilled mapmakers in the army – both the regular army and colonial regiments – and many of the great maps of colonial America were made by these men.

This map, the most important survey of the Virginia colony from the colonial period, was surveyed by Joshua Fry, late Commander of the Virginian Regiment, and Peter Jefferson, Deputy Surveyor of Albemarle County. They were commissioned by the Lords of Trade France and Plantations, apparently anxious for better information for the interior, particularly for the Ohio Valley, in view of impending war.

This is the first map to give a passable accurate delineation of the Appalachian Mountains, and their Lordships approving of the draught, the manuscript was passed to Jefferys for publication.

In this later state, further information on the interior was added, from the diaries and notes of John Dalrymple, including the table of distances.

TEGNING til Byen

FRIDERICHS-STÆD

164

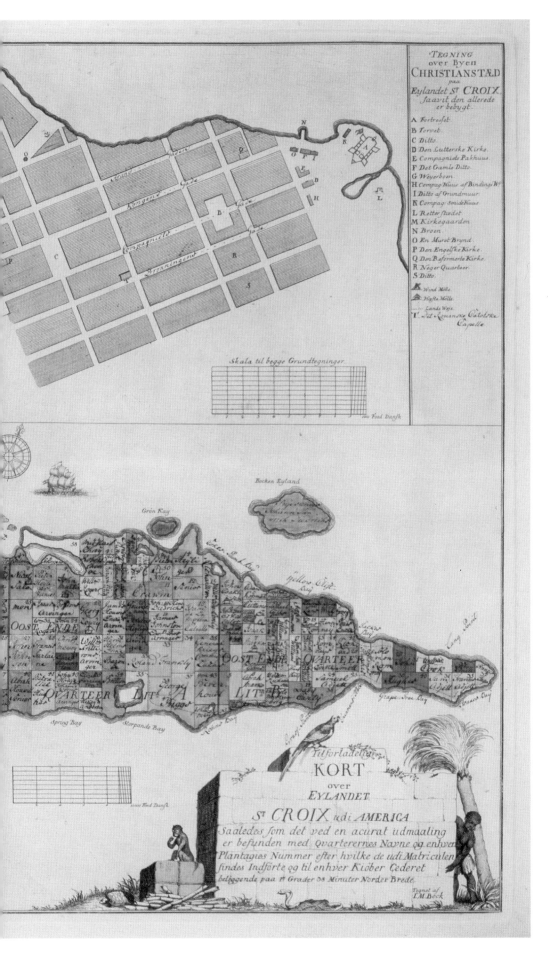

1754

'Tilforladelig Kort Over Eylandet St Croix udi America …'

Jens Michelsen Beck
Separate publication,
Copenhagen, 1754.
475 x 730 mm

Jens Michelsen Beck was a Danish settler on the island of St Croix in the West Indies. He settled there in 1742 and was employed by the Danish West India Company, between 1749 and 1753, as official surveyor for the island. He left St Croix in 1753 under suspicion of corruption, and returned to Copenhagen where, the following year, he published this map of the island.

Beck's map bears a certain similarity with Johann Cronenberg and Johann von Jaegersberg's survey of 1750, a manuscript copy of which is preserved in the archives of the Nautical Charts Department.

The map shows the island divided into cadastral lots, with the names of the quarters and numbers for each plantation. The purpose of the map is to record the current settlement pattern for the island; natural geographical features are treated as secondary elements, with relief entirely omitted for example, and limited place names, particularly for the coastal features. The emphasis is entirely economic: roads, windmills and such are accurately recorded, as are unoccupied lots, particularly in the northwest of the island.

'A Map of the British Colonies in North America, with the Roads, Distances, Limits, and Extent of the Settlements…'

John Mitchell
Separate publication,
William Faden Jr., *c.* 1777.
Copper engraving, 1350 x 1930 mm

John Mitchell's map of the British colonies in North America is widely regarded as the most important single map in American history, and the most comprehensive general map of the region from the colonial period. The map is an all the more remarkable achievement as it was the only map made by Mitchell, and there is little in his background to explain how he was able to produce such a remarkable map, even with the patronage and materials of the Board of Trade and Plantations in London.

The map was first published immediately prior to the outbreak of the French and Indian War, and revised frequently thereafter, for example adding the panels of text visible in the North Atlantic.

The state of the map illustrated here was published *circa* 1777, at the height of the American Revolutionary War. It was an example of this map that was used by the rival commissioners to settle the boundaries of the United States during the negotiations for the Treaty of Paris, which ended the war.

The example of the map, actually used in the negotiations, was owned by George III and is in the King's Topographical Collection in the British Library. The map illustrated here has had the original manuscript annotations inserted, possibly in relation to a boundary dispute between Canada and the United States in 1898. The map has also been frequently consulted in disputes between individual US States, even in recent times.

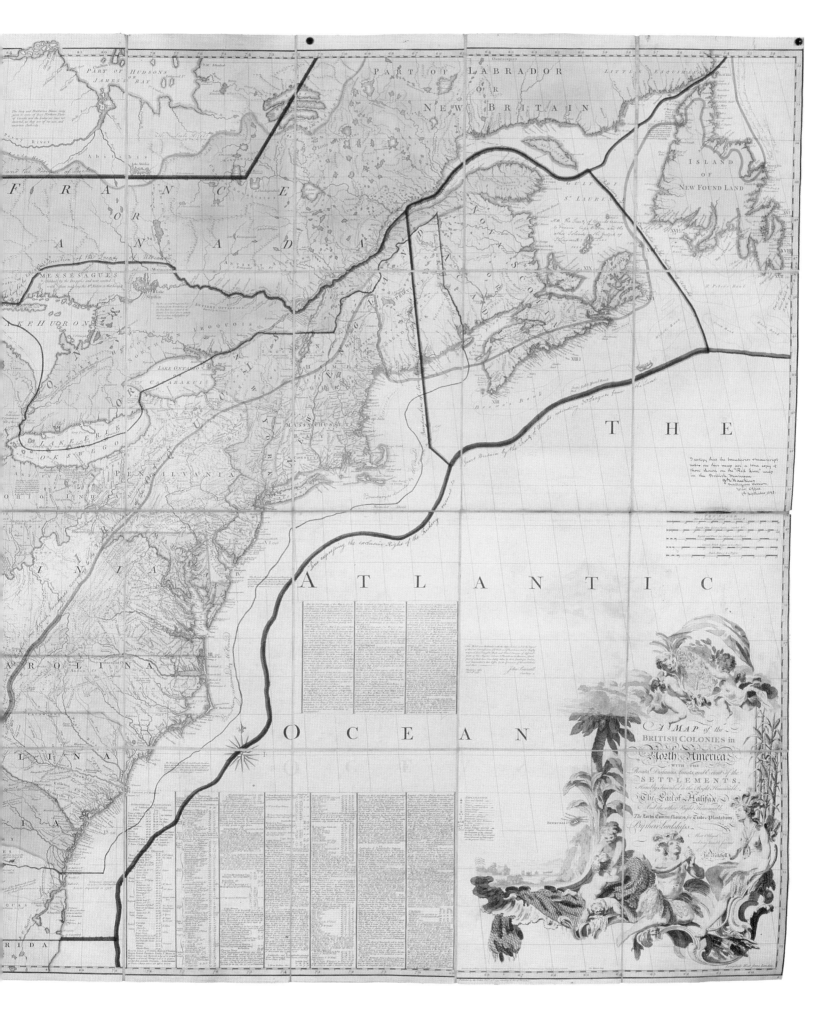

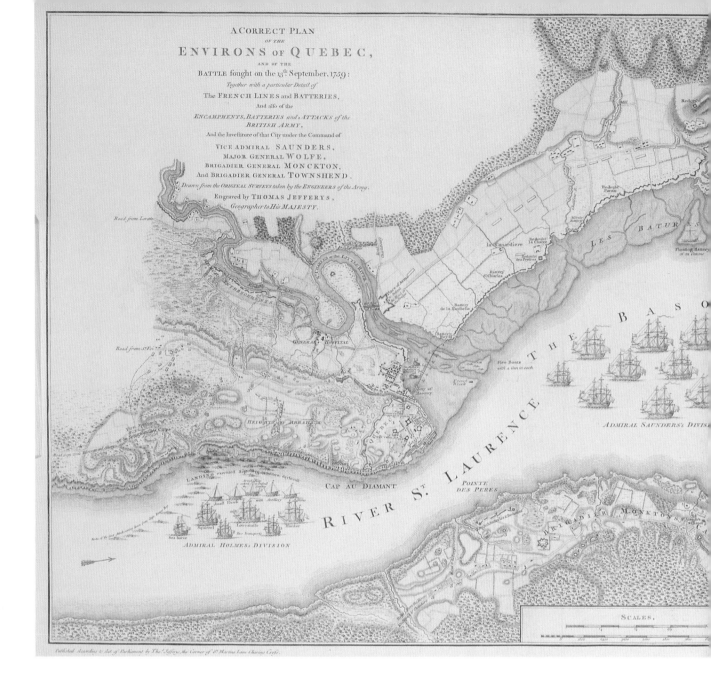

A CORRECT PLAN
OF THE
ENVIRONS OF QUEBEC,
AND OF THE
BATTLE fought on the 13th September, 1759:
Together with a particular Detail of
The FRENCH LINES and BATTERIES,
And also of the
ENCAMPMENTS, BATTERIES and ATTACKS of the
BRITISH ARMY,
And the Investiture of that City under the Command of
VICE ADMIRAL SAUNDERS,
MAJOR GENERAL WOLFE,
BRIGADIER GENERAL MONCKTON,
And BRIGADIER GENERAL TOWNSHEND.
Drawn from the ORIGINAL SURVEYS taken by the ENGINEERS of the Army.
Engraved by THOMAS JEFFERYS,
Geographer to His MAJESTY.

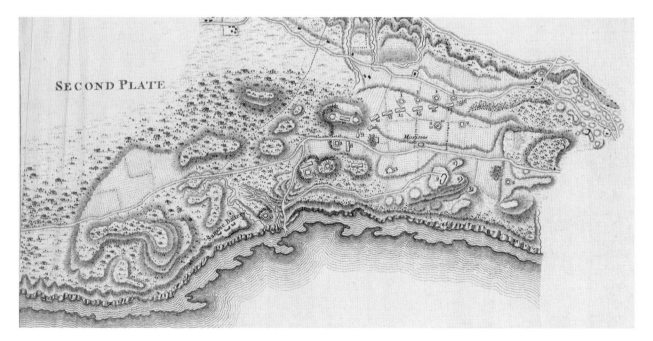

SECOND PLATE

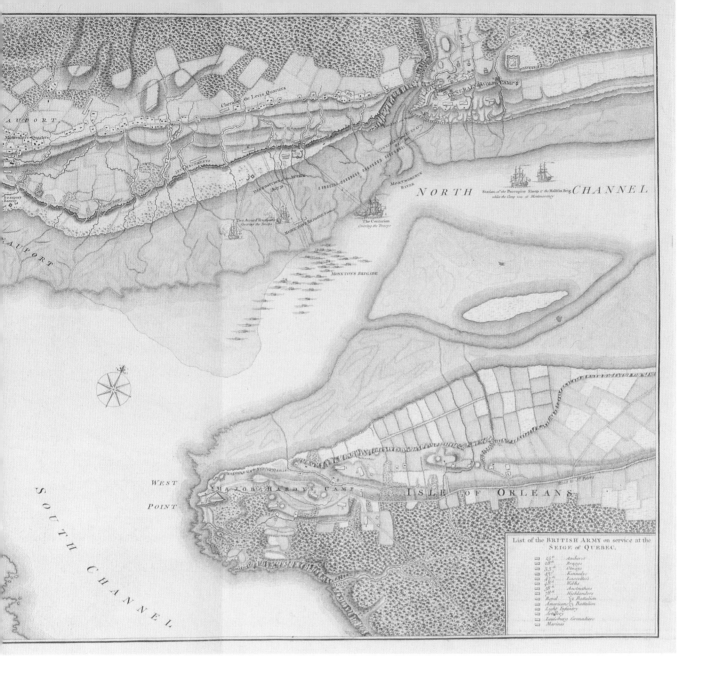

c. 1760

'A Correct Plan of the Environs of Quebec, and of the Battle fought on the 13th September, 1759…'

Thomas Jefferys Sr.
Separate publication,
London, *c.* 1760.
Copper engraving, 410 x 885 mm

The British capture of Quebec was the turning point in the French and Indian War, which culminated in the British wresting control of Canada from the French. This is the great contemporary printed plan of the siege of Quebec in 1759.

The map was sold separately, but could also be accompanied by a pamphlet, referred to in this entry from a Jefferys catalogue of *circa* 1763: 'A Correct Plan of the Environs of Quebec and of the Battle fought on the 13th of September… with a Journal of the Siege. Price 5s.'

The plan is also interesting as an example of the difficulties in showing unfolding events on a single map, and for the way that Jefferys has adapted to the challenge. There is a second map pasted as an overlay, over the battle on the Heights of Abraham at the left. The main map shows the two armies drawn up in line of battle; the overlay shows the final phase with the British troops in possession of the field of battle.

c. 1763

'A New and Accurate Map of the British Dominions in America, according to the Treaty of 1763…'

Thomas Kitchin Sr.
Separate publication,
London, *c.* 1763.
Copper engraving, 525 x 630 mm

The British captured Canada by force of arms during the French and Indian War, and this victory was officially recognized in the Treaty of Paris, which ended the war, signed in 1763. An important part of the provisions was the territorial settlement, with France formally ceding Canada to the British, retaining St Pierre and Miquelon and fishing rights along the Newfoundland coast, and also Louisiana, the land west of the Mississippi.

Within Canada, the British created the province of Quebec, the first province to be established in Canada, stretching along the banks of the St Lawrence River, as can be seen on this map. The Treaty of Paris also established reserves for the First Nations and further restricted settlement in western Canada. It was not until the Quebec Act of 1774 that the Province of Canada was expanded to include the Great Lakes region.

Kitchin's map is one of several that were quickly published to show the boundaries established in the treaty. A notable feature of the map is the boundaries of the southern American colonies, which were laid down in the seventeenth century, when the Crown thought that the Pacific Ocean was a relatively short march, perhaps ten days inland from the Atlantic. The boundaries were therefore laid out as straight lines extending from the Atlantic coasts to the Pacific coast, a notion modified when it became clear the Pacific was rather further away than thought, and with the French establishing control of the Mississippi river system.

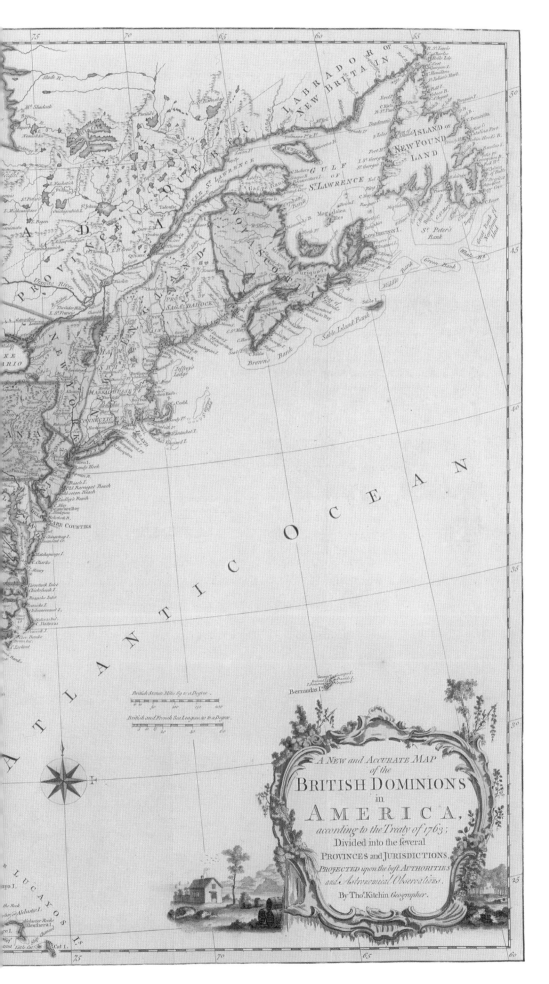

'Mappe-Monde Physique Politique et Mathématique ou Nouvelle Manière de considérer la Terre…'

Louis Denis
Separate publication, Paris, 1764.
Copper engraving, 1270 x 640 mm

In the mid-eighteenth century, French mapmakers led the interest in the physical nature of the earth. One of the pioneers in the study of the earth – nowadays termed thematic mapping – was Philippe Buache, appointed Premier Géographe du Roi in 1729, and elected to the Academy of Sciences in 1730.

Buache believed that the mountains of the world were linked, with the mountain systems not only running across the surface of the Continents, but also across the Ocean floors before emerging on the far side, and he sought to prove this theory by linking in the rivers systems of the world, studying the origins of the rivers, and also the mineralogy of the countries of the world. His evolving theories were illustrated in a series of maps printed in the proceedings of the Academy of Sciences.

Louis Denis's world view is amongst the most bizarre looking of all world maps; he has incorporated into the map Buache's theories on the mountains, the chains clearly visible in the Pacific Ocean for example, but he has also incorporated other speculative geography, including a quite unique depiction of Antarctica as a group of islands, reminiscent of Mercator's North Pole (pp.54–5) and Admiral de la Fonte's fictional 'Mar du Ouest', and other curious waterways, in western North America. While much of the geography is wrong, it is still encouraging evidence of early scientific enquiry into the nature of the earth.

(see overleaf) ↓

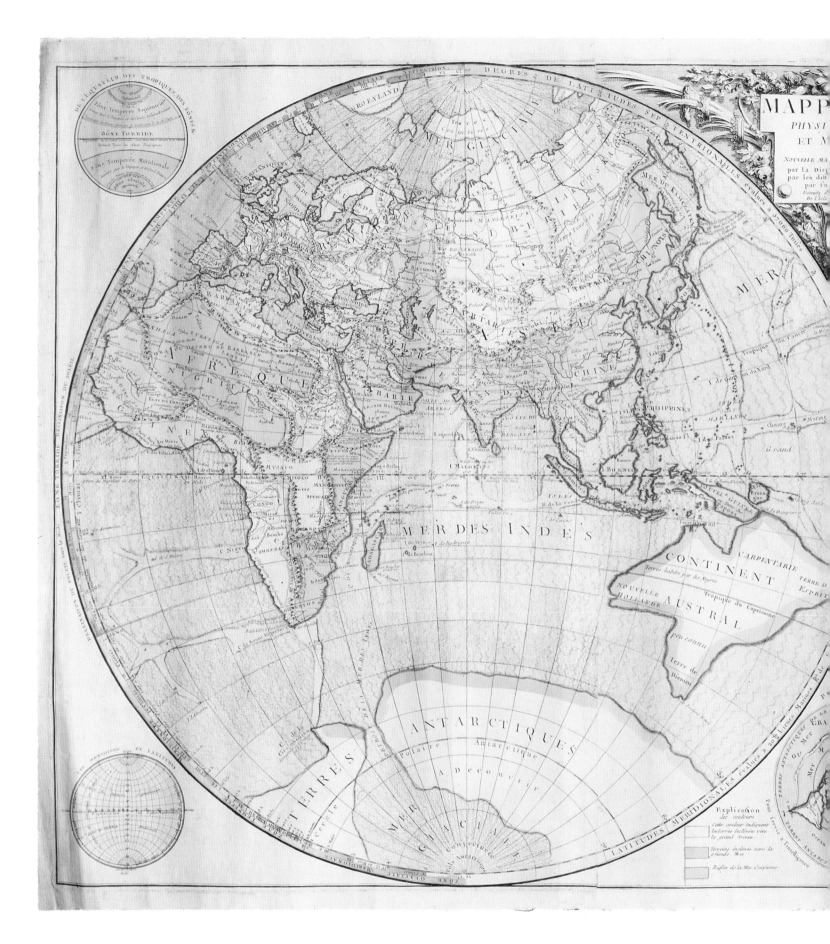

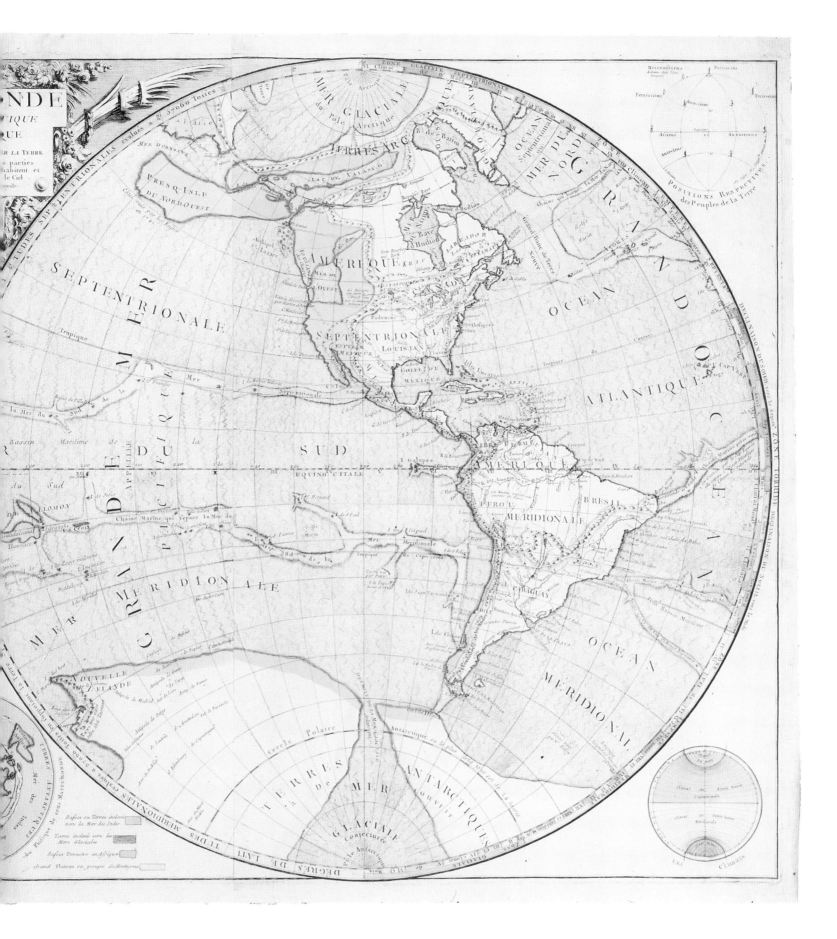

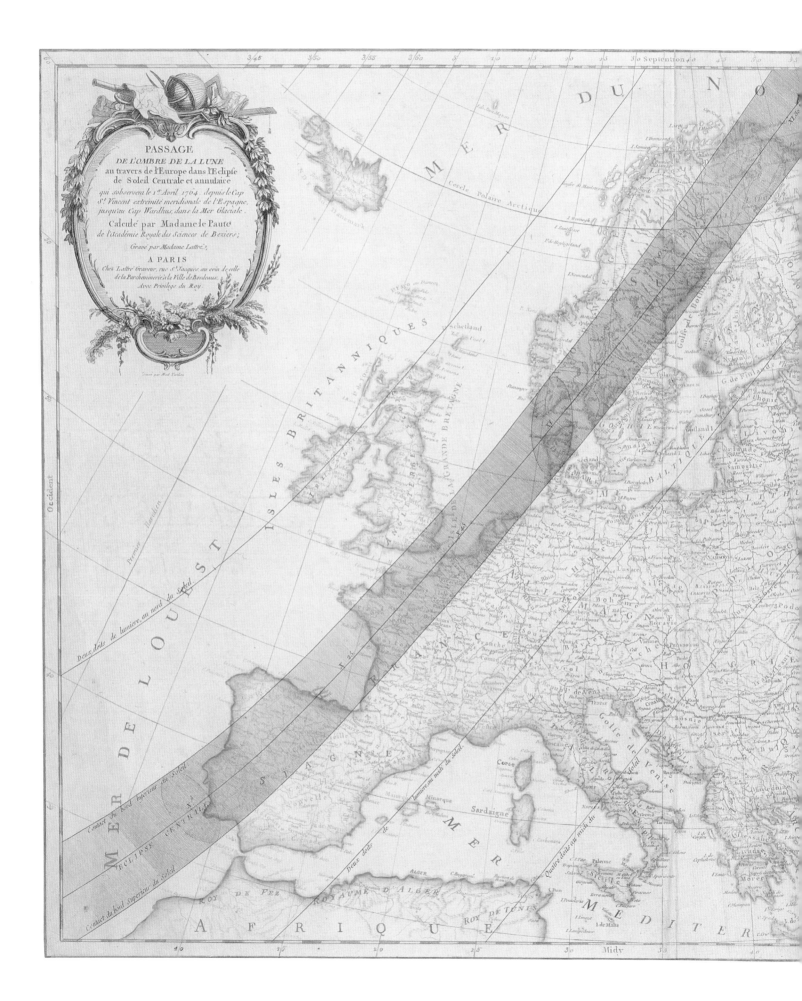

PASSAGE
DE L'OMBRE DE LA LUNE
au travers de l'Europe dans l'Eclipse
de Soleil Centrale et annulaire
qui s'observera le 1.er Avril 1764. depuis le Cap
St Vincent extrémité méridionale de l'Espagne,
jusqu'au Cap Wardhus, dans la Mer Glaciale.

Calculé par Madame le Pauté
de l'Académie Royale des Sciences de Beziers;

Gravé par Madame Lattré;

A PARIS
Chez Lattré Graveur, rue St Jacques, au coin de celle
de la Parcheminerie à la Ville de Bordeaux.
Avec Privilège du Roy.

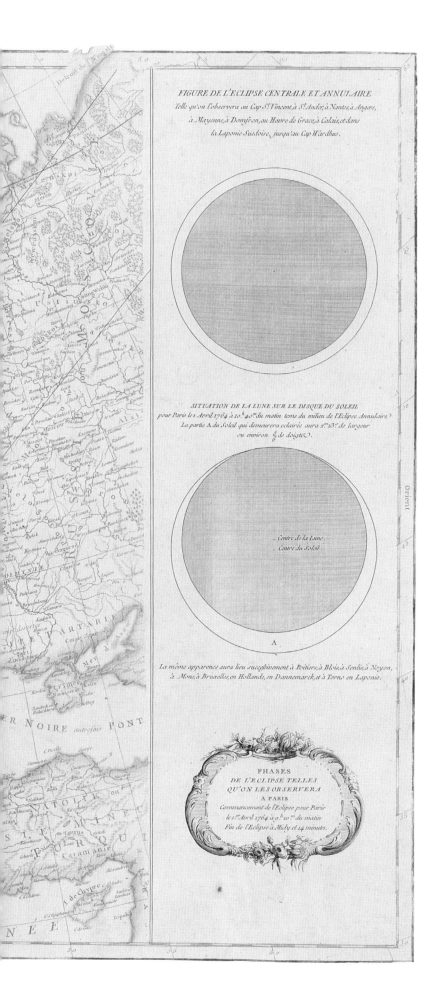

1764

'Passage de l'Ombre
de la Lune au travers
de l'Europe…'

Madame le Pauté Dagelet
Separate publication,
Madame Lattré, Paris, 1764.
Copper engraving, 470 x 640 mm

In the eighteenth century scientific mapmakers, such as Edmond Halley in England, began to publish maps of the path of eclipses. Then, and this is all the more remarkable in view of what they had at their disposal, such men began to publish maps that predicted the date and path of future eclipses.

A particularly interesting example of the type is this map of Europe recording the passage of the lunar eclipse in April 1764. The map is printed in sepia, with the eclipse information over-printed in black ink, creating a most striking image.

However, it is in the individuals involved that the interest lies. The map was drawn by Madame le Pauté Dagelet, an astronomer and member of the Académie Royale des Sciences de Béziers; the title cartouche was etched and engraved by Elizabeth Claire Tardieu, and the main map engraved by Madame Lattré, wife of Jean Lattré.

At the time both the science and publishing of cartography were dominated by men; this is a remarkable – perhaps unique – example of a map drawn and engraved entirely by women.

PART OF SOUTH CAROLINA

1770

'A Compleat Map of
North Carolina from
an actual Survey…'

John Abraham Collet
Separate publication,
Samuel Hooper, London, 1770.
Copper engraving, 760 x 1100 mm

Captain John Collet was a Swiss-born military engineer serving in the British army in North America. Sometime before 1767, he was appointed Commander of Fort Johnston, at Cape Fear, with orders to rebuild it. In 1768, he drew an important manuscript map of the back country of North Carolina, which he dedicated to George III.

This map served as the basis for Collet's map of North Carolina, published in 1770. It is surprising that Collet chose Samuel Hooper, who was not well known as a map-publisher to produce this map, rather than Thomas Jefferys Sr., who published almost every other major map of North America in the 1760s and early 1770s.

Collet's map was the definitive map of North Carolina from the colonial period, superior in accuracy to any other map of the time, and recording the developing settlements in the western part of the province. Indeed, it served as the standard delineation of North Carolina until John Price and John Strother published their map of the state in 1808.

c. 1775

Untitled Map of the Battle of Bunker Hill

Anonymous
From: *Gentleman's and London Magazine*, John Exshaw (I),
Dublin, 1775.
Copper engraving, 110 x 130 mm

This attractive plan/view of the Battle of Bunker Hill was issued in the *Gentleman's and London Magazine* for September 1775. The accompanying text (not present here) refers to 'A View of the Attack on Charles Town, and the Lines erected by the Provincials on Bunker's Hill, which were forced by his Majesty's Forces, under the Command of Major General Howe.'

Unusually, this seems to be an original map as there does not appear to have been an equivalent magazine map issued in London.

The Battle of Bunker Hill, the first set-piece engagement of the American Revolutionary War, captured popular imagination. Although the British won the day, their casualties were very heavy, and the tenacity of the Americans suggested that crushing the rebellion might not be as simple as some thought, and so it was to prove.

See page 613.

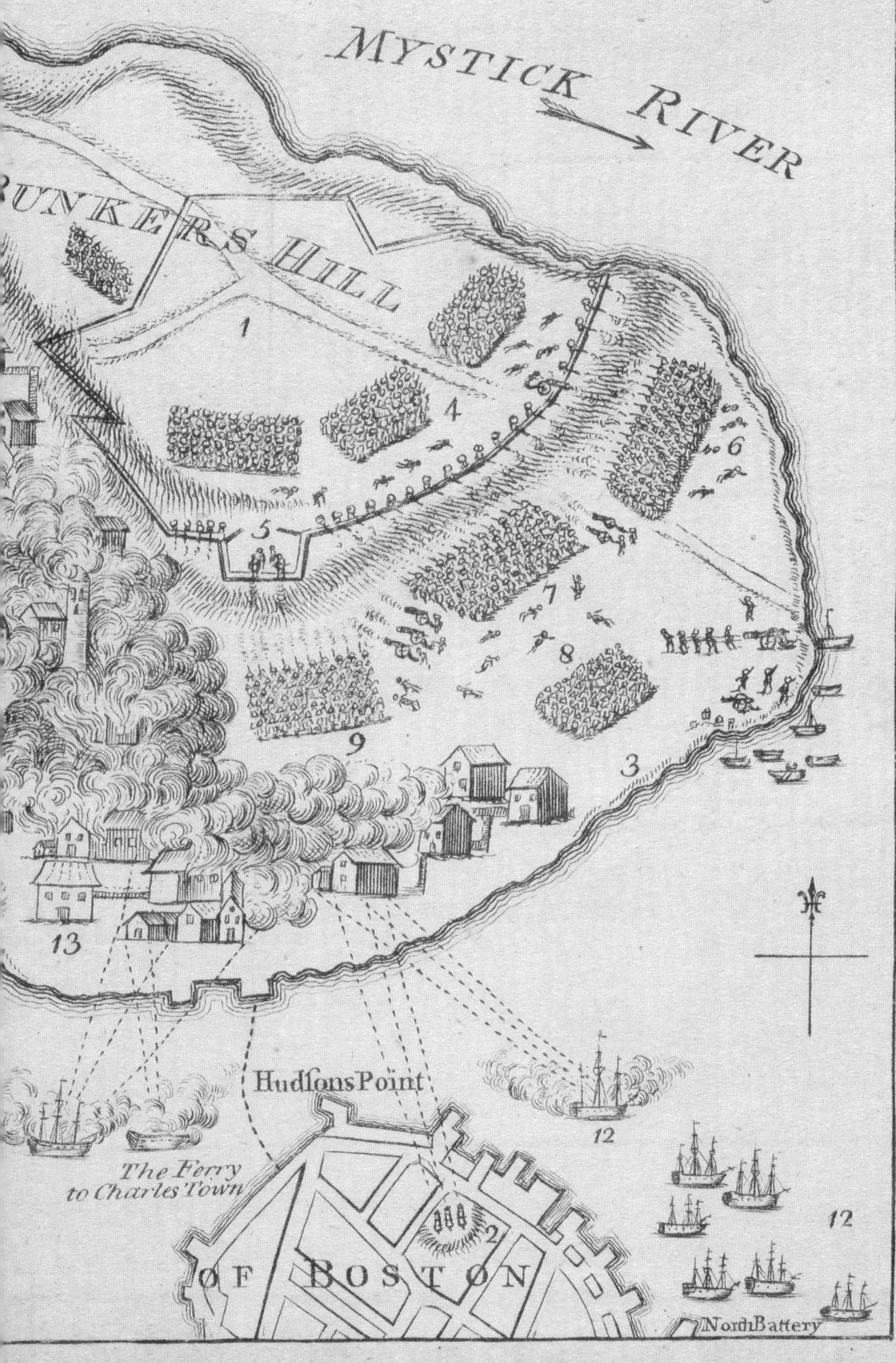

MYSTICK RIVER

BUNKERS HILL

1

4

6

5

7

8

9

3

13

Hudsons Point

12

The Ferry
to Charles Town

2

OF BOSTON

12

North Battery

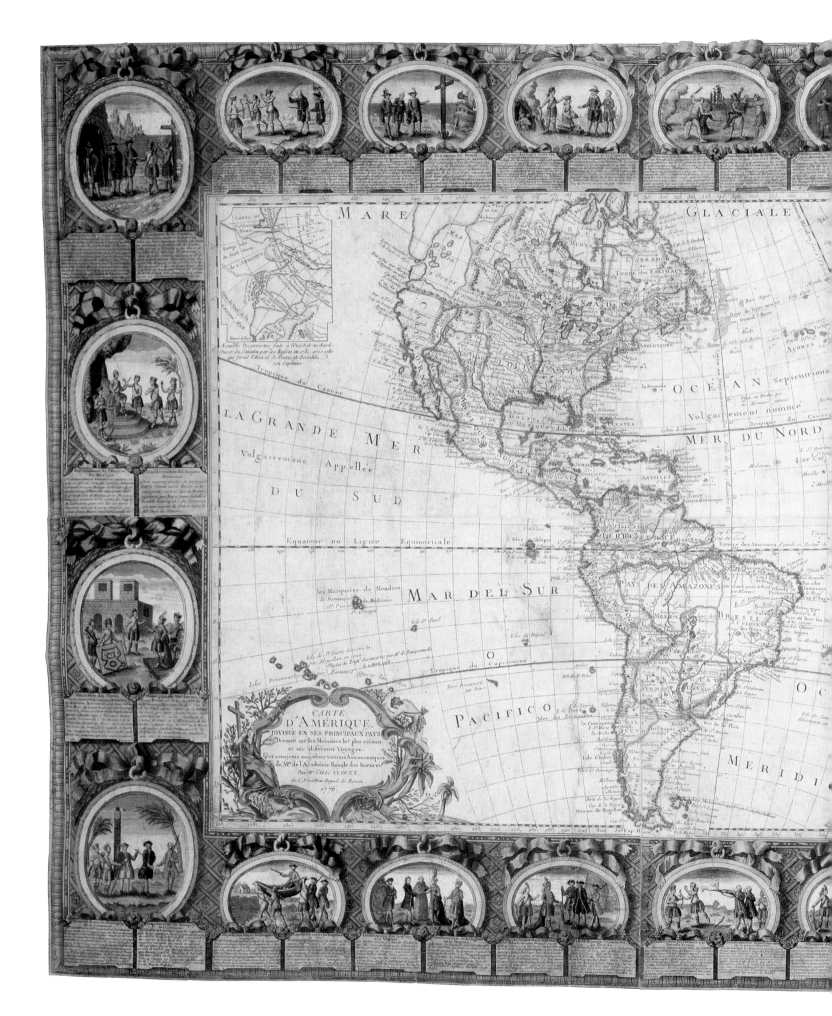

1776

'Carte d'Amérique divisée en ses principaux pays…'

Jean-Baptiste-Louis Clouet
Separate publication, Paris, 1776.
Copper engraving, 121 x 920 mm

In a similar style to Nolin's wall-maps are a series of maps of the continents drawn by l'abbé Clouet and published by Louis Mondhare in 1776.

If the point could be made that the emphasis on Nolin's wall-maps was on the decorative rather than geographical element, then how much more so it is in the case of Clouet's map of the Americas. The boundaries depicted for the English colonies seem to be more French wishful thinking than actual reality, giving the impression that the map is geographically about 15 years out of date, with French Louisiana dominating the interior of the modern United States.

Clouet's map is also notable for the very fanciful geography of western Canada, with the large Mer du Ouest visible on the western seaboard and the largely imaginary network of rivers, including the 'Rivière longue' extending westwards from the Great Lakes. This misconception originated with the Baron Lahontan, *circa* 1703, but was actively sought in the 1740s by leading French explorers such as Pierre Gaultier la Varenne de la Vérendrye, as a means of reaching the Pacific coast.

Around the map are 20 elaborate vignettes from the history of the Americas, each scene engraved so as to appear set in a frame, and with each frame suspended from a ribbon as if in a display. Each scene is captioned both in French and Spanish, and indeed the title is also given in Spanish.

1777

'The Harbour of Charles Town in South Carolina…'

Joseph Frederick Wallet des Barres
From: des Barres's *The Atlantic Neptune*, London, 1777.
Copperplate engraving and etching, 850 x 630 mm

Joseph des Barres was the pre-eminent chart-maker of colonial America. Originally from Switzerland, des Barres joined the British army as an engineer, and served in North America for over 20 years. If he proved himself as a surveyor, he also proved to have a problem with authority, which greatly handicapped his career. His *Atlantic Neptune*, considered one of the finest sea-atlases ever published, is an outstanding series of charts of the coastal waters of Canada, New England and New York, prepared shortly before, and during the early years of the American Revolutionary War. However, the survey work was discontinued as the war progressed. South of the Delaware, des Barres was only able to publish a small number of general charts.

This particular chart is taken from a survey by Captain James Wallace, RN, supplemented from other sources, and is probably the finest chart/view of Charleston from the colonial era, enlivened with the fine etched, but rather distant view, of Charleston from across the harbour.

Charleston was one of the principal centres of the war in the southern colonies and was captured by the British in May 1780, towards the war's end.

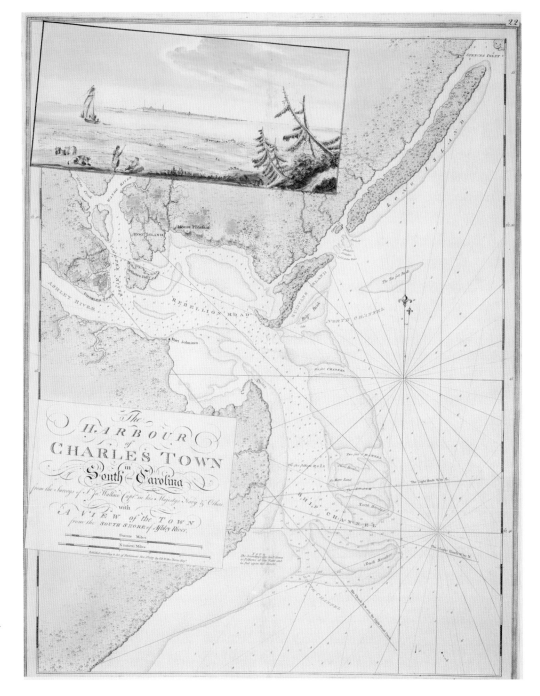

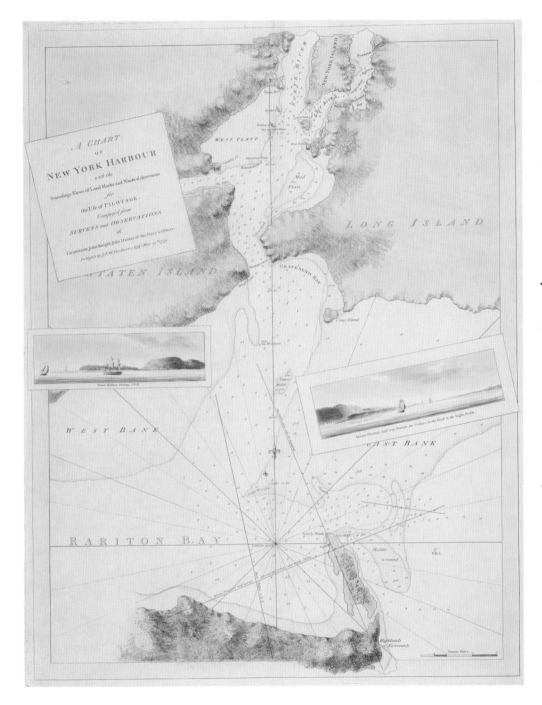

1777

'A Chart of New York Harbour with the Soundings, Views of Land Marks and Nautical directions for the Use of Pilotage...'

Joseph Frederick Wallet des Barres
From: des Barres's *The Atlantic Neptune*, London, 1777. Copperplate engraving and etching, 850 x 630 mm

For a description of the Barres *Atlantic Neptune* see the previous entry.

Des Barres's chart of New York harbour is from a survey by Captain John Knight and John Hunter RN, and is one of the finest, and most attractive charts of the mouth of New York harbour, and approaches to New York itself, from the colonial period.

Within the blank area of the bay are two coastal profiles, designed as an aid to pilots to help them orientate themselves within the bay. They could use the profiles to locate themselves in preparation for approaching the neck of the harbour, and thus avoid the two shoals on the seaward side.

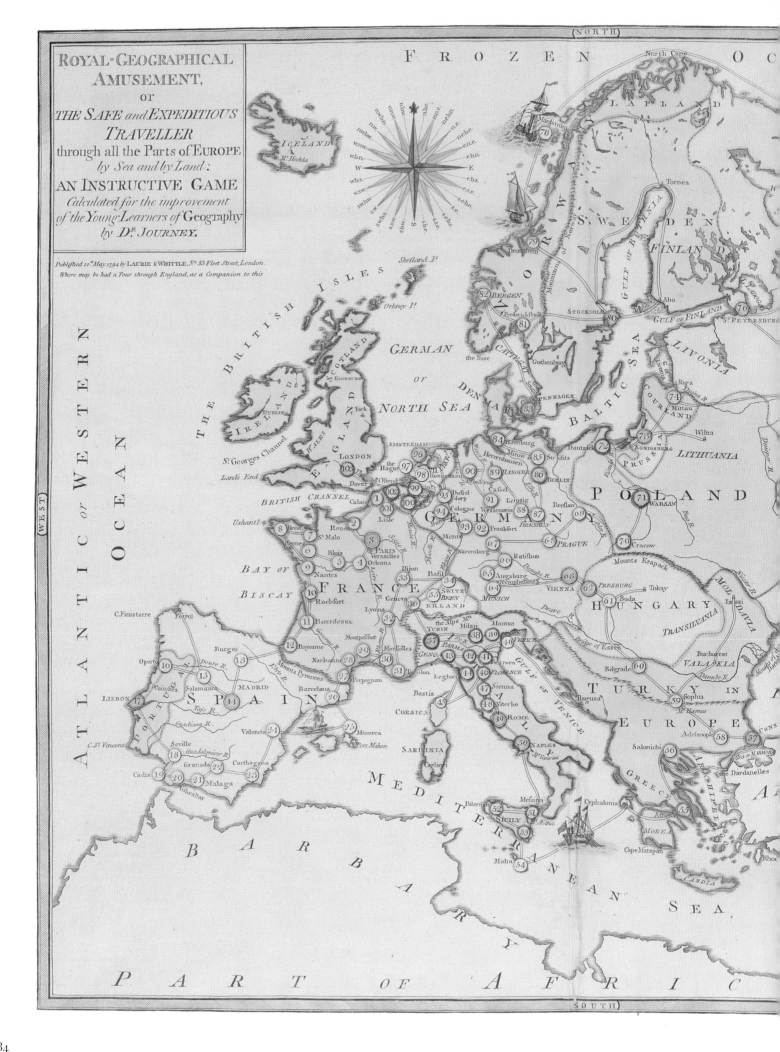

ROYAL-GEOGRAPHICAL
AMUSEMENT,
or
THE SAFE and EXPEDITIOUS
TRAVELLER
through all the Parts of EUROPE
by Sea and by Land:
AN INSTRUCTIVE GAME
Calculated for the improvement
of the Young Learners of Geography
by Dr. JOURNEY.

Publifhed 12th May 1794 by LAURIE & WHITTLE, No 53 Fleet Street, London.
Where may be had a Tour through England, as a Companion to this

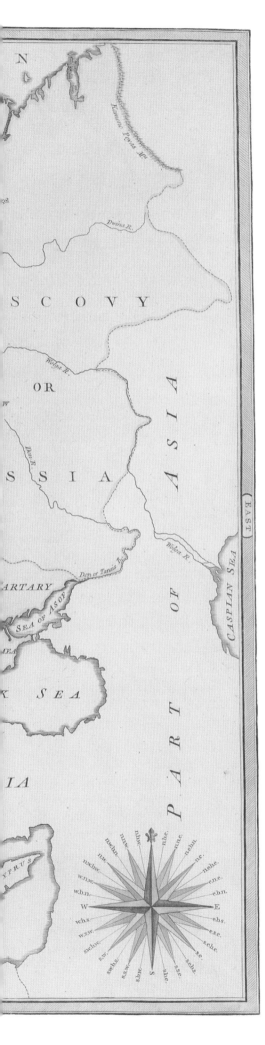

1787

'Royal-Geographical Amusement or the Safe and Expeditious Traveller through all the Parts of Europe…'

Robert Sayer, Robert Laurie and James Whittle
Separate publication,
London, 1794.
Copper engraving, 460 x 510 mm, with letterpress rule sheet

The game is a Grand Tour around Europe, with 102 locations, starting at Calais and going as far as Constantinople before returning to London. This is a rare game map, attributed to Dr. Journey, evidently a pseudonym for Robert Sayer, the original publisher, who first issued the map in 1787. This example was printed by his heirs Robert Laurie and James Whittle shortly after they took control of the firm.

In the game, the distance travelled is decided by a throw of the dice; the accompanying rules describe the location and list penalties for landing there. For example, a player would have to stay in Venice three turns 'to see St Mark's and the Arsenal, to take the diversions of the carnival, and to go to Ragusa, a little republican city in the Gulf of Venice'. It is ironic that the more interesting a place, the less desirable it is to land there.

Game maps of this kind are generally found dissected and mounted on a cloth backing, with the rules pasted along the side borders, to make them easily folded for storage. It is most unusual to see a game map in its sheet form, uncut, as here.

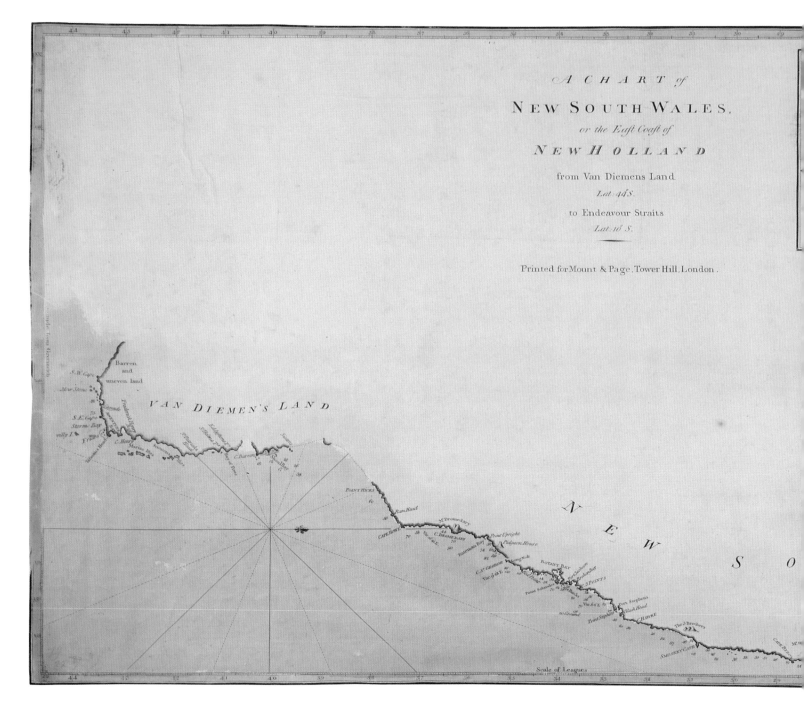

A CHART of
NEW SOUTH WALES,
or the East Coast of
NEW HOLLAND
from Van Diemens Land
Lat. 44 S.
to Endeavour Straits
Lat. 16 S.

Printed for Mount & Page, Tower Hill, London.

VAN DIEMEN'S LAND

c. 1790

'A Chart of New South Wales or the East Coast of New Holland...'

Mount & Page Separate publication,
London, *c.* 1790.
Copper engraving, 260 x 790 mm

Mount and Page published this very scarce chart of New South Wales, orientated with north to the right. It extends from Tasmania in the south northwards to the Endeavour Strait (between Cape York Peninsula and Prince of Wales Island) on the right, with insets of 'Endeavour Bay' and Botany Bay. The map is based on the 'official' chart drawn by Cook from the survey that he made on board *HMS Endeavour* in 1770, which was the first printed chart of the east coast of Australia. Although Cook made a major contribution to the mapping of Australia, there were still questions that he left unresolved:

Tasmania's relationship to the mainland was still unknown, as was Torres Strait, which divides Australia from New Guinea.

Cook's voyage opened up Australia for British colonialism: one of the insets is a chart of Botany Bay, the famous penal colony, a site recommended by Cook. Cook landed at Botany Bay in April 1770, renamed as a consequence of the number and variety of flowers blooming at the time, but it was to prove an inhospitable home for a settlement. Transportation had long been a way of keeping Britain's prison population down, but because of the American Revolutionary War, 1775–83, the Americas were closed to

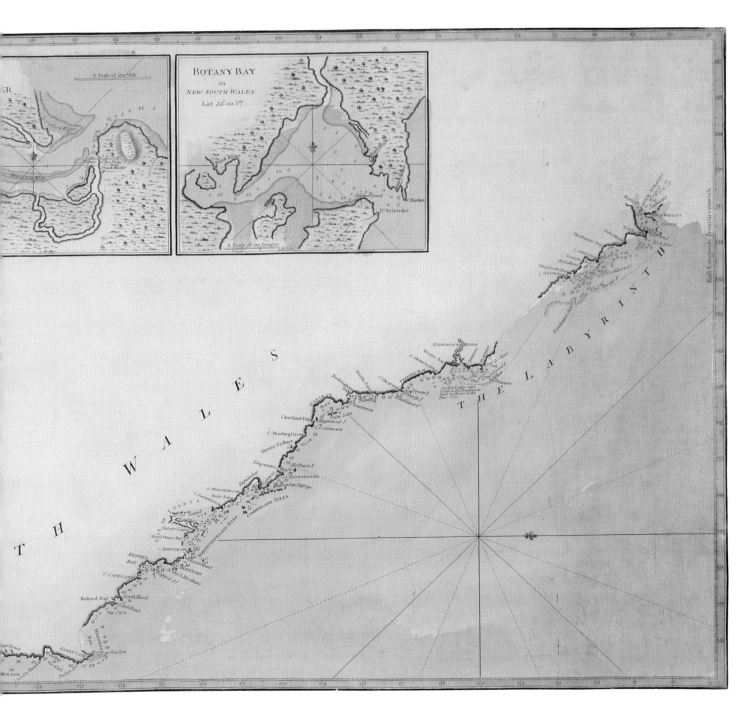

convicts. Australia was the logical alternative.

The 11 ships of the First Fleet sailed from Portsmouth in 1787, with at least 1,350 people, of whom 780 were convicts and 570 were freemen, women and children, and four companies of marines. The oldest convict was 82 and about 20 per cent were women. The fleet arrived in Botany Bay in 1788, but the landing party was not impressed with the site. They moved the fleet to Port Jackson and settled in Sydney Cove. The last shiploads of convicts would go to the fledgling settlement in Western Australia in 1868.

c. 1795

'Geography Bewitched!
or, a droll Caricature Map
of Scotland'

Robert Dighton
Pen, ink and wash colour,
186 x 161 mm

Dighton was a well-known painter of portraits and caricatures as well as decorative subjects, who is regarded as one of the most talented social caricaturists of the late eighteenth and early nineteenth centuries. This drawing is believed to be Dighton's original design for his caricature map of Scotland, published by Henry Carington Bowles (Carington Bowles's son) and Samuel Carver, in partnership as Bowles and Carver, *circa* 1795.

Many of Dighton's works were issued anonymously, and published by Carington Bowles (fl.1752–93). Carington Bowles worked initially with his father, John Bowles, before leaving to take over his uncle, Thomas Bowles (II)'s, business, *c.* 1762. Carington Bowles was among the most active print- and map-sellers and publishers of his day in London, as can be seen in the extensive catalogues of his issued in 1782, 1784, 1790 and in 1795 (by his successors Bowles and Carver).

Dighton's drawing is one of the most attractive caricature maps of Scotland, giving 'Jock' a rather more pleasant demeanour than some later English caricaturists.

1796

'The Kingdom of France is
represented under the form of
a Ship...'

Anonymous
Separate publication,
London, 1796.
Copper engraving, 480 x 620 mm

Published three years after the execution by guillotine of Louis XVI and Marie-Antoinette, and a year after the death of the Dauphin in prison, the English publisher of this very decorative, and rare, engraving apparently still saw hope for the restoration of the monarchy.

In the map the ship represents that part of France supportive of the republic and the land (Brittany, Normandy and the Pyrenees) those areas not yet subdued. Yet the country is shown divided into the *départements*, the administrative areas set up by the National Convention in 1790 to break up the old and corrupt system of counties.

In the Bay of Biscay is a broken mast carrying the Royal Crest and a lifeboat filled with royalists. A suggestion that the revolution is not going well is the ship's anchor is shown with a broken chain, suggesting aimless drift – three years later Napoleon Bonaparte was able to declare himself First Consul and, later still, Emperor.

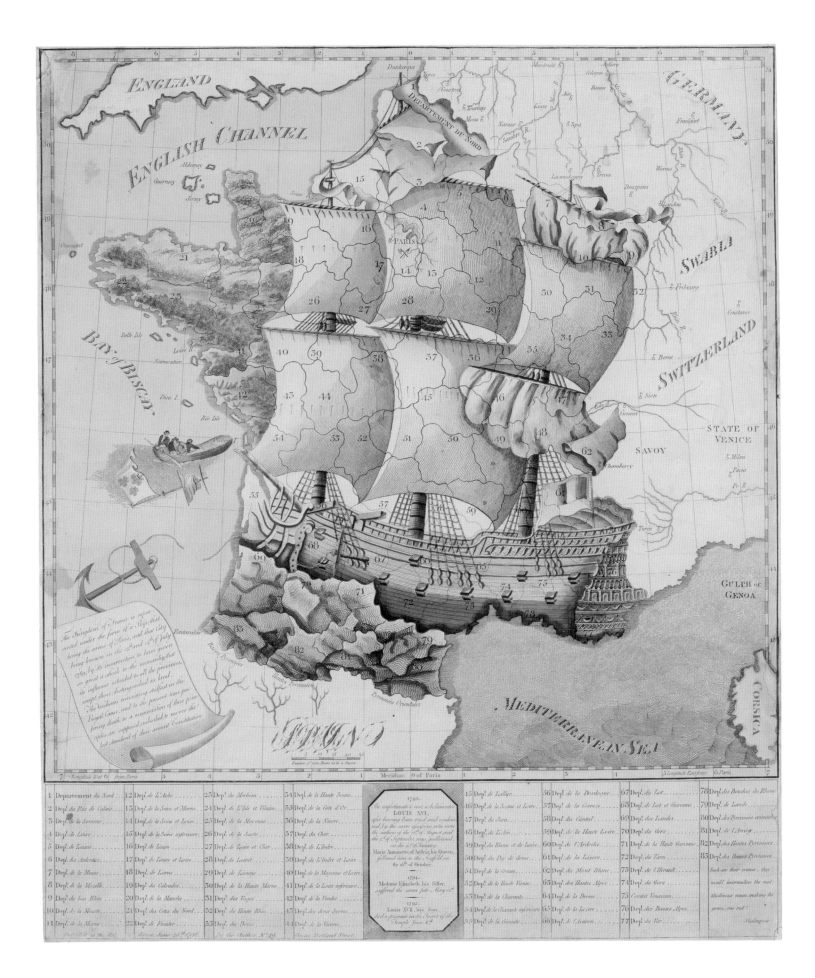

1798

'La Nuova Olanda e la Nuova Guinea...'

Giovanni Maria Cassini
From: Cassini's *Nuovo Atlante Geografico Universale*, Rome, 1798.
Copper engraving, 365 x 490 mm

An Italian map of Australia and New Guinea, published in Rome, the emphasis is on Captain Cook's charting down the east coast of Australia. Most of the marked features are those named by Cook and his crew between the Torres Strait and Tasmania. Cook left two blanks: as he travelled north he did not assertain the relationship of Tasmania to the mainland, so it is shown here with lines suggesting it is part of the mainland; further north, close to the Torres Strait, is another unmapped region, with a region of sea that Cook called 'The Labyrinth', now called the Coral Sea. Having already run aground once on a coral reef, causing considerable damage to the *Endeavour*, he chose not to take the risk and stayed outside the reefs, unable to see or chart the shore.

The title is within a decorative cartouche with two natives: not only do they look more like American Indians, but also one carries a bow, which the Australian aborigines never developed.

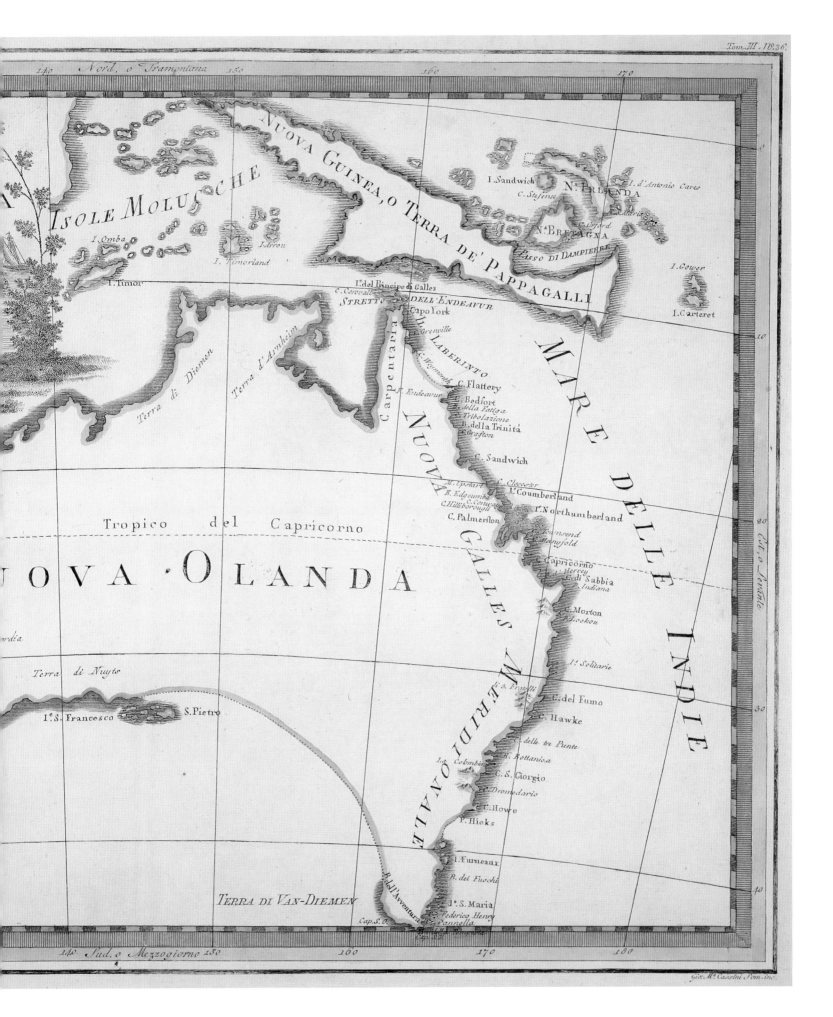

140　Nord, o Tramontana　150　　　　　160　　　　　170

ISOLE MOLUCCHE

NUOVA GUINEA, O TERRA DE' PAPPAGALLI

N. IRLANDA

I. Sandwich

C. Stefense

N. BRETAGNA

Passo di Dampierre

I. d'Antonio Caves

I. Orford

I. Gower

I. Carteret

I. Omba

I. Arrou

I. Timorland

I. Timor

I. del Principe di Galles

C. Corwall

STRETTO DELL'ENDEAVUR

Capo York

C. Grenville

Terra di Diemen

Terra d'Arnheim

LABERINTO

C. Weymouth

F. Endeavur

C. Flattery

C. Bedfort

I. della Fatiga

C. Tribolazione

B. della Trinità

C. Grafton

Carpentaria

C. Sandwich

MARE DELLE INDIE

NUOVA

M. Upstart

B. Edgeumbe

C. Conway

C. Hillsborough

C. Palmerston

C. Gloecester

I. Coumberland

I. Northumberland

C. Townsend

C. Manifold

Tropico　del　Capricorno

NUOVA · OLANDA

GALLES

Capricorno

I. Hervey

C. di Sabbia

C. Indiana

C. Morton

I. Lookou

MERIDIONALE

Est, o Levante

I. Solitarie

Terra di Nuyts

I. 3 Fratelli

C. del Fumo

C. Hawke

I.e S. Francesco

S. Pietro

C. delle tre Punte

B. Rottanica

La Colombia

C. S. Giorgio

C. Dromedario

C. Howe

P. Hicks

I. Furneaux

B. dei Fuochi

TERRA DI VAN-DIEMEN

B. dell'Avventura

I.e S. Maria

Cap. S. O...

Federico Henry

C. Pannella

140　Sud, o Mezzogiorno 150　　　　160　　　　　170　　　　　180

Gio. M.a Cassini Sen. inc.

191

1801

'The Toper's Atlas
from the newest
Observations…'

Giles Grinagain
Separate publication,
London, 1801.
Copper engraving, 215 x 180 mm

The *bon viveur* in this early nineteenth-century
caricature is holding up a wall-map showing
only those areas of the world that interest
him: countries that produce fine wines and
spirits. On the mainland are the famous wine
regions, including Champagne, Burgundy
and Shiraz, surrounding the river Rhine; in
the river are islands that produce stronger
fare, including the Canaries and Jamaica.

The *bon viveur* has the dazed look and red
cheeks of a man used to drink: however the
pock-marks suggest his vices were not limited
to alcohol.

'Giles Grinagain' was the pseudonym for
Samuel Howitt, a famous sporting artist and
illustrator, who preferred to publish such low
caricatures anonymously.

THE TOPERS ATLAS.

A MAP intended to illustrate the *threatened* INVASION of ENGLAND by BONAPARTE.

AMSTERDAM. ROTTERDAM. FLUSHING. SLUYS. ANTWERP. OSTEND. NIEUPORT. DUNKIRK. GRAVELINES.

A
Complete Representation of the
COAST of ENGLAND,
together with the
INTERIOR, divided into COUNTIES and MILITARY DISTRICTS,
Also the COAST of FRANCE and HOLLAND from the *Texel* to *Brest*
With the *Bearings* from LONDON, and the *Distance*, in Miles,
from *Port* to *Port*;
To which is annexed EIGHTEEN PLANS of the PORTS of
THE ENEMY,
The PRINCIPAL DEPÔTS of the FLOTILLA
intended for the
INVASION of ENGLAND.
By John Luffman, Geog[r].

References to the Military Districts.

1. Western	7. Severn	
2. South West	8. North Inland	
3. Southern	9. York	
4. South Inland	10. North West	
5. Home	11. Northern	
6. Eastern	12. London Comprising London and Westminster, the Tower hamlets Rotherhith, Lambeth and all the Parishes within the Bills of Mortality.	

Cities are thus described, as ● LONDON
Cities being also County towns ● EXETER
County towns ● Hertford
Great towns ● Leeds
Small towns and villages . . . Rye
The Figures annexed to places as BATH 6 shew their rank in the Population of England. These places which are without figures have a population under seven thousand each.

A Plan of the
Coast of France
from Cape Gris-nez
to Portel, with all
the Batteries.

Bay
of
Boulogne

CALAIS. BOULOGNE. DIEPPE. HAVRE. CHERBOURG. GRANVILLE. St MALO. MORLAIX. BREST.

Engrav'd & Publish'd Jan[y] 19, 1804, by John Luffman, N[o] 28, Little Bell Alley, Coleman Street, London. Price 3s. 6d. Col[d] 4s. 6 in a case. Of whom may be had all the principal Sea Ports of Holland, France, Spain, Portugal & Italy. The Population of England, Scotland & Wales

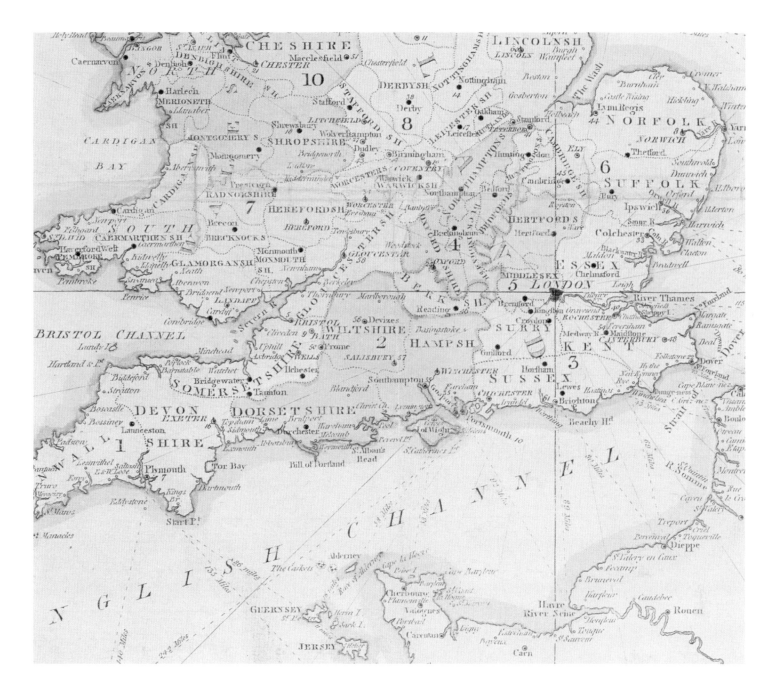

1803

'A Map intended to illustrate
the threatened Invasion of
England by Bonaparte'

John Luffman
Separate publication,
London, 1803.
Copper engraving, 415 x 355 mm

John Luffman published this very scarce
broadsheet map of England and Wales at the
height of British fear of an invasion by
Napoleon. In the upper and lower margins
are insets of 18 continental ports from which
such an invasion would be launched. Within
the map, straight lines give the distances from
these ports to potential landing sites.

   Part of the purpose of the map, as
noted in the text 'To my Countrymen',
is Luffman's advocacy of the seizure of
strategic islands along the coast of the Low
Countries, to deny Napoleon the use of
the ports of the region.

   This map sold originally for 1s. 6d. in black
and white, or 2s. 6d. for a coloured version
like this example.

Publish'd Dec.ʳ 6. 1806, by LAURIE & WHITTLE, *53. Fleet Street, London.*

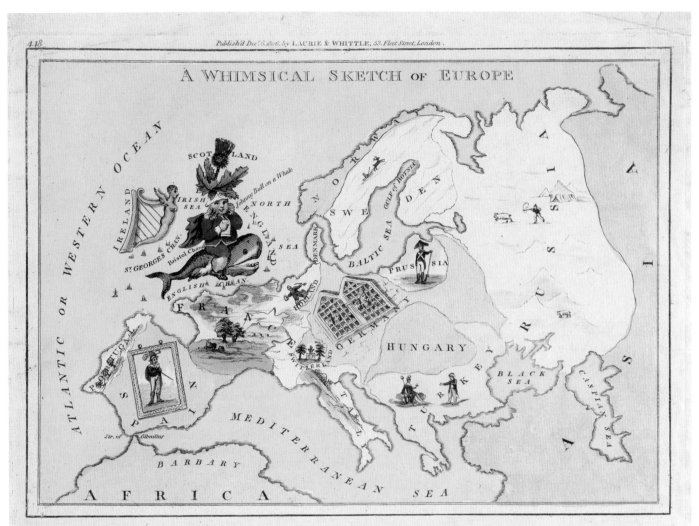

A WHIMSICAL SKETCH OF EUROPE

A POETICAL DESCRIPTION OF THE MAP.

OFT we see in the shops, a print set up for sale,
England colour'd, an *old fellow striding a whale:*
Yes! Old England's a picture; the sea forms its frame;
And Hibernia and Scotia they class with the same.
Would you ask me what chrystal, so clear; 'tis before?
'Tis the large lens of liberty plates them all o'er.
See Hibernia! a *harp*, gilt with industry's gold:
And the *seed-spreading thistle* is Scotia we're told.
Whilst crown'd with the thistle, the harp on his side,
He hangs o'er the ocean, protector, and pride.
See! the rude hand of time has not dar'd to assail
Yet " the sturdy old fellow astride on his whale."

There's a picture just by these, all tatter'd and torn;
One all *blood-smear'd and red*; that is France I'd be sworn,
What's that covers its surface, all shining like wax?
'Tis the varnish of tyranny; see how it cracks!
There's a portrait beside of a *drunken old sot*;
That is Holland: how mildew'd and eat with the rot!
And its station, alas! by the very first glance,
We may see does not suit; for its crowded by France.
See! these cast such a shadow throughout the whole space,
That they seem to distort every natural grace,
Save with those where their shadows don't reach to prevail,
And " the sturdy old fellow's astride on his whale,"

Yon *rich landscape* behold! it has seen better days;
And illumin'd was once with bright liberty's rays:
That is Switzerland; fam'd for its picturesque views;
But France now clouds its prospects; its *vines* turns to *yews*.
View that one to the right; that to France very near:
That bore once brightest colours, transparent and clear;

A tint most harmonious; like opening dawn:
That is Italy; mark how its colours are gone!
It no longer can boast of its olive retreat,
Now its large lumb'ring neighbour so elbows its seat!
Yon *vineyard-scene's* Portugal: some tints still prevail,
Like " the sturdy old fellow's astride on his whale."

See that *portrait!* away to the left, in the rear;
Descriptive of jealousy, anguish, and fear;
That which tremblingly hangs by its slight golden string;
And seems ready to drop from its great gilded ring:
That poor portrait is Spain; and the ring is its crown:
See! the motions of France almost shatter it down!
Yon's a picture surrounded by some smaller ones,
Which seems like a *debtor that's haunted by duns:*
That is Germany, tended by all its small states,
And it looks tow'rds France like a pris'ner through grates.
They're so shadow'd by France not a ray can prevail,
Like " the sturdy old fellow's astride on his whale."

The next portrait is Prussia; a *soldier* afar,
Just arous'd into action; and rushing to war.
Look again tow'rds the right: see! *three snow-scenes* appear,
See! their shadows diminish; their colours grow clear:
Russia, Sweden, and Denmark, distinguish these three,
Still there's one distant picture o'erlook'd you may see:
It is Turkey; and see it tow'rds England advance;
For its terribly lately been shadow'd by France.
Now to tell you, as showman, it falls to our lot,
Who plac'd these around in each singular spot,
'Twas the hand of that master, which long shall prevail,
For " the sturdy old fellow's astride on his whale."

1806

'A Whimsical Sketch of Europe'

Laurie & Whittle
Separate publication,
London, 1806.
Copper engraving,
image: 250 x 185 mm

A caricature map of Europe at the height of the Napoleonic Wars is shown here, with 'A Poetical Description of the Map' underneath. Unlike later versions, for example the Rose map of 1899 included later, only the caricatures of England, Ireland and Scotland form the outlines of their countries; the other countries just have illustrations n them.

England is John Bull astride a whale, representing British naval power the year after Trafalgar. From his head grows the 'seed-spreading thistle' and at his back is Ireland as a harp. Both countries played a great part in Britain's military successes.

On the Continent, France is represented by a blood-smeared painting. Holland, who aggravated Britain by becoming France's partner in the 'Continental System' trade embargo against them, is a 'drunken old sot'. Prussia, the only German state independent of Napoleon (and Britain's ally against Napoleon at Waterloo less then ten years later) is a smartly dressed soldier. The other German states are prisoners peering through a grate, 'so shadowed by France not a ray can prevail'. Lastly, in the Balkans, a Turk makes friendly approaches to Britannia, hoping to gain an ally against French incursions.

The Napoleonic Wars had nearly another decade to run.

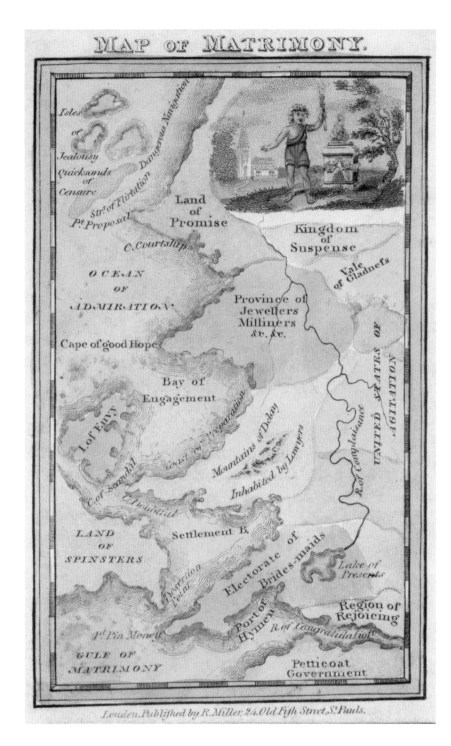

c. 1810

'Map of Matrimony'

William Miller
Separate publication,
London, c. 1810.
Copperplate engraving, 100 x 65 mm

The bookseller William Miller published this scarce miniature allegorical version of the 'Map of Matrimony'.

Due to the small format used, Miller has reduced many of the negative elements; although the 'Mountains of Delay Inhabited by Lawyers' is prominent at the centre of the map, 'Petticoat Government' and 'Land of Spinsters' are relegated to the outer reaches of the map.

It is noticeable however, that there is no land of 'Happy Ever After'.

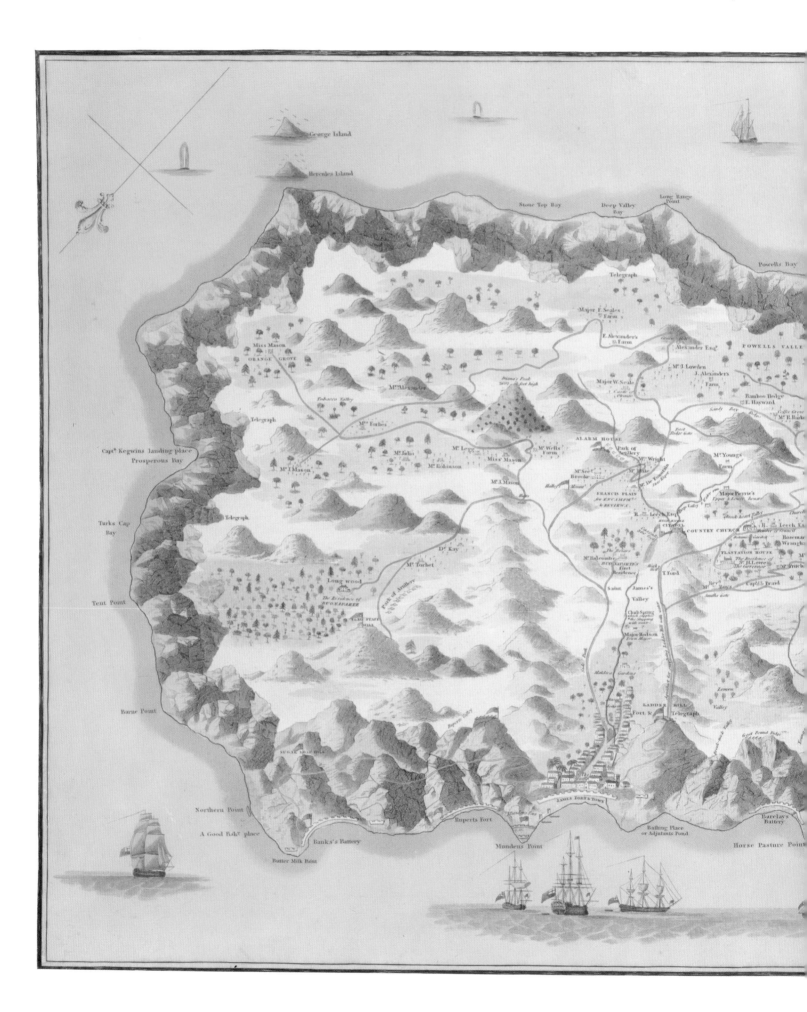

George Island

Berentes Island

Stone Top Bay
Deep Valley Bay
Long Range Point

Powells Bay

Telegraph

Major F. Seales Farm

E. Alexander's Farm

Alexander Esq.
POWELLS VALLEY

Miss Mason
ORANGE GROVE

Mr J. Lowden

J. Alexanders Farm

Bamboo Hedge
E. Hayward

Mrs Alexander

Diana's Peak

Major W. Seale

Mr R. Barke

Tobacco Valley

Sandy Bay

Telegraph

Mrs Forbes

ALARM HOUSE

Park of Artillery

Mr Wright

Mr Youngs Farm

Capt. Kegwins landing place
Prosperous Bay

Mr J. Mason

Mr Julia

Mr Lee

Mr Robinson

Miss Mason

Mr Wells Farm

Mr Seel Brooke

Mr De Fountain

Major Pettie's

FRANCIS PLAIN for ENCAMPM & REVIEWS

R. Leech Esq.

CITADEL

COUNTRY CHURCH

Leech Est.

Rosemary Wrought

Turks Cap Bay

Telegraph

Mr J. Mason

Mr Balcombe

BUONAPARTE'S First Residence

PLANTATION HOUSE

The Residence of J. H. Lowe
Lt Governor

Dr Kay

Mr Turbet

Saint

James's Valley

T. Ford

Capt. Brad

Tent Point

Long wood

Park of Artillery

The Residence of BUONAPARTE

Chub Spring which supplies the Shipping with water

Major Hodson late a Major

Lemon Valley

FLAG STAFF HILL

LADDER HILL Fort S.

Telegraph

Barne Point

SUGAR LOAF HILL

Northern Point

JAMES FORT & TOWN

Ruperts Fort

Barclay's Battery

A Good Fishg place

Bathing Place or Adjutants Pond

Horse Pasture Point

Banks's Battery

Butter Milk Point

Mundens Point

'This Geographical Plan of
THE ISLAND & FORTS OF
SAINT HELENA
is Dedicated by permission to
Field. Marshal His R.l Highness
The Duke of Kent and Strathearn
By Lieu.t R. P. Read.'

Point

Sandy Bay

Potatoe Bay

LIMESTONE QUARRY

Lou Wifes Beach

Needles & Speery

Thos Bagleys Farm

Col. Greentree

J. Bagleys Farm

Lots Wife

Horse

Lieut Scale

Manate Bay

HIGH PEAK

THOMSON'S WOOD

Greentrees

Mr. Alexander

J. Knipe's Farm

Major

R. Mason's Farm

De Fountain

Mrs. Fs Knipe's Farm Half Moon

Sam. Knipe Esq. Horse Pasture Farm

G. Leech Esq.

Grounds

Good Fishing Ground

Granny Marys House

HIGH HILL

Lemon Garden

Old Womans Valley

S.W. Point
Man & Horse Point

Egg Island

Bird Island

Good Fishing Ground

Rocks

Scale of Miles

Fac Simile of Napoleon Buonapartes Signature

When First Consul

Bonaparte

When Emperor

Napoleon

1815

'This Geographical Plan
of the Island & Forts
of St Helena…'

Lieut. R.P. Reid
Separate publication,
London, 1815–1816.
Copper engraving, 570 x 440 mm

Despite seeming to be an insignificant
island in the South Atlantic, St Helena
was a possession of the British East India
Company from 1651, who used it as a staging
post on the way to the Far East; the island
came to the world's attention when the
British chose it as the new place of exile for
Napoleon Bonaparte after his final defeat
at the Battle of Waterloo in 1815.

This was Napoleon's second exile: in 1814
he had been forced to abdicate and had been
sent to the Italian island of Elba. This proved
to be too easy to escape from: after less than
ten months he slipped away, returning to
France in an unsuccessful attempt to regain
his throne.

St Helena was a very different proposition:
not only was it far more remote, but most of
the island was ringed with high cliffs. The
only landing point was the heavily fortified
James Town and Fort on the south of the
island, so it was impossible for a rescue party
to land unnoticed, and Napoleon remained
there until his death in 1821.

Today the island is an overseas territory of
the UK, although the land Napoleon lived on
and the valley he was buried in (before being
returned to Paris in 1840) are French territory.

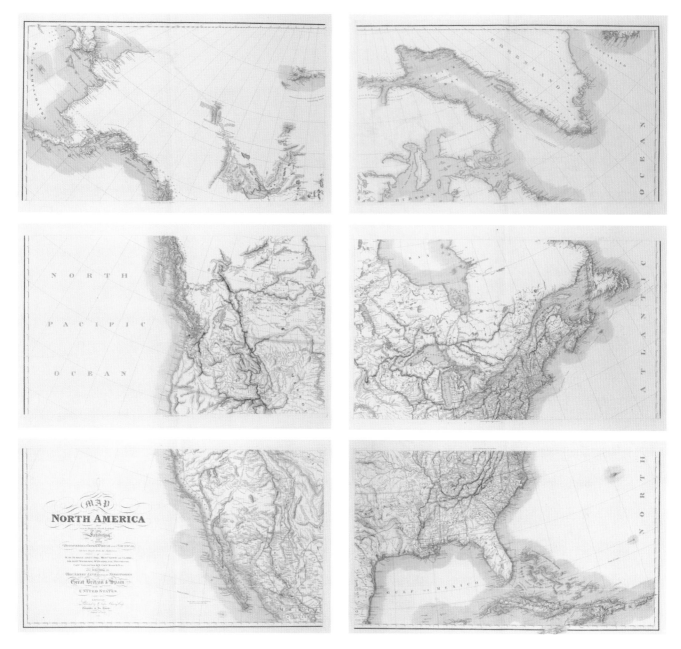

1820

'Map of North America … exhibiting the recent discoveries … . [&] boundary lines between the territories of Great Britain & Spain with the United States…'

William Faden Jr.
Separate publication,
London, 1820.
Copper engraving. 6 sheets;
TL: 480 x 820 mm; TR: 480 x 825 mm; LC: 480 x 825 mm; RC: 485 x 825 mm; BL: 483 x 825 mm; BR: 500 x 825 mm

On six sheets, the first edition of this very rare and important wall-map of the Americas was among the largest maps of North America published at the time. It incorporates considerable new information from the accounts of the most recent explorations of the regions of North America, including Humboldt in the southwest, Lewis and Clark in the west, Hearne and Mackenzie in Canada and Vancouver along the Pacific Coast.

As such, it is probably the most important map of North America of its time; in the hands of Faden's successor James Wyld Sr., and his successors, the map was reprinted, with additions and amendments, as late as 1874.

This map is not found in the Library of Congress or British Library, or other British institutions, and is all the more unusual as being issued uncut, rather than dissected and laid on linen for folding into a slipcase.

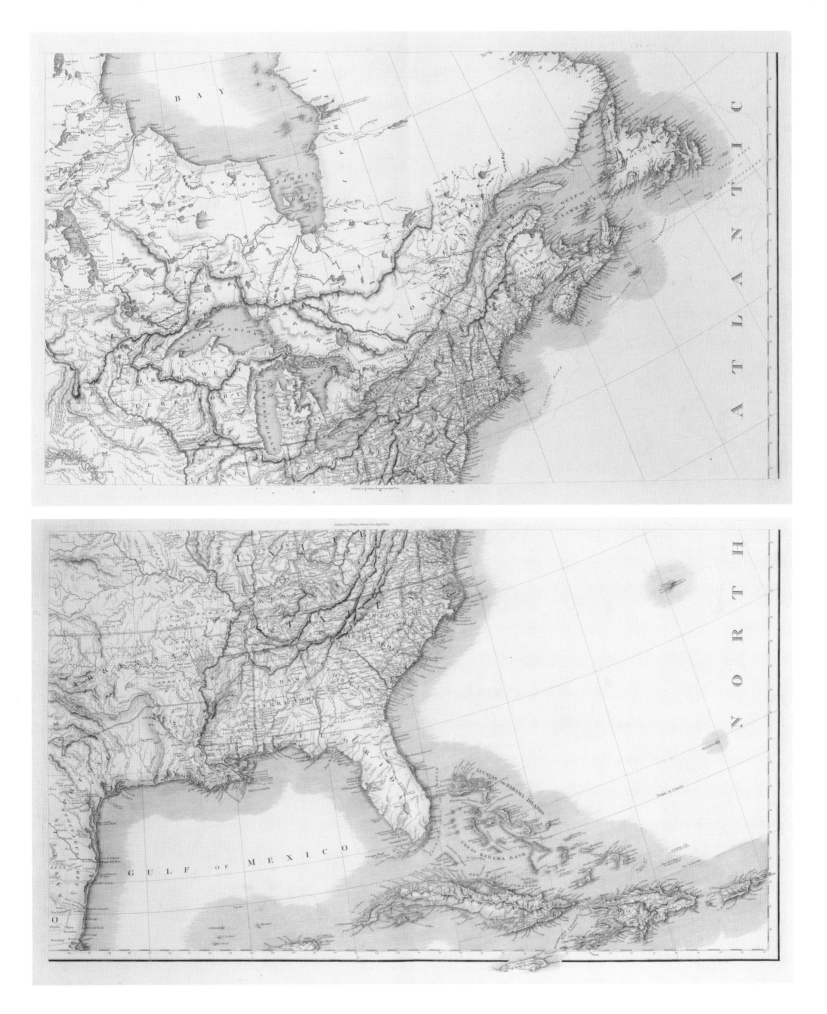

ASIEN

CHINA

ASEN

NIPHON

DAS COREANISCHE MEER

JAPANISCHE INSELN

OST-CHINESISCHES MEER

GELBE MEER

KIANG NANKIN

TONQUIN

CAMBODSHA

CHINESISCHES MEER

DIE MANILLISCHEN oder PHILIPPINISCHEN INSELN

LUZON

Mindoro

Samar

Leyta

Palawan

Paragoa

MAGINDAO

BORNEO

SUMATRA

LADRONISCHE od. MARIANISCHE INSELN

I Guahan

Byrons Fahrt 1765

Wallis Fahrt 1767

Cap. Marshalls Fahrt 1788

PALAOS od. PELEW INSELN

DIE CAROLINISCHEN INSELN

DER AEQUATOR

NEU GUINEA oder LAND der PAPUS

Neu Hanover

Neu Irland

Neu Britanien

Bougainvilles Fahrt 1768

SALOMON INSELN

Torres Strasse 1606

Endeavour Strasse

KOENIGIN CHARLOTTENS INSELN

Egmonds od. Sta Cruz

DIE NEUEN HEBRIDEN

Heil Geist Land

Arnhems Land

Carpentaria

G. F. de Witts Land 1628 entd.

NEU HOLLAND

WENDECIRKEL DES STEINBOCKS

Endracht Land

Edels Land 1619 entd.

Löwins Land

Peter Nuyts Land

NEU CALEDONIEN

Botany I.

Botany Bay

BASSES STRASSE

Van Diemens Land

Tasmans Fahrt 1642

Auf dieser Karte sind die drei Seereisen des Capt. Cook, und anderer Weltumsegler angezeigt; um die Richtung zu sehen, nach welcher sie hinsegelten, wurden den Punkten, welche die Reisen bezeichnen, kleine Pfeile beygefügt.

Oestliche Laenge von der Insel Ferro.

TAVAI POENAMMOO

Cooks erste Fahrt

Cooks zweite Fahrt

Cooks dritte Fahrt vom Vorg. der guten Hoffnung kommend

1830

'Australien (Südland) auch Polynesien oder Inselwelt...'

Johann Walch
Separate publication,
Augsburg, 1830.
Copper engraving, 470 x 590 mm

Published in Augsburg the year after the British formally claimed the western part of Australia (1829), this is a German map of Australasia. However the English presence is limited here to New South Wales, with Sydney Cove, Port Jackson and Botany Bay all named, but in the west Dutch names still predominate.

Elsewhere the routes of Captain Cook in the 1770s were still considered important enough to be marked. Walch has also attempted to colour-code the islands to show which European country controlled them.

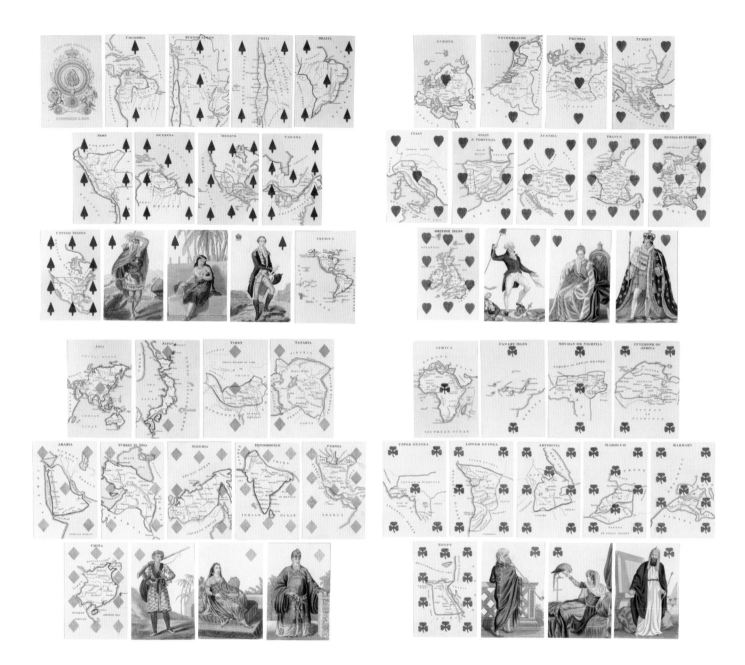

1840

Playing card maps

James Head Stopforth
Copper engravings, each card
approx. 100 x 65 mm

A fine pack of playing cards, each suit represents a continent, with portraits for the court cards. The cards are modelled on René Janet's *Boston de l'Univers* pack (Paris, 1825). Europe is hearts, spades the Americas, diamonds Asia and clubs Africa, each suit with the symbol coloured by hand.

Each suit includes portraits for the court (or face) cards. In the case of Europe these are William IV of England as king, Catherine II of Russia as queen and Robespierre of France as knave. America has George Washington, Queen Neala of Canada and Telasco of Mexico. Within the suits each country is graded according to

its importance in the group, so the British Isles are shown as the most valuable card in hearts, the United States in spades and China in diamonds, while Egypt has the pre-eminent position in clubs.

James Head Stopforth, working in partnership with his son, published a number of packs of playing cards, from standard decks to deluxe sets such as this. Because the maps had to be printed, hand coloured, and over-stamped with the suit marks, the production would have been expensive, so it is likely that most sets would have been bought by collectors rather than for use but, even so, such sets are only rarely found.

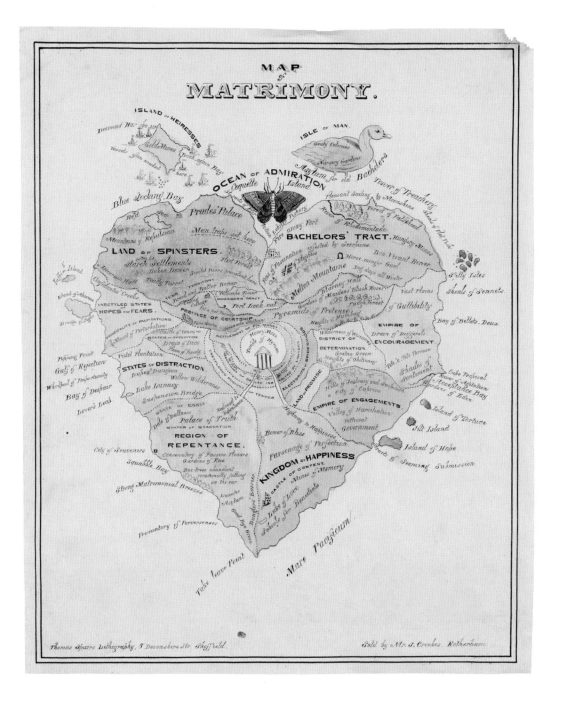

1840

'Map of Matrimony'

Thomas Spurrs
Separate publication,
Sheffield, *c.* 1840.
Lithograph, 290 x 225 mm

The mythical island of Matrimony owes more than a little to John Bunyan's *Pilgrim's Progress*, with allegorical lands representing the difficult routes through life en route to Heaven. Here there are the 'Land of Spinsters' and 'Bachelor's Tract' from which the first objective is to pass through 'Province of Courtship' to the 'Honeymoon', placed at the centre of the map. From there lead the 'Railroad to Repentance' and 'Road to Happiness'. Off the northern coast is the 'Island of Heiresses', with gold mines in the interior but also a warning 'Vessels often wrecked here'; and 'Isle of Man', shaped like a goose, with an 'Asylum of Old Bachelors' and 'Gouty Colonies'. This map was published early in the reign of Queen Victoria and, while it doesn't have a romantic view of love, it exhibits a great deal of Victorian morality: a less restrained Italian version has the 'Province of Cuckolds', 'Mountains of in-laws' and 'Bigamy Island'.

1842

'Map of Texas from
the most recent authorities…'

C.S. Williams
Separate publication,
Philadelphia, 1845.
Lithograph, 310 x 380 mm

C.S. Williams published this map of the
short-lived Republic of Texas, with an inset
showing the area north of the Red River.

Texas had rebelled from Mexican control
in 1835, and, after a war that included the
heroic stand at the Alamo mission, had its
status as an independent country recognized
by Mexico in 1840. However at the time this
map was published the end was already in
sight: the United States had announced that it
intended to absorb Texas, contrary to the
1840 treaty, resulting in the Mexicans
declaring war again. Although Texas joined
the Union in 1846 the war continued, with
Mexico also losing New Mexico before
admitting defeat in 1848.

As so few were published during the short
span of the republic, maps of independent
Texas are in great demand.

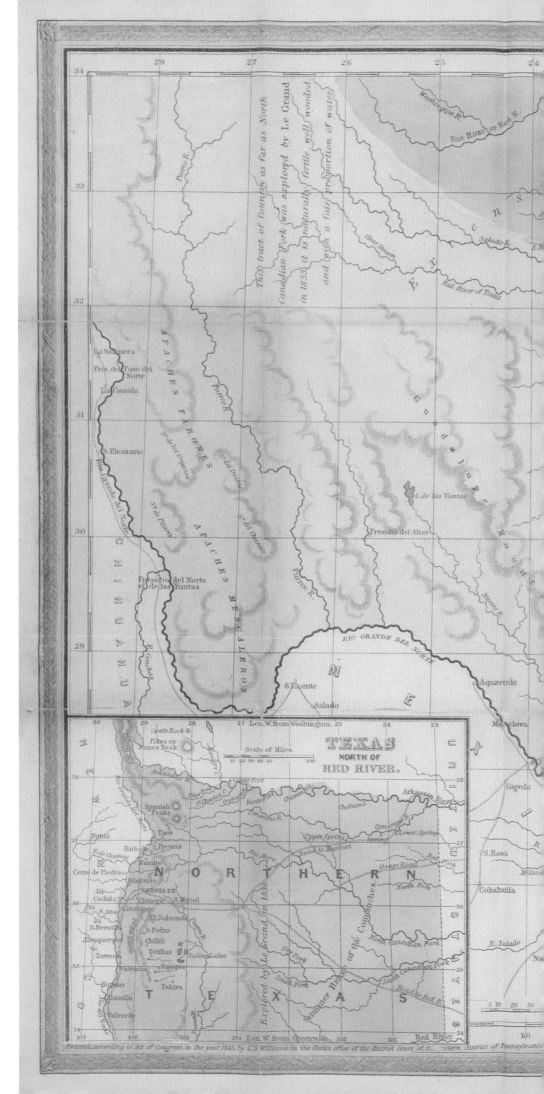

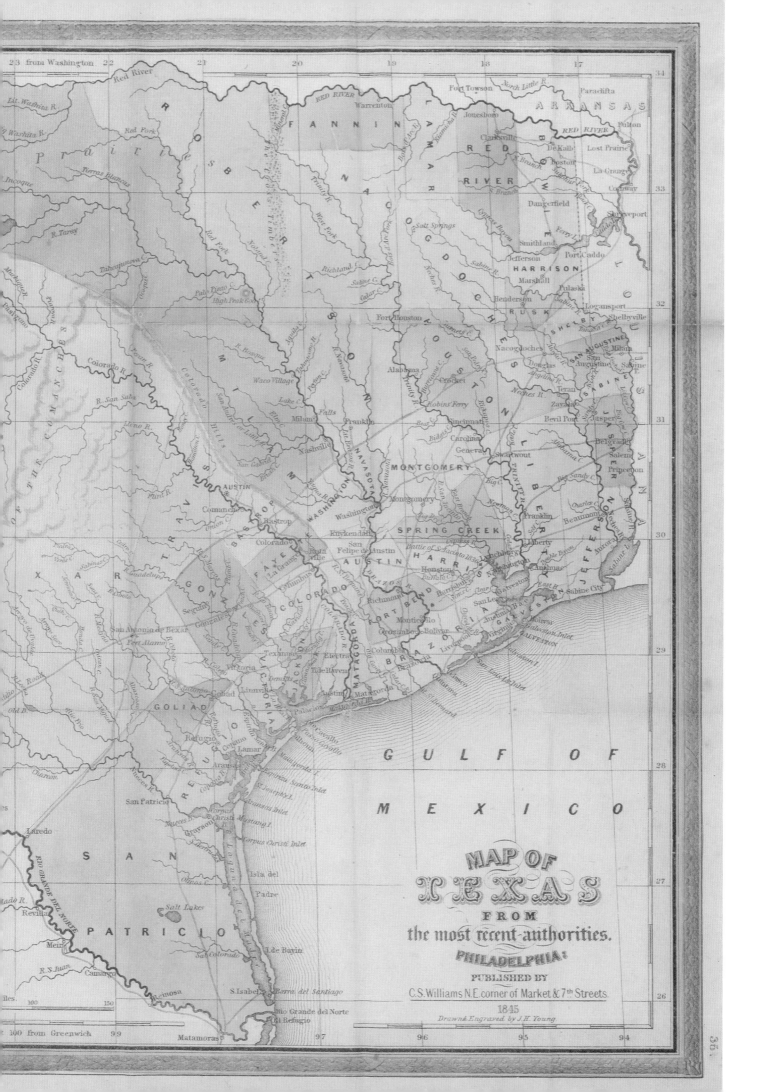

MAP OF
TEXAS
FROM
the most recent authorities.
PHILADELPHIA:
PUBLISHED BY
C.S. Williams N.E. corner of Market & 7th Streets.
1845
Drawn & Engraved by J.H. Young.

1851

'Eastern Hemisphere'

John Tallis
From: R. Montgomery Martin's
*The British Colonies; Their History,
Extent, Condition and Resources,*
London, 1851.
Steel engraving, 260 x 350 mm

R. Montgomery Martin's book was a
celebration of the British Empire near its
height. As such, in a period when printing
processes were becoming more efficient and
the market for cheaper atlases was opening
up, it is one of the last decorative atlases.

The finely engraved borders show some
of the more remarkable sights in the Eastern
hemisphere: camels, kangaroos and giraffes;
costume vignettes include a Maori in a cloak
of feathers.

On the map there is a blue line marking
the mail route from England to the furthest
reaches of the empire – India, Australia
and Hong Kong. It runs past Gibraltar
and Malta, both British possessions in the
Mediterranean; across Suez (two decades
before the opening of the canal) and down
the Red Sea, across the Indian Ocean to
Bombay and Calcutta, then Singapore
and the final destinations.

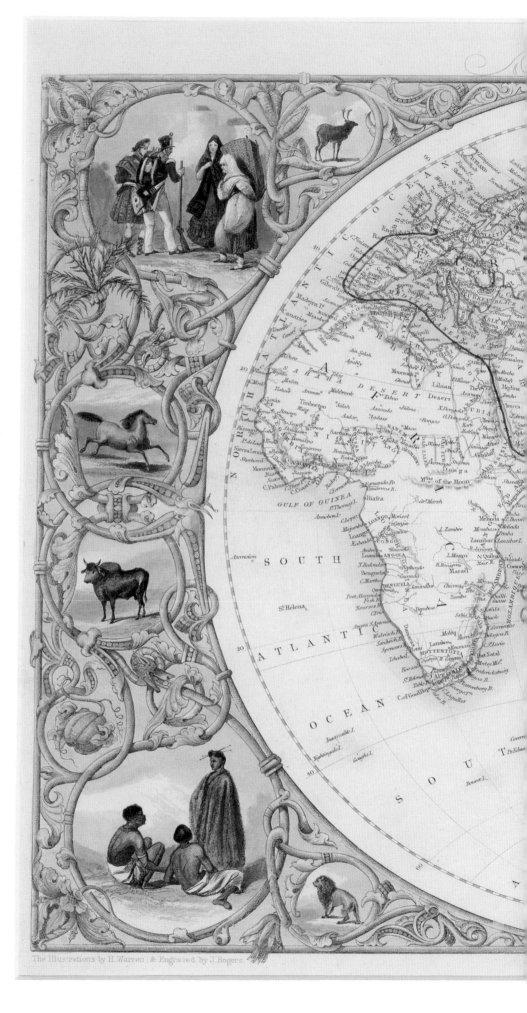

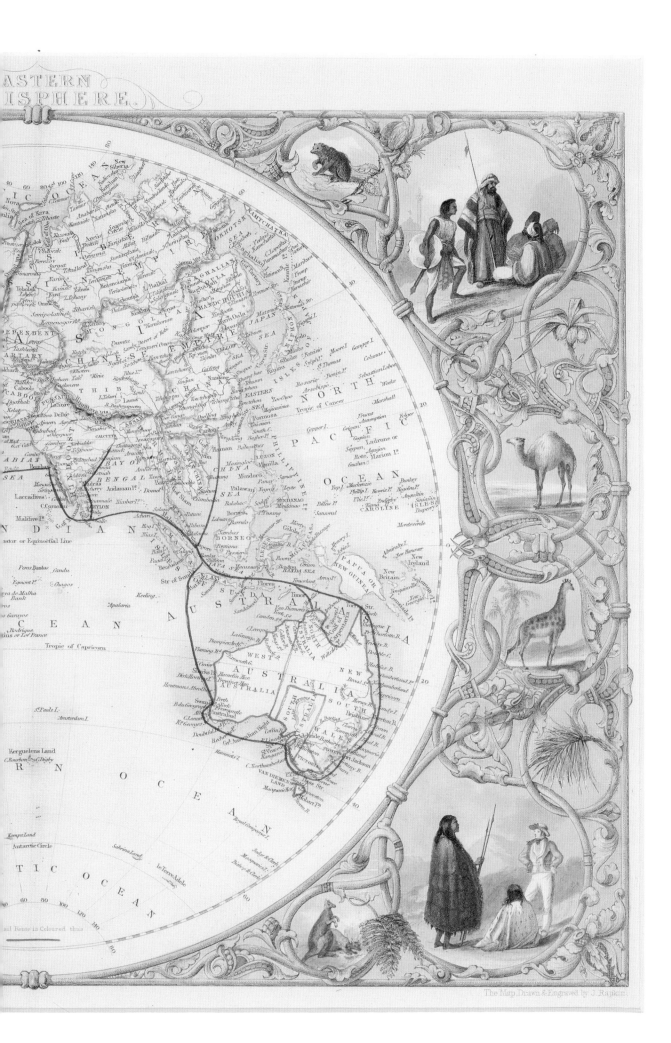

1860

'British Empire Throughout the World Exhibited In One View'

John Bartholomew
From: Bartholomew's *The Royal Illustrated Atlas*,
Edinburgh, *c.* 1860. Steel
engraving, 440 x 530 mm

The world in Victorian times is shown in this engraving, with the British Empire marked in red.

Both above and below the map are representations of the different dress of British subjects on five continents. There are Africans; Europeans include a Scot in a kilt, a guardsman wearing his bearskin and Greeks from the Aegean islands; Americans include Canadian Indians and Eskimos; Chinese and Indians represent the Asians; and Aborigines and Maoris the Australians.

This is a symbolically happy montage of the blessings and benefits brought by British rule.

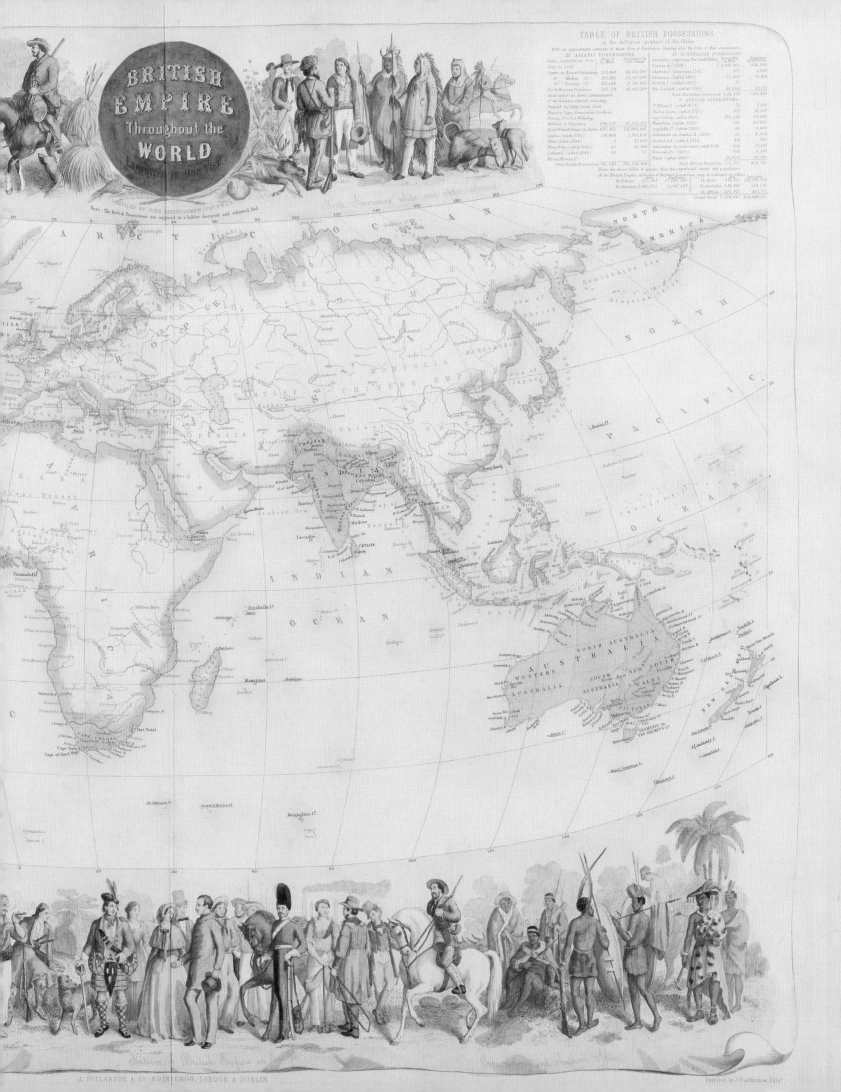

ADAMANTIA

THE

DIAMOND & GOLD FIELDS

OF

SOUTH AFRICA

BY

JAMES WYLD

GEOGRAPHER TO THE QUEEN

REFERENCE

Postal
Roads
Railways
British Territory
DIAMOND DISTRICT
GOLD   Dᵒ
Routes to Dᵒ
Telegraph Lines

COMPLETED
NOW IN
CONSTRUCTION

English Miles

The latest Explorations of Dr Thomas Baines, F.R.G.S.
are included in this Map.

Published by James Wyld, Geographer to the Queen, 457 Strand, 11 & 12 Charing Cross & 2 Royal Exchange, London.

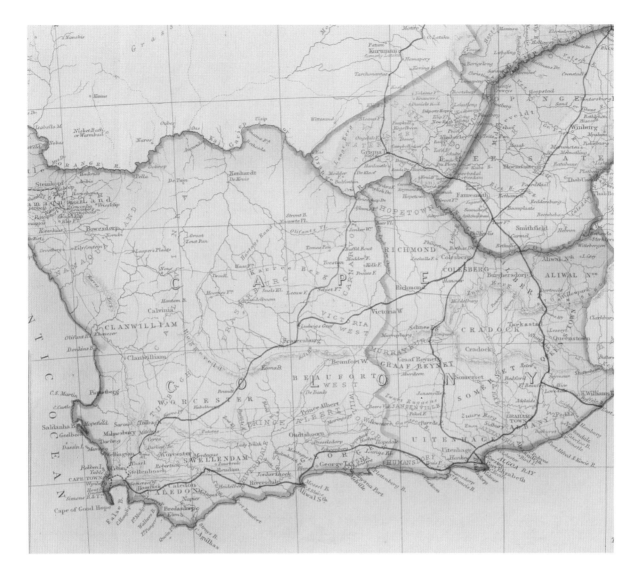

1871

'Adamantia. The Diamond & Gold Fields of South Africa...'

James Wyld Jr.
Separate publication.
Steel engraving,
widest: 538 x 390 mm

The 'Diggers' Republic of Adamantia existed for only a few months in 1870, but made enough of an impression that this map was published. After the discovery of diamond and gold deposits in the northern reaches of South Africa there was the inevitable gold rush of fierce, independently minded diggers. They set up a 'Mutual Protection Association' under the leadership of Stafford Parker, a local general trader and owner of a saloon. When the Dutch governments of both the Free State and Transvaal laid claim to the area the Diggers declared themselves a republic.

This very scarce broadsheet map of South Africa was prepared to show the newly discovered goldfields in the Transvaal and to the north, in the Matabele, Mashona and Manica tribal areas.

The dispute over the deposits turned into another episode in the long-running struggle between the British and Dutch settlers in South Africa. The British governor of the Cape of Good Hope intervened on the side of the miners, strengthening Britain's hold on the area.

The next, modest gold rush in South Africa took place in 1873 when payable gold was discovered on Geelhoutboom farm near the town of Sabie, on the Mpumalanga escarpment. President Burgers, who visited the site, named the camp 'Mac Mac' and declared the area the New Caledonia gold fields due to the Scottish extraction of many of the prospectors.

These early finds were only a prelude to the great Witwatersrand Gold Rush of 1886, which brought a huge influx of prospectors into the Transvaal. Within ten years the newly established city of Johannesburg had a larger population than Cape Town, established several centuries earlier. Indeed, it is believed that as much as 40 per cent of all the gold ever mined came from here.

EL IBRAHIMIYEH   ABUKEBIR

MEHIVEH

EL KARAIM

KASSAS

KISHLAK

ABASSA   TEL EL KEBIR

ZAGAZIG   KAFR
Ru of   MAXK
BUBASTIS   ABU HAMMAB   PITHAM

EL-ZENKELUN

BURDEN

MINIE EL KAMB   MIT BESHAR   BELBEIS   DESERT
Lock

MITBEREH   SHALSHALAMUN

EZ ZAUAMES

BENHA EL ASL   SHEBLENCEH   EL MENAIR   JEBEL DIMESHK

ESHSHEMUT   ROUTE TAKEN

MUTSHTAHIR   SHEBIN EZ KANATIR   D

SUBT ED DAK   ABU ZABEL

TUKH EL MELK   EL KHANKAH   DISUSED   RAILWAY

ES STRXAKUS
Lock

KALYUB   HELIOPOLIS
TELLHASAN

MOKATTAM

SHUBRA
JEBEL

EL ABBASIYEH   CAIRO

EL BL MENASHI   BULAK   CITADEL

CANAL   OLD CAIRO   BABYLON

EL GHIZEH

SPHINX

PYRAMIDS OF GHIZEH

BIRDS EYE VIEW
OF
CAIRO
LOOKING NORTH EAST.

1882

'Bird's Eye View of Cairo Looking North East'

The Graphic
Separate publication,
London, 1882.
Chromolithograph, 390 x 550 mm

The Graphic newspaper published this decorative map-view of Cairo and the surrounding desert in a 'Special Gratis Supplement' on 23 September 1882.

In the foreground are the Sphinx and Pyramids of Giza; in the top right corner 'The Great Bitter Lake' is part of the Suez Canal. The balloon over the desert nearby suggests that one was used to prepare this view.

The view was published just after Great Britain had reluctantly sent troops to Egypt to protect its interests, primarily the Suez Canal. British and French companies had funded the building of the canal, which opened to traffic in 1869. However the ruler of Egypt, Isma'il Pasha, developed such huge debts that he was forced to sell his country's share to Britain for £400,000 in 1875.

This cash was not enough, and increasing instability caused the mobilization of the British troops, who defeated the Egyptians at the battle of Tel-el-Kebir, establishing their control over the canal. The Convention of Constantinople in 1888 declared the canal a neutral zone under the protection of the British.

Surprisingly, considering British power, the passage of the British forces to Egypt was entrusted by the government to a private travel company, one Thomas Cook.

1894

'Plano de Manila y sus Arrabales...'

Anonymous
Separate publication,
[Manila], 1894.
Lithograph, 905 x 1365 mm

Manila 'and its Suburbs' are shown in this folding street map. The Spanish founded this colony in 1571 with the construction of a fort by López de Legaspi. The fort's original outline can still be seen on the right of the river at centre, marked 'Intramuros' (within the walls).

This detailed plan was published less than five years before the city was seized by the United States in 1898, as part of the Spanish–American War. It was not until 1901 that Filipino resistance had died down enough for a civil government to be established.

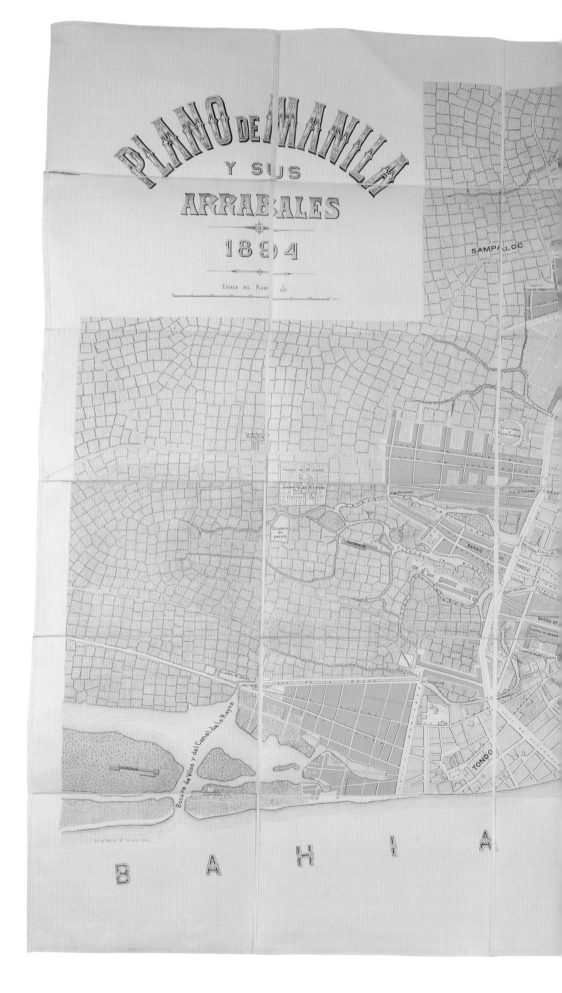

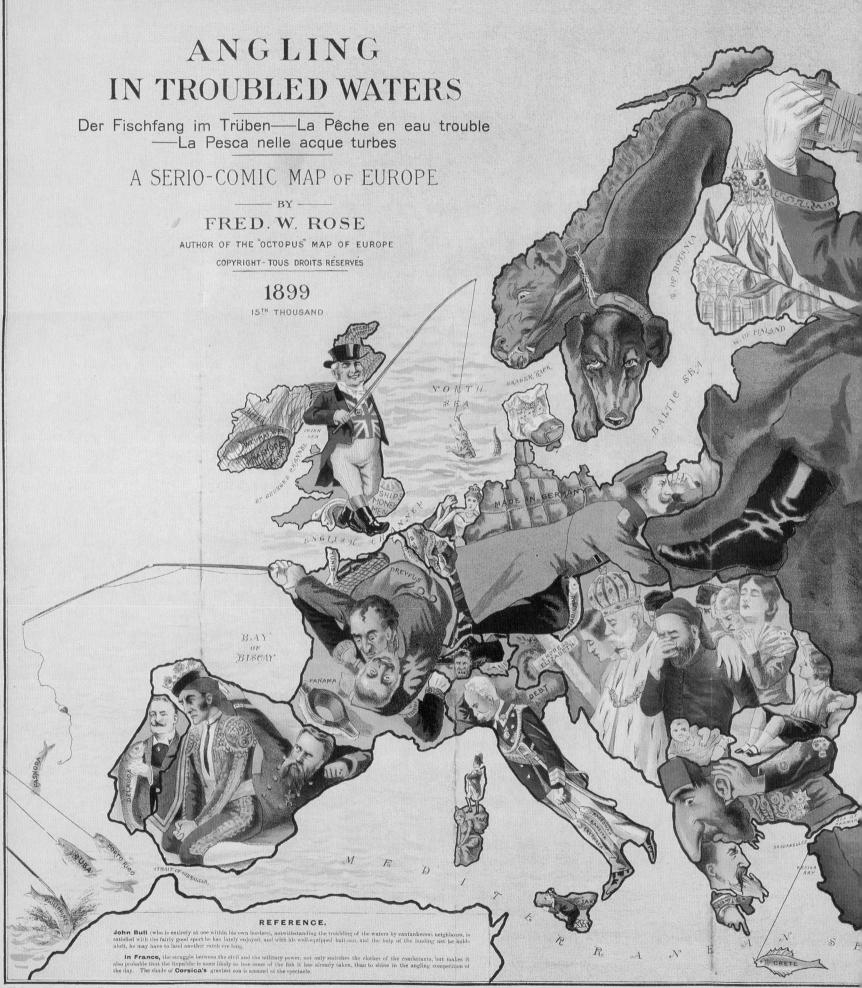

ANGLING
IN TROUBLED WATERS

Der Fischfang im Trüben——La Pêche en eau trouble
——La Pesca nelle acque turbes

A SERIO-COMIC MAP of EUROPE

— BY —

FRED. W. ROSE

AUTHOR OF THE "OCTOPUS" MAP OF EUROPE

COPYRIGHT - TOUS DROITS RÉSERVÉS

1899

15TH THOUSAND

REFERENCE.

John Bull (who is entirely at one within his own borders), notwithstanding the troubling of the waters by cantankerous neighbours, is satisfied with the fairly good sport he has lately enjoyed, and with his well-equipped bait-can, and the help of the landing net be holds aloft, he may have to land another catch ere long.

In France, the struggle between the civil and the military power, not only switches the clothes of the combatants, but makes it also probable that the Republic is more likely to lose some of the fish it has already taken, than to shine in the angling competition of the day. The shade of **Corsica's** greatest son is amazed at the spectacle.

G. W. Bacon & Co., Ltd., 127, Strand, London.

1899

'Angling In Troubled Waters.
A Serio-Comic Map Of
Europe By Fred W. Rose…'

Fred W. Rose
Separate publication,
London, 1899.
Wood engraving, 700 x 490 mm

The political turmoil of Europe as the twentieth century approaches is shown in this classic caricature map. Each country is portrayed as a fisherman, with their lines an allegory for their interference elsewhere, with the more successful with their catch in bags.

Most prominent is Russia, depicted as Tsar Nicholas II, whose line is cast eastwards into Asia: having increased Russian influence in Manchuria, including the acquisition of a lease to the important port of Port Arthur, Nicholas has reason to look pleased, but the disastrous war with Japan is less than a decade away.

Britain is shown as John Bull rather than a real character. Although his line is cast into the North Sea, on the other end is a crocodile marked Egypt, a catch he would rather not have made. Britain had to join France in an expedition to secure the Suez Canal during the period of domestic upheaval 17 years previously, resulting in the British military occupation of Egypt that lasted until 1936.

Elsewhere: France, despite the internal wrestling between civil and military power, has still hooked African 'fish'; Spain, a matador, looks on as unseen fishermen in America are catching three fish marked 'Porto Rico', 'Cuba' and 'Philippines', all former colonial possessions of Spain; Kaiser Wilhelm of Germany carries sacks of coal on his back, symbolizing their increasing industrial muscle; the Austro-Hungarian Empire is mourning after the assassination of Empress Elizabeth in September 1898; and Turkey has hooked Crete, referring to the Greco-Turkish War of 1897.

Rose made a career out of drawing these caricature maps: the 'Octopus' map mentioned in the map's title was published in 1877, showing Russia with grasping tentacles.

Sources for Antique Maps

Here follows a brief, selective, listing of dealers and auctioneers in old maps. Telephone numbers are given without international codes, assuming the reader is dialling from within the country concerned.

DEALERS

Altea Gallery

35 Saint George St
London W1S 2FN
UK

Telephone: 020 7491 0010
Email: info@alteagallery.com
Website: www.alteagallery.com

W. Graham Arader III

29 East 72nd St
New York, NY 10021
USA

Telephone: 212 628 3668
Email: info@aradergalleries.com
Website: www.aradergalleries.com

Argosy Gallery

116 East 59th St
New York, NY 10022
USA

Telephone: 212 753 4455
Email: gallery@argosybooks.com
Website: www.argosybooks.com

Richard B. Arkway, Inc.

59 East 54th St
Suite 62
New York, NY 10022
USA

Telephone: 212 751 8135
Email: arkway@mindspring.com
Website: www.arkway.com

Roderick M. Barron

Antique Map Specialist
POBox 67
Sevenoaks
Kent
TN13 3WW
UK

Telephone: 01732 742558
Email: rod@barron.co.uk
Website: www.barron.co.uk

The Baynton-Williams Gallery

37a High St
Arundel
West Sussex
BN18 9AG
UK

Telephone: 01903 883588
Email: gallery@baynton-williams.freeserve.co.uk
Website: www.baynton-williams.com

Tim Bryars Ltd.

8 Cecil Court
London WC2N 4HE
UK

Telephone: 020 7836 1901
Email: tim@timbryars.co.uk
Website: www.timbryars.co.uk

Clive A. Burden Ltd.

Elmcote House
The Green
Croxley Green
Rickmansworth
Herts
WD3 3HN
UK

Telephone: 01923 772387
Email: philip@caburden.com
Website: www.caburden.com

Jo-Ann & Richard Casten

4 Dodge Lane
Old Field, NY 11733
USA

Telephone: 631 689 3018
Email: jrcasten@castenmaps.com
Website: www.castenmaps.com

Cohen & Taliaferro Inc.

59 East 54th St
Suite 62
New York, NY 10022
USA

Telephone: 212 751 8135
Email: henry@arkway.com
Website: www.arkway.com

Frame

c/o Jaime Armero
General Pardinas 69
28006 Madrid
Spain

Telephone: 091 564 1519
Email: info@frame.es
Website: www.frames.es

J.A.L. Franks & Co.

7 Allington St
London SW1E 5EB
UK

Telephone: 020 7233 8433
Email: jalfranks@btinternet.com
Website: www.jalfranks.btinternet.co.uk

Garwood & Voigt

55 Bayham Road
Sevenoaks
Kent
TN13 3XE
UK

Telephone: 01732 460025
Email: maps@garwood-voigt.com
Website: www.garwood-voigt.com

Gowrie Galleries

316 Oxford St
Woollahra
NSW 2025
Australia

Telephone: 02 9387 4581
Email: maps@sydney.net
Website: www.gowrie-galleries.com.au

Hemispheres Antique Maps

PO Box 355
Stoddard, NH 03464
USA

Telephone: 603 446 7181
Email: betz@betzmaps.com
Website: www.betzmaps.com

Murray Hudson

PO Box 163
109 S. Church St
Halls, TN 38040
USA

Telephone: 731 836 9057
Email: mapman@ecsis.net
Website: www.murrayhudson.com

Imago Mundi

Antique Maps Ltd
40a Museum St
London WC1A 1LU
UK

Telephone: 020 7405 7477
Email: info@imagomundi.co.uk
Website: www.imagomundi.co.uk

Intercol

43 Templars Crescent
Finchley
London N3 3QR
UK

Telephone: 020 8349 2207
Email: yasha@Intercol.co.uk
Website: www.intercol.co.uk

Iris Antique Globes b.v.

Dorpsstraat 31b
7218 AB Almen
The Netherlands

Telephone: 0575 439440
Email: info@irisglobes.nl
Website: www.irisglobes.nl

Lee Jackson

Antique Maps & Prints
Suite 53
176 Finchley Road
London NW3 6BT
UK

Telephone: 020 7625 2157
Email: leejackson@btinternet.com
Website: www.leejacksonmaps.com

Loeb-Larocque

31 Rue de Tolbiac
75013 Paris
France

Telephone: 01 4424 8580
Email: info@loeb-larocque.com
Website: www.loeb-larocque.com

The Map House

54 Beauchamp Place
Knightsbridge
London SW3 1NY
UK

Telephone: 020 7589 4325
Email: maps@themaphouse.com
Website: www.themaphouse.com

Martayan Lan Inc.

The Heron Tower
70 East 55th St, 6th Floor
New York, NY 10022
USA

Telephone: 212 308 0018
Email: info@martayanlan.com
Website: www.martayanlan.com

Kenneth Nebenzahl Inc.

PO Box 370
Glencoe, IL 60022
USA

Telephone: 847 835 0515
Email: knebenzahl@msn.com

The Neptune

Shankill Castle
Shankill
County Dublin
Republic of Ireland

Telephone: 01 282 2139
Email: abl@nep.ie

The Old Print Shop Inc.

150 Lexington Avenue at 30th St
New York, NY 10016
USA

Telephone: 212 683 3950
Email: info@oldprintshop.com
Website: www.oldprintshop.com

F. Pettinaroli Sas

Piazza San Fedele, 2
20121 Milano
Italy

Telephone: 02 8646 4642
Website:
www.pettinarolimapsandprints.com

The Philadelphia Print Shop, Ltd.

8441 Germantown Avenue
Philadelphia, PA 19118
USA

Telephone: 215 242 4750
Email:
PhilaPrint@PhilaPrintShop.com
Website: www.philaprintshop.com

Jonathan Potter Ltd.

125 New Bond St
London W1S 1DY
UK

Telephone: 020 7491 3520
Email: jpmaps@attglobal.net
Website: www.jpmaps.co.uk

Barry Lawrence Ruderman

Antique Maps Inc.
1298 Prospect St
Suite 2C
La Jolla, CA 92037
USA

Telephone: 858 551 8500
Email: blr@raremaps.com
Website: www.raremaps.com

Antiquariat Sanderus

Nederkouter 32
B-9000 Gent
Belgium

Telephone: 09 223 3590
Email: sanderus@sanderusmaps.com
Website: www.sanderusmaps.com

Paulus Swaen

31 Rue de Tolbiac
75013 Paris
France

Telephone: 01 4424 8580
Email: paulus@swaen.com
Website: www.swaen.com

Tooley Adams & Co.

PO Box 174
Wallingford D.O.
Oxon
OX10 0YT
UK

Telephone: 01491 838298
Email: steve@tooleys.co.uk
Website: www.tooleys.co.uk

World View Antique Maps

2 Keeler Lane & Route 121
North Salem, NY 10560
USA

Telephone: 914 669 8695
E-mail: info@worldviewmaps.com
Website: www.worldviewmaps.com

AUCTIONEERS

Old World Auctions

PO Box 2224
Sedona, AZ 86339
USA

Sotheby's

c/o Cathy Slowther
Book Department
34-35 New Bond St
London W1A 2AA
UK

Telephone: 020 7293 5291
Email:
catherine.slowther@sothebys.com
Website: www.sothebys.com

Swann Galleries

104 East 25th St
New York, NY 10010
USA

Telephone: 212 254 4710
Email: swann@swanngalleries.com
Website: www.swanngalleries.com

Dominic Winter Book Auctions

Mallard House
Broadway Lane
South Cerney
near Cirencester
Gloucestershire
GL7 5UQ
UK

Telephone: 01285 860006
Email: info@dominic-winter.co.uk
Website: www.dominic-winter.co.uk

BIBLIOGRAPHY

As might be expected, there is an extensive bibliography relating to old maps and their makers, but any sort of comprehensive listing is beyond the remit of this volume. There follows a brief listing of some of the more useful general introductions to antique maps, in English. There is, obviously, no substitute for seeing the real thing.

Bagrow, Leo. *History of Cartography. Revised and enlarged by R.A. Skelton.* London: C.A. Watts & Co., 1964.

Baynton-Williams, Roger. *Investing in Maps.* London: Barrie & Rockcliff, 1969.

Campbell, Tony. *The Earliest Printed Maps 1472–1500.* London: The British Library, 1987. [map no. 214]

Crone, G.R. *Maps and their Makers. An Introduction to the History of Cartography.* London: Hutchinson University Library, 1966.

Gohm, Douglas. *Antique Maps of Europe, the Americas, West Indies, Australasia, Africa, the Orient.* London: Octopus Book, 1972.

Goss, John. *The Mapmaker's Art. A History of Cartography.* London: Studio Editions Ltd., 1993.

Howegego, James. *Printed Maps of London circa 1553–1850* Second Edition. Folkestone (Kent): Dawson, 1978. [Map no. 9]

Jolly, David C. *Maps in British Periodicals.* Brookline (Massachusetts): David C. Jolly, 1991. [Vol. II, GAL-107 (*Gentleman's & London Magazine*)]

Lister, John. *How to identify Old Maps and Globes.* London: G. Bell & Sons, 1965.

Manasek, F.J. *Collecting Old Maps.* Norwich (Vermont): Terra Nova Press, 1998.

MapForum. Quarterly magazine devoted to antique maps. Interalia, each issue contains a 'beginner's guide' describing one aspect of maps and mapmaking. London: MapForum Ltd. 2004 to date. www.mapforum.com

Moreland, Carl & Bannister, David. *Antique Maps.* London: Phaidon Press Ltd., 1989.

Potter, Jonathan. *Collecting Antique Maps – A New Edition With Price Guide An Introduction To Cartography.* London: Jonathan Potter Ltd, 1999.

Shirley, Rodney W. *The Mapping of the World.* London: Holland Press Cartographica, 1984. [Map no. 605]

Skelton, R.A. *Decorative Printed Maps of the 15th to 18th Centuries.* London: Spring Books, 1952.

Tooley, R.V. *Maps and Mapmakers.* London: B.T. Batsford, 1978.

Tooley, R.V., Bricker, Charles & Crone, Gerard. *Landmarks of Mapmaking An illustrated survey of Maps and Mapmakers.* Oxford: Phaidon Press, 1976.

INDEX

PICTURE CREDITS

Quercus
21 Bloomsbury Square
London
WC1A 2NS

First published in 2008

Copyright © Quercus Editions Ltd.
2008